McCoy POTTERY

VOLUME II

COLLECTOR'S REFERENCE & VALUE GUIDE

FEATURING THE TOP 100 FINDABLES

BOB HANSON, CRAIG NISSEN, and MARGARET HANSON

Floral arrangement in Basketweave Jardiniere
7½", no mark, $65.00 – 80.00.

COLLECTOR BOOKS
A Division of Schroeder Publishing Co., Inc.

The current values in this book should be used only as a guide. They are not intended to set prices, which vary from one section of the country to another. Auction prices as well as dealer prices vary greatly and are affected by condition as well as demand. Neither the authors nor the publisher assumes responsibility for any losses that might be incurred as a result of consulting this guide.

SEARCHING FOR A PUBLISHER?

We are always looking for knowledgeable people considered to be experts within their fields. If you feel that there is a real need for a book on your collectible subject and have a large comprehensive collection, contact Collector Books.

On the front cover:

Leaves and Berries Jardiniere & Pedestal, page 32;
Happy Face Cookie Jar, page 269;
Apple Cookie Jar, page 270;
Mac Dog Cookie Jar, page 260;
Chipmunk Cookie Jar, page 246;
Pink Poppy Planter, page 142;
Koala Bear Cookie Jar, page 288;
Kitten on Basketweave Cookie Jar, page 239;
Woodsy Owl Savings Bank, page 168;
Green Onyx Table, page 10.

On the back cover:

Christmas Tree Cookie Jar, page 248;
Coalby Cat Cookie Jar, page 260;
Traffic Light Cookie Jar, page 286;
Pumpkin Cookie Jar, page 237;
Hobnail Cookie Jar, page 233;
Two Kittens in Basket Cookie Jar, page 237.

Book design: Sherry Kraus
Cover design: Beth Summers

McCoy Umbrella Stands and Sand Jar.
See pages 130 & 151, respectively.

COLLECTOR BOOKS
P.O. Box 3009
Paducah, KY 42002–3009
or

Bob Hanson
P.O. Box 1945
Woodinville, WA 98072

Craig Nissen
P.O. Box 223
Grafton, WI 53024

CONTENTS

Pages from booklet sold with several pieces in 1970s.

Bob, Craig, and Margaret are long-time collectors of Nelson McCoy Pottery. Their collecting began when McCoy was usually the pottery on the floor at an antique show or in the grass at a flea market. It was one of the "other" potteries. However, part of the attraction to McCoy then was that you could find it as well as afford it. These factors are major reasons that the collections of the Hansons and Nissens have grown to a combined total of more than 5,000 pieces.

Bob and Margaret are interested in a variety of collections in addition to McCoy, including Brush-McCoy, and J.W. McCoy as well as many pieces from the "Arts & Crafts Era." In addition to pottery, they collect reverse paintings and trays, silhouette pictures, vintage whimsical plastic pins, and electric novelty clocks. Bob and Margaret have four children and live in the Seattle, Washington, area.

Craig, and his wife Pat, also enjoy collecting a number of other things in addition to the Nelson McCoy pottery. They have a modest collection of Van Briggle and Roseville pottery. They also collect Aladdin electric lamps, beaded "sugar" shade lamps from the '20s, cupid photos, rug and pillow beaters, "Chandler" pastels, and fruit and vegetable wall pockets. Craig and Pat have one daughter and are located in the greater Milwaukee area of Wisconsin.

Vintage items included in many photographs throughout the book are used to enhance a piece or to demonstrate a particular way of displaying pieces and are part of the authors' collections. Both the Hansons and the Nissens have a primary "obsession" of collecting McCoy pottery.

Margaret Hanson (holding Fergie), Craig Nissen, and Bob Hanson

DEDICATION

This Volume II is dedicated, as was Volume I, to all the past, present
and future collectors of Nelson McCoy Pottery.

*May you have as much fun and enjoyment
in your collecting as we have had in ours.*

PREFACE

This, our second reference book on the topic, is again exclusively about the pottery made by the Nelson McCoy Pottery Company from 1910 through the Lancaster years of ownership in the 1980s. In this volume we have also included the complete line of Nelson McCoy Pottery cookie jars.

We have again presented the content of the pottery information from the perspective of a collector. Being collectors ourselves, we have hopefully been successful in that goal. The order of presentation of the pieces is in a general chronological order. This is also true of the cookie jar section. We have also included brief facts and/or opinions on some of the individual pieces and cookie jars that are bits of information we have picked up during our period of collecting or are valuable additions received from other collectors. We hope you enjoy the book and will find the information useful as you seek to add to your own collections.

ACKNOWLEDGMENTS

We have so many people to acknowledge and thank for their help with this project. We truly could not have accomplished this without their assistance, from sharing information, shipping pieces with risk of loss or damage, allowing us to come into their home and photograph their collection, or simply giving that important moral support. All of these efforts have been greatly appreciated and have meant a great deal.

The following collectors pictured as well as those listed are the people responsible for all this assistance. It is with no small recognition of gratitude that we include them in this book of Nelson McCoy Pottery. Again, thank you!

Chiquita & Dewey Prestwood, North Carolina

Sandra Burdette, South Carolina
Jim Burnette & Charlie Blunt,
   North Carolina
Jean Bushnell, Colorado
Lillian Conesa, Florida
Craig Cooper, North Carolina

Evelyn Drews, Washington
Doug Dreher, Texas
Opal Dunne, Ohio
Edward Franklin, North Carolina
Bob & Sharon Huxford, Indiana
Jack & Nancy Koehler, Washington

Jan Lahti, Washington
Randy Lyon, Washington
Jim & Nea Miller, Wisconsin
Pat Nissen, Wisconsin
Bill Ornstein, Florida
Frank Poolas, New Jersey

ACKNOWLEDGMENTS

Shelley & Dave Perry, Pennsylvania
Joyce Roerig, South Carolina
Dennis Roth, New Jersey
Larry & Sharon Skillman, Ohio

Mark Sluga, Washington
Don & Becky Snyder, North Carolina
Al Sowers, Ohio
Debra Thorson, Minnesota

Bee Williams, North Carolina
George & Adena Williams, North Carolina,
Jan Witsoe, Washington

John & Polly Sweetman and daughter
Katie Phillips, Delaware

Mark & Marilyn Cooley, Wisconsin

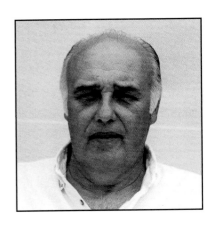

Jerry Downey, Ohio

Brian Donaldson, Ohio

Gerald Donaldson, Ohio

Charles & Virginia Ness, Washington

Carol Seman, Ohio

Dan Eggert, Ohio

Mary Proctor, Washington

Louise Francis, Washington

Sharon & Herb Klaviter, Oregon

Stan Gracyalny, Wisconsin

Dewayne & Audrey Imsand, Alabama

Kathy & Steve Anderson, Washington

Roy & Nancy Demory, Virginia

Jean Burmeister, Wisconsin

Margaret Tucker,
South Carolina

Kathy Durnell, Washington

K.C. Heylin, California

Pat & Royal Ritchey, Alabama

As we noted in Volume I, the history of "McCoy" pottery is actually quite complex. The following is a summary of our historical content from Volume I.

• In 1899 J.W. McCoy organized the J.W. McCoy Pottery company in Roseville, Ohio. In addition to crock type products made initially, one of the early lines was the Loy-Nel-Art line which was named after his three sons, Lloyd, Nelson, and Arthur.

• In 1911, J.W. McCoy Pottery merged with other small pottery companies and became the Brush-McCoy Pottery Company. J.W. McCoy remained with the company as a principal stockholder. In 1925, after the McCoy family sold their interest in the company, Brush-McCoy Pottery became Brush Pottery.

• Meanwhile, in 1910, Nelson McCoy, one of the three sons of J.W. McCoy, started the Nelson McCoy Sanitary Stoneware Company in Roseville, Ohio, with his father's financial help. This company was in competition with the Brush-McCoy Company.

• In 1933, the company reorganized and renamed itself the Nelson McCoy Pottery Company.

• Nelson McCoy Pottery flourished in the 1940s. In 1945, Nelson McCoy died and was replaced as president by his nephew, Nelson McCoy Melick. In 1950, all the manufacturing buildings were destroyed by fire, but the McCoy family decided to rebuild, utilizing the latest technology which helped position the company for the future. They were the largest producer of pottery in the U.S. by the end of the decade, shipping millions of pieces annually. Mr. Melick remained as president until his death in 1954. At that time, Nelson McCoy Jr., who had joined the company in 1948 after serving in WWII, became president, a position he held for almost three decades.

• In 1967, the company was sold to David Chase of the Mount Clemens Pottery Company. Some pieces from this era can be identified by an "MCP" on the bottom.

• In 1974, Mr. Chase sold the company to Lancaster Colony Corporation. Through this entire period, Nelson McCoy Jr. remained as president and the pottery continued to carry the Nelson McCoy Pottery name.

• In 1981, Nelson McCoy left the company after over 30 years of service.

• In 1985, Lancaster sold to Designer Accents who merged the company with two other small companies but was not very successful and closed the doors around 1990.

Billie and Nelson McCoy Jr.
We would like to thank them again so much for their continued support and generosity, especially for allowing us to photograph some of their wonderful rare Nelson McCoy cookie jars.

Below you will find two charts showing a timeline of the Nelson McCoy Pottery Company and the Brush McCoy/Brush Pottery Company. Both our Volumes are exclusively about the Nelson McCoy Pottery Company.

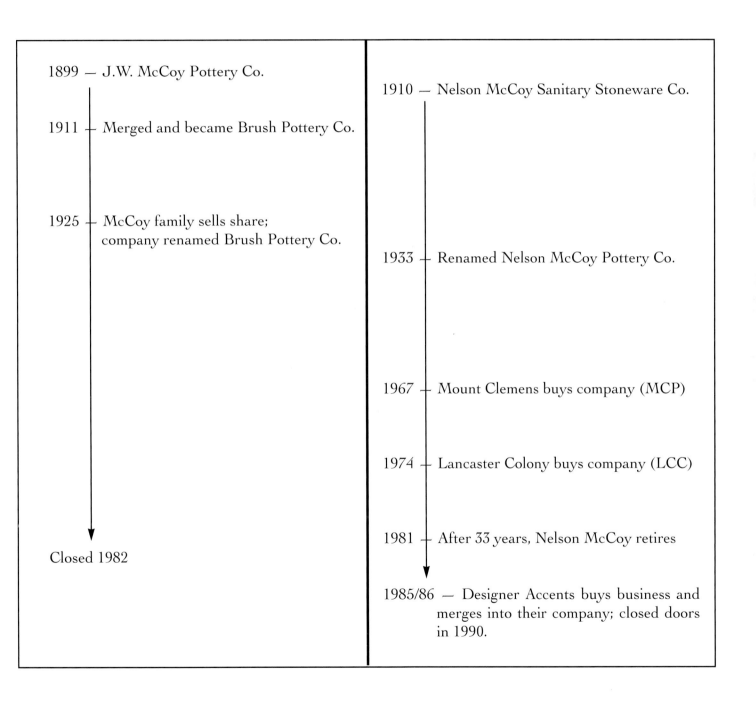

1899 — J.W. McCoy Pottery Co.

1911 — Merged and became Brush Pottery Co.

1925 — McCoy family sells share; company renamed Brush Pottery Co.

Closed 1982

1910 — Nelson McCoy Sanitary Stoneware Co.

1933 — Renamed Nelson McCoy Pottery Co.

1967 — Mount Clemens buys company (MCP)

1974 — Lancaster Colony buys company (LCC)

1981 — After 33 years, Nelson McCoy retires

1985/86 — Designer Accents buys business and merges into their company; closed doors in 1990.

The values indicated throughout this book are again based on pieces without any damage. This means no hairlines, chips, cracks, crazing, or flakes. What continues not as clear in affecting value is defects in original manufacture. Some collectors feel that, depending on the defect, these pieces can actually be more valuable. For example, a chip that was glazed over when the piece was originally made may seem to add character as well as a degree of rarity and may therefore make the piece more valuable. We continue to leave those decisions to the preference of the individual collector.

The value range shown accounts for variation in prices throughout the country. It also considers that one particular piece may have a sharper look than another sample of the same piece, due to the color of the same glaze or the crispness of the piece out of the mold. As a mold is used over and over, the sharpness of its pattern, especially if very detailed and finely designed, starts to fade or dull in appearance. This is how you can tell if a particular piece was "early" out of the mold or made near the end of the mold's life. The number of years of manufacture of many of the pieces will also have an effect on the value. More years, of production, of course, also give a higher probability of finding a particular piece.

There are a number of pieces that were made for several years but with a variety of glazes used over that time. In some of these examples, the marking of the piece may also have changed. This is especially true of several pieces initially made in the late 1920s to early 1930s. They were available in one or more of the glazes of that era and then continued to be manufactured in the pastel glazes of the late 1930s and 1940s. A few actually were still being made into the early 1950s. The example of the lower sand butterfly porch jar is still a good one. The early pieces were not marked and had matte glazes. The later pieces had gloss finishes and were marked McCoy. The manufacture of this piece covered the better part of 20 years! Other later examples of pieces with a long production life are some of the turtle and frog pieces that were all made originally in the same green color and were made in other glazes several years later. The values of these types of pieces can vary greatly. We have again tried to cover these issues in the development of the values of these pieces in the book. However, some of these issues can be subtle, and thought should be given to this area, when applicable, before making a purchase.

Several pieces were hand decorated over the glaze in a method commonly described as "cold paint." This paint was not very durable and pieces are commonly found with much of the paint missing or none at all remaining. A piece complete with all the original cold paint will command a premium price over one with no paint at all. The value ranges in the book again have taken this variation into consideration. However, this topic remains one that relates to the personal preference of the individual collector in terms of the amount of additional value the cold paint should add to a piece.

20" Onyx Table. Only a few are known to exist, $1,800.00 – 2,000.00.
Sophie, Hallie Hanson's Shih Tzu pup, wonders if there is a cookie on top of the table.

Several paper labels were used on a number of lines. They were usually attached to the side of the piece. If a piece in the book has a label, this again has NOT been considered in the value. If the label is in good condition, you should add $5.00 – $15.00 to the value of the piece. This range covers slight variation in acceptable condition as well as the rarity of the label. (See the Marks and Labels section for photo examples of these labels.)

Throughout the book, we have included additional information on all pieces. Size of a pictured piece is included as well as other sizes of that same style. Generally, jardinieres are sized by the width of the opening at the top, and vases by their height. We have also included information on other glazes offered on pieces not pictured. The difference between cataloged glazes and other unusual or rare glazes found by collectors is noted. An estimate of the original year or era of manufacture of a piece is also included although we remind you of the earlier point made that some pieces were made for many years after initially produced.

Finally, we have included an indication of whether or not a piece is usually marked. If usually marked, we have listed the type of mark style used by category indicated in the Marks and Labels section. We have noted where we know a piece that has been found both with and without a mark or if it has been found with more than one style of mark, such as "NM" and "McCoy."

The Roseville and Crooksville road signs, photographed in spring of 1998. As you can see, these towns seem to compete a bit as to which is "the" pottery town. One fact is sure, they have both played a major role in the development and making of Ohio pottery.

The following are examples of some of the marks used on the bottom of the pottery throughout the history of the Nelson McCoy Pottery Company. There are many different styles of these marks. Variations exist on letter style, position of the "USA" or "Made in USA" mark in respect to the McCoy name, location of mark, etc., but the content should be similar. The following examples provide a range of those styles so that you can make an identification. As we indicate the presence or absence of a mark, you will see that we do it by general style. In addition to a "no mark" indication, we will use either "old mark" for the first style group shown, "NM" for any variation of that mark and "McCoy," if any style of "McCoy" is used. For Floraline, we will indicate as such. We have also included photo examples of labels as reviewed in the Pricing Information section.

Old Stoneware Marks (1920s) _____

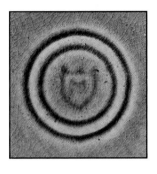   

"NM" Marks (Late '30s and '40s) – Small "NM" mark shown on bottom side of piece is typical of the mark used on many of the smaller pieces of this era. _____

  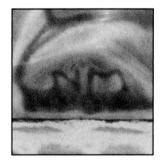 

"McCoy" Marks ('40s through the late '60s) _____

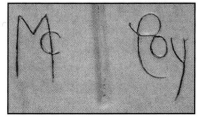

Later Marks ('70s and '80s)

Floraline Marks ('40s through the late '70s)

Labels

STONEWARE 1920s – 1940s

Pedestal from "Glazing Globe" Set. 1920s. Globe was 14" in diameter. Pedestal came in two heights: 23" & 28". No mark. $150.00 – 200.00. Pictured with shorter vase. 8½". See below.

Below: Selection of similar Vases. 1920s. 8½" & 10½" height. No marks. $85.00 – 110.00.

Jardiniere with Fine Mahogany Finish. No mark. 1920s. Came in four sizes: 7", 8", 9", and 10". $75.00 – 150.00.

Fern Pattern Jardinere & Pedestal. 1920s. 7" Jardinere, 7" Pedestal. No mark. $150.00 – 200.00.

Mug. 1926. Shield mark. Green color is more common. Black with cold paint is unusual. $25.00 – 30.00.

Blue & White Good Luck Salt. 1920s. No mark. May not be original cover. Right: Cream & Green Daisy Butter. 1920s. No mark. $75.00 – 125.00 each.

Jardiniere and Pedestal Set (41"). 1920s. No mark. $900.00 – 1,100.00. Top portion of the pedestal is actually a separate piece attached at the factory to the bottom pedestal. Hanging out in the beautiful jardiniere is Summer (poodle), who is part of the Sweetman family.

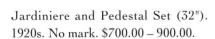

Jardiniere and Pedestal Set (32").
1920s. No mark. $700.00 – 900.00.

Jardiniere and Pedestal Set: Jardiniere 9", Pedestal 13". No mark. Hard-to-find glaze. Set, $450.00 – 500.00. Also pictured: same size pedestal in different pattern, same glaze. Sold with same size jardiniere. Set, $450.00 – 500.00.

Same Jardiniere and Pedestal Set as pictured above. Hard-to-find glaze. Set, $450.00 – 500.00.

Left: 1920s V2 Vase, 7½", marked "V2", $60.00 – 80.00.
Center: 1920s Pot Jardiniere, 4½", shield mark, $40.00 – 50.00.
Right: 1920s Ringed Vase, 7½", shield mark, $60.00 – 80.00.

Brown Doe & Fawn Pitcher. 8½" tall. No mark. $125.00 – 175.00.

6" size of Pot Jardiniere shown in top photo, with cold paint decoration. $60.00 – 75.00.

Caution: Other companies made this style of product; if pieces are not marked, they may not be McCoy.

Left: Pitcher, No mark. $60.00 – 80.00.

Right: Ringed Vase with Handles. 7½". Shield mark. $60.00 – 80.00.

Buccaneer Mug in uncommon glaze. 4¾". Shield mark. $30.00 – 35.00.

Same Ringed Vase with Handles as pictured above, showing different glaze colors.

Green Mugs shown in two sizes: 5" & 4½" heights. Shield mark. $20.00 – 30.00.

Pictured above is a wonderful set of Mixing Bowls. They are marked with the shield style mark – see below right. Values range from $50.00 – $150.00, depending on size.

Left: Pretzel Jar. Shield mark. $90.00 – 110.00.
Right: Tobacco Humidor. No mark. $75.00 – 100.00.

Mixing Bowl shield mark from above.

1920s – 1940s

Cameo Jardiniere & Pedestals Sets:
Smaller Set: Jardiniere 8½", Pedestal 12½", $250.00 – 350.00.
Larger Set: (Rare) Jardiniere 10", Pedestal 18½", $600.00 – 700.00.

Jardiniere & Pedestal Sets:
Smaller Set: Jardiniere 10", Pedestal 18½", $450.00 – 550.00.
Larger Sets: (Rare) Jardiniere 12½", Pedestal 20½", $550.00 – 650.00.

Larger Jardiniere with Handles 10". No mark. $90.00–110.00.
Small Jardinieres 4½", pictured in a variety of glaze colors. $30.00 – 50.00.

Jardiniere and Pedestal Sets: Jardinieres 10½". Pedestals 18½". No mark. Note difference in styles of jardinieres; same pedestal with each set. Set, $450.00 – 550.00.

Jardiniere and Pedestal Sets. Jardinieres 10½". Pedestals 18". No mark. Set, $450.00 – 550.00.

Pictured above are two 12" Oil Jars and one 15" Oil Jar with Handles. All the jars have what was cataloged as a "chromoveil decoration." Base colors with this decoration were yellow, maroon, or green. The 12" jars are valued at $250.00 each. The 15" jar is valued at $400.00. This finish was cataloged in the 1950s.

Left: 18" Oil Jar. No mark. $350.00 – 400.00.
Right: 15" Oil Jar with handles. No mark. $250.00 – 300.00.

7" Jardinieres. Shown in gloss and matte blended glazes. Both have the shield mark. $50.00 – 60.00.

7" Jardinieres. Shown in different gloss and matte blended glazes. Both also have the shield mark. $50.00 – 60.00.

7" Jardinieres in an onyx glaze. 4" Pot with saucer, green glaze. Both have the shield mark. 7", $50.00 – 60.00; 4", $30.00 – 40.00.

Above: Duck Pitcher shown in four glaze colors. Late 1930s. No mark. $80.00 – 100.00.

Duck Pitcher shown in blue glaze color. Same as above pitchers. Leaves & Berries 5" Teapot in same blue glaze. Late 1930s. No mark. $75.00 – 100.00.

Leaves & Berries Teapot Set. Same teapot as shown above. $75.00 – 100.00.
Sugar & Creamer. No marks. $40.00 – 50.00 each.

Left: 8" Vase in matte blue. No mark. $70.00 – 85.00.
Center & Right: 7" Vases in matte blue and brown. No mark. $80.00 – 100.00.

These pieces all have the hand decoration in the leaves and berries area. Vases with this decoration were part of the Nelson McCoy Company "Loy–Nel–Art" line. The name of this line was actually a copy of the name of a line that Nelson's father, J.W. McCoy, used for his pottery company in earlier years. The name of the line came from his three sons' names, Lloyd, Nelson, and Arthur.

8" Vase in light yellow. No mark. $70.00 – 85.00.
6" Vase in light yellow. No mark. $60.00 – 80.00.

Right: 6¼" vase in blue. No mark. $70.00 – 85.00.
Left: Centerpiece Planter in Blue. No mark. $50.00 – 70.00.

Vase shown in the four sizes produced. Variety of glaze colors. No mark. 10" Vase, $90.00 – 125.00; 8" Vase, $50.00 – 90.00; 6" Vase, $40.00 – 75.00; 5" Vase, $40.00 – 75.00.

Above & below: 7" Vase in rainbow of colors. No mark. $90.00 – 125.00.

THE NELSON McCOY POTTERY COMPANY
ROSEVILLE, OHIO

No. 4. Jardiniere
Blended Glazes
4½", 3 doz. Ctn., 45 lbs.
7½", 1 doz. Ctn., 42 lbs.

No. 20. Jardiniere
White, Rose & Green Mats
4", 3 doz. Ctn., 35 lbs.
7½", 1 doz. Ctn., 45 lbs.

No. 21. Jardiniere
White, Rose & Green Mats
4½", 3 doz. Ctn., 45 lbs.
7½", 1 doz. Ctn., 45 lbs.

No. 24. Jardiniere
White, Rose & Green Mats
4½", 3 doz. Ctn., 45 lbs.
7½", 1 doz. Ctn., 45 lbs.

No. 25. Jardiniere
White, Rose & Green Mats
4½", 3 doz. Ctn., 45 lbs.
7½", 1 doz. Ctn., 45 lbs.

No. 10. Vase, 7 x 6"
1 doz. Ctn., 33 lbs.

No. 11.
Jard. Vase, 6 x 7"
1 doz. Ctn., 35 lbs.

No. 12.
Vase, 8¼ x 5"
1 doz. Ctn., 30 lbs.

No. 15. Vase
6", 3 doz. Ctn., 40 lbs.
8", 1 doz. Ctn., 30 lbs.

No. 81. Vase
6", 3 doz. Ctn., 40 lbs.
8", 1 doz. Ctn., 30 lbs.

No. 83. Vase
6", 3 doz. Ctn., 40 lbs.
8", 1 doz. Ctn., 30 lbs.

White, Rose, Green & Blue Mats

White, Green & Rose Mats

No. 94. Flower Pot & Saucer
White, Green & Rose Mats
4", 3 doz. Ctn., 42 lbs.
5½", 1 doz. Ctn., 26 lbs.
6½", 1 doz. Ctn., 38 lbs.

No. 27
7" Hanging Basket
Green Glaze
1 doz. Ctn., 30 lbs.

No. 28. 7½" Hanging Basket
White, Rose & Green Mats
1 doz. Ctn., 30 lbs.

No. 29. 6" Hanging Basket
White, Rose & Green Mats
1 doz. Ctn., 25 lbs.

No. 20
6½" Pedestal or Vase
White, Green & Rose Mats
1 doz. Ctn., 42 lbs.

No. 63 Bulb Bowl
White, Drip Green & Drip Brown
5½", 3 doz. Ctn., 36 lbs.
7½", 2 doz. Ctn., 55 lbs.

No. 87. Garden Dish
Green Glaze
8", 2 doz. Ctn., 60 lbs.

No. 125
20 oz. Pitcher
Green & Walnut Glazes
3 doz. Ctn., 40 lbs.

No. 122. 42 oz. Pitcher
Lt. Green & Lt.
Blue Semi-Mats
1 doz. Ctn., 30 lbs.

Dog Feeders
Green & Brown Glazes
No. 1. 5", 3 doz. Ctn., 45 lbs.
No. 3. 7½", 2 doz. Ctn., 53 lbs.

No. 4G. 8½" Bowl, Green
No. 4Y. 8½" Bowl, Yellow
2 doz. Ctn., 55 lbs.

No. 4G. 9½" Bowl, Green
No. 4Y. 9½" Bowl, Yellow
1½ doz. Ctn., 55 lbs.

No. 4G. 10½" Bowl, Green
No. 4Y. 10½" Bowl, Yellow
1 doz. Ctn., 50 lbs.

No. 4G. 11½" Bowl, Green
No. 4Y. 11½" Bowl, Yellow
1 doz. Ctn., 55 lbs.

Vases shown in three sizes made. Variety of glaze colors. No mark. 9" Vase, $100.00 – 125.00; 8" Vase, $70.00 – 90.00 ; 6" Vase, $50.00 – 75.00.

6½" Jardiniere with little handles. Shown in two matte glazes. No mark. $75.00 – 100.00.

Jardiniere 6½". No mark. $90.00 – 125.00.

Decorative Bowl shown with matching Candleholders. Made in variety of glaze colors. No marks. Bowl, $50.00 – 75.00; Pair of Candleholders, $40.00 – 60.00.

Jardiniere shown in four sizes made. Variety of glaze colors. No mark. *7½",* $90.00 – 125.00; *7",* $50.00 – 90.00; *5",* $40.00 – 75.00; *4",* $40.00 – 75.00.

Flower pots in three sizes. Gloss blue is very uncommon. No mark. 4", $40.00 – 75.00; 3", $40.00 – 75.00; 6", $50.00 – 90.00.

"Swallows" Jardinieres shown in two sizes. Gloss brown is very uncommon. No mark. *7",* $85.00 – 125.00; *4",* $45.00 – 65.00.

Leaves & Berries family of Jardiniere and Pedestal Sets. No marks. 10½" Jardiniere, 18½" Pedestal (rare), $600.00 – 700.00.
8½" Jardiniere, 12½" Pedestal, $250.00 – 350.00.
7" Jardiniere, 6½" Pedestal, $200.00 – 250.00.

Green Onyx Jardiniere and Pedestal set on the cover is the same size as the large set in this photo. $600.00 – 700.00.

Bottom left: 12" Vase with handles. No marks. $100.00 – 150.00.
12" Vase without handles. NM mark. Rare. $250.00 – 300.00.

Below right: NM mark on white vase at left.

Jardiniere 7" with floral display. No mark. Matte glazes. $85.00 – 110.00.

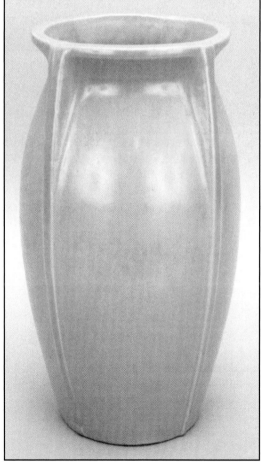

14" Vase shown in two standard glazes. No mark. $250.00 – 350.00. 7" Jardiniere. No mark. $80.00 – 100.00.

Same 14" Vase as pictured at left, shown in matte blue. Has also been found in white and brown/green matte glaze. Same value range.

Morning Glory Jardinere and Pedestal Set in Brown Onyx glaze. No mark. 8" Jardinere with 12½" Pedestal, $300.00 – 350.00.
Green Onyx Pedestal only, $150.00 – 200.00.
7" Jardiniere in foreground. No mark. $75.00 – 100.00.

This set has not been verified by catalog information as McCoy, but collector consensus is that it is a Nelson McCoy product.

Above: 10" Vase. No mark. $80.00 – 100.00.

6¼" Vase. No mark. $70.00 – 85.00.
4½" Jardiniere. No mark. $35.00 – 50.00.
7" Jardiniere. No mark. $85.00 – 125.00.

Left: 10½" Jardinere, 18½" Pedestal (rare). $600.00 – 700.00.
Right: 8½" Jardinere, 12½" Pedestal. $250.00 – 350.00.

Above: Pedestal and Jardinere Set in Brown Onyx. 8½" Jardinere, 12½" Pedestal. $300.00 – 350.00.

7" Bowls. No marks. $60.00 – 80.00.

Large 10" Jardiniere with saucer. Onyx glaze. No mark. $125.00 – 150.00.
4½" Jardiniere. Onyx glaze. No mark. $40.00 – 55.00.

Below: Holly Jardiniere family. Wide range of glaze colors. No mark.
Left to right: 10½" Jardiniere. $100.00 – 125.00.
8½" Jardiniere. $75.00 – 90.00.
7½" Jardiniere. $50.00 – 75.00.
4" Jardiniere. $25.00 – 50.00.

4½" & 7½" Jardinieres. No mark.
4½", $40.00 – 55.00.
7½", $70.00 – 85.00.

8" Burgundy Vase. Early 1940s. McCoy mark. $50.00 – 65.00.

Pictured with very special Bud Vase, also 8" tall. Shown in brown/green matte glaze but with same McCoy mark found on burgundy Vase. Extremely unusual to find this glaze on a vase with this mark. (Note mark in upper right photo.) In addition, it is also extremely unusual to find a piece with a mark of this style on the bottom with no glaze on the bottom! On top of all that, this bud vase is also very rare. $250.00– 300.00.

An example of the bottom of an umbrella stand made by the Nelson McCoy Pottery Co. Note the unfinished ring around the outer edge with the entire center covered with glaze. Also, the center area will be slightly concave. Having these features does not assure you that it is Nelson McCoy, but if you find an umbrella stand and are unsure, finding all these characteristics allows it to be considered.

6½" Vase. Early 1940s. No mark. Variety of gloss glazes. $50.00 – 75.00.

8" Cobalt Blue Vase. Early 1940s. McCoy mark. Wide variety of glaze colors. $50.00 – 65.00.

4" x 7" Fernery. Early 1940s. Shown in blue color glaze. NM mark. $45.00 – 60.00.
10" Vases. Early 1940s. McCoy mark. Variety of gloss glazes. $80.00 – 110.00.

3" x 5" Planter. Early 1940s.
No mark. Variety of colors.
$35.00 – 50.00.

Right: Two Vases pictured in beautiful cobalt blue glaze. Both vases were made in several glaze colors. Both pieces are found with McCoy mark or "dry bottom," no mark.
Left vase: 7" tall. $35.00 – 50.00.
Right vase: 6" tall. $40.00 – 60.00.

Pitcher 7". 1940s. Again, examples of the wonderful cobalt blue glaze. Variety of other glaze colors made. Lower photo shows piece made with NM & McCoy marks. $85.00 – 125.00.

18" Vase. Early 1940s. No mark. Rare. Variety of colors. $250.00 – 300.00.

Same 9" Vase as pictured in lower left photo. Hand decorated under glaze. $200.00 – 300.00.

9" Vase. Early 1940s. McCoy mark. Made in a variety of gloss glazes. Matte lavender example is very uncommon. $50.00 – 90.00.

Jardiniere. Early 1940s. USA mark. Variety of gloss colors. Three sizes.
3¾", $30.00 – 40.00.
5", $35.00 – 50.00.
7½", $55.00 – 70.00.

Pitcher. 7" tall. 1939 – 1940s. Variety of colors. Mark and no mark. This piece is engraved: "Treasure Island – San Francisco; 1939." $30.00 – 45.00.

Flower Bowl. 8¼" wide. NM mark. Early 1940s. Variety of colors. $30.00 – 45.00.

Vase shown in matte aqua glaze with vivid color flowers. 6" tall. Early 1940s. Variety of colors made as pictured in photo below, including a gloss green. McCoy mark. $30.00 – 50.00.

Lamb Planter. 6" wide. 4½" x 3". Early 1940s. NM mark. $50.00 – 60.00.

Vase 5½" tall. Early 1940s. No mark. Variety of gloss colors. Left vase in white glaze is example of standard product. Vase pictured on right is hand decorated under glaze with signature. Production vase, $90.00 – 125.00; decorated vase, $125.00 – 150.00.

Pictured are two Vases with similar styles of markings on the bottom. Left is "USA C"; right is "USA A." Early 1940s. 5" tall. These vases have been found by several collectors in the typical McCoy gloss glaze colors of the early 1940s pieces. We could find no information to verify that they are indeed McCoy, but with the majority opinion of collectors being yes, we have included them for your information. $25.00 – 40.00.

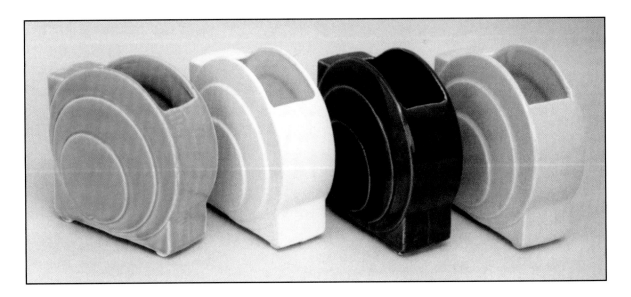

Vase. 6¾" tall. Early 1940s. USA mark. Wide variety of glaze colors. One of the more Art Deco style pieces made. $80.00 – 100.00.

Below: Basketweave pattern pieces. 1940s. No mark. Left to right: 7" Jardiniere, $50.00 – 65.00. 3½" Flower Pot, $35.00 – 45.00. 5½" Vase, $30.00 – 40.00. 8" Vase, $45.00 – 60.00. 12" Vase, $75.00– 90.00.

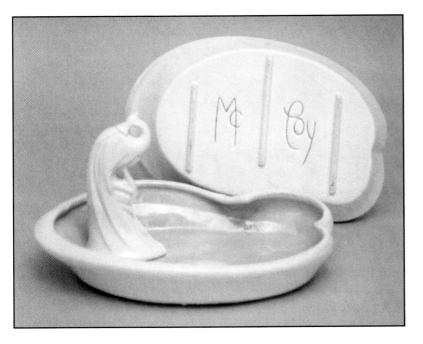

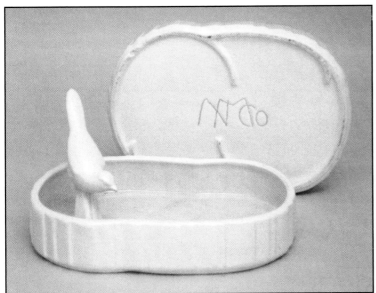

In the late 1930s and early 1940s, the white figural Flower Bowl Ornaments were cataloged on the same page with two styles of Flower Bowls. The intention was that a customer would purchase a Flower Bowl and an Ornament to go in it. In the two photos to the left, we have pictured the two styles of Flower Bowls that were offered with a sample Flower Bowl Ornament. We also show the bottom marks of each Bowl because they have very unique style markings. Both Flower Bowls were offered in all white, or white outside with an option of turquoise or yellow inside as shown.

Top photo: Flower Bowl. 9½". $35.00 – 50.00.
Peacock Ornament. 4¾". $80.00 – 100.00.

Bottom photo: Flower Bowl. 9½". $30.00 – 40.00.
Wren Ornament. 4¼". $60.00 – 80.00.

Top right photo: Flower Holders: Pitcher 4" x 3¼" on left with hand decoration and Vase 3½" x 3¼" shown in the production white color. NM mark on both but frequently difficult to see. Wide variety of colors for both. Pitchers, $30.00 – 60.00; Vases, $30.00 – 60.00.

Bottom right photo: Flower Holder, "Hands of Friendship" shown in the production rose color and a white example with hand decoration. 4" x 3". Late 1930s and early 1940s. NM mark. Wide variety of colors. $60.00 – 150.00.

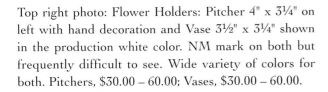

Donkey Planters. Early 1940s. Both sizes shown: 7" x 7½" and 6½" x 6". No mark. Variety of glaze colors. 7" x 7½", $30.00 – 40.00; 6½" x 6", $25.00 – 30.00.

Gnome (Hillbilly) and Witch. Both pieces are 3" tall. Both pictured in yellow glaze which is rare in these already rare pieces. Available in a variety of gloss colors. Gnome, $250.00 – 400.00; Witch, $400.00 – 500.00.

Small Stretch Lion shown in rare cobalt blue glaze. 5¼" x 4". Early 1940s. No mark. Variety of matte pastel colors most commonly found. $200.00 – 300.00.

Cat Bowl. 6½". 1940s. McCoy mark. Inscription on side: "Pussy Cat, Pussy Cat – Where Have You Been?" $70.00 – 100.00.

Vase. 6½". Early 1940s. No mark. Variety of colors. $40.00 – 60.00.

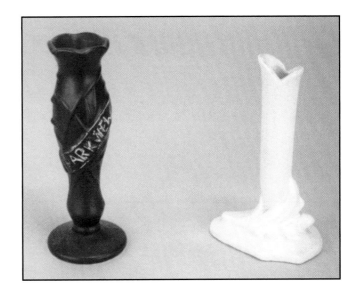

Left: Bud Vase. 6½". 1950s. McCoy mark. Shown with unusual "Parkview" name highlighting. Right: Bud Vase. 5". Late 1930s, early 1940s. Early McCoy mark. 6½", $25.00 – 35.00; 5", $100.00 – 125.00.

Flower Holder Pitcher (See page 45) and Frog with Lotus planter. 1940s. No mark. Both pieces have unusual markings on bottoms with a similar style. May have been a coding used in production for glaze coloring.
"X149" Pitcher. $75.00 – 100.00.
Standard Frog Planter. $15.00 – 20.00.
"HX7" Frog Planter. $50.00 – 60.00.

Fish Flower Holder. 4¼" x 3¼". NM mark. Shown in the rose glaze on the right and the rare coral glaze on the left. Production glazes, $80.00 – 200.00; Coral glaze, $250.00 – 300.00.

12" Oil Jar, hand decorated in a beautiful floral design. We cannot determine whether or not these hand decorated pieces were always "factory," but they are certainly in demand by many McCoy collectors and their value greatly varies from piece to piece. It is for that reason that we will not value this decorated example. For the Oil Jar value, see below.

Garden Dish. Shown in two styles. 7¾" x 6". NM mark on both. The matte aqua example with the three resting points/legs is the most commonly found. The gloss green style is quite uncommon. Variety of colors in each style. Three-point style, $50.00 – 60.00; uncommon style, $70.00 – 80.00.

Oil Jar. 12" tall. Late 1930s, early 1940s. NM mark. The blue inside color glaze is very unusual. The white is commonly all white. Variety of glaze colors. $125.00 – 200.00.

Planters. 3½". 1940s. NM mark. Variety of colors. Pictured in most common form in center with unusual examples on the outside with a "tab" section in the top edge "V" area. Standard Planter, $30.00 – 40.00; Tab Planter, $50.00 – 65.00.

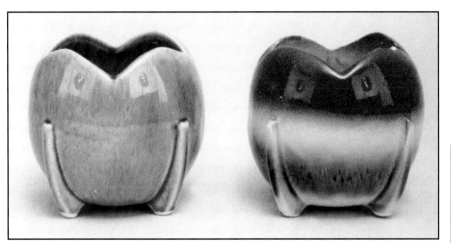

Uncommon glaze examples of brown & multicolors. Brown piece has some glaze coding on bottom. Brown, $75.00 – 100.00; Multicolor glaze, $50.00 – 60.00.

6" Bowl. Early 1940s. NM mark. $50.00 – 60.00.

Another example of a multicolored planter. $50.00 – 60.00.

V-Vase. 7¾" tall. 1940s. NM mark shown at left. Rare. $500.00 – 650.00.

Candleholder/Planter. 1940s. 8" x 6" x 2". NM mark shown at left. Rare. $250.00 – 300.00.

Elephant Pitcher. Both sides shown. 7" tall. Early 1940s. NM mark. Variety of colors. Very rare. $400.00 – 500.00.

Vase. 6". 1940s. Variety of colors. Marked NM. Pictured in cobalt blue. $60.00 – 100.00.

Hat Flower Holder. 4". Early 1940s. Variety of colors, also shown in cobalt blue. $25.00 – 40.00.

Pig pitcher. 5" tall. 1940s. Marked McCoy. Variety of colors. Very rare. $500.00 – 600.00.

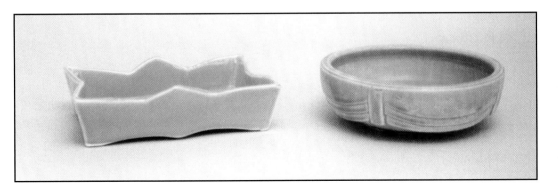

Planter. 8" x 5½". Early 1940s. NM mark. Variety of colors. $40.00 – 60.00.
Bulbs Bowl. Early 1940s. NM mark. Variety of colors. Three sizes: 6", 7½", 8¼". Any size, $35.00 – 60.00.

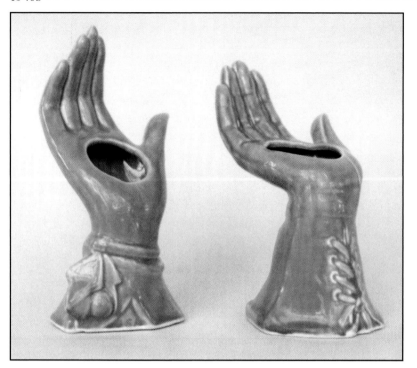

Hand vases. Early 1940s. 8¼" tall. NM mark or no mark (dry bottom). Variety of colors.
Left vase pictured is more commonly found. $35.00 – 60.00. Right Hand Vase is quite rare and called the "Glove Vase." $175.00 – 250.00.

Novelty Trays. Early 1940s. Left: more common tray, 5¾". NM mark. Variety of colors. $35.00 – 50.00.
Right: very rare tray, 5¾". No mark. Variety of colors. $125.00 – 150.00.

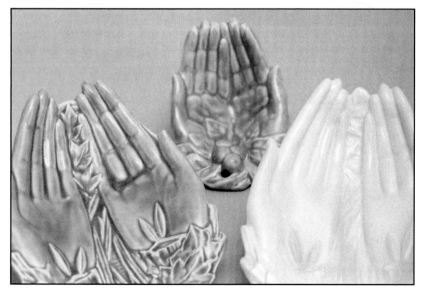

Large Hands Novelty Trays. 8½". Early 1940s. NM mark. Variety of colors. $100.00 – 125.00 (Pictured with one of the smaller size hand trays shown above.)

NOTE: The large trays came from two different tools. If you look closely, the leaf design slightly covers the little fingers on the green one while the same fingers on the white tray are untouched.

These three vases are all pictured in yellow glaze on page 58 of Vol. I. We have had frequent questions asking to verify if they are really Nelson McCoy. We show them here in the beautiful blue glazes and want to assure collectors that they all are the "Real McCoy." Early 1940s. All USA marked. Variety of colors. Left to right: 10" Vase, $85.00 – 110.00; 12" Vase, $110.00 – 140.00; 10" Vase, $85.00 – 110.00.

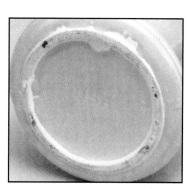

Bottom of vase with fine handles. You will find similar vases with this shape but the bottom will be different.

Flower Pot. Early 1940s. NM mark. Made in three sizes. 3¾" & 5" shown, and 6" size not shown. Variety of colors. 3¾", $25.00 – 35.00; 5", $30.00 – 40.00; 6", $40.00 – 50.00.

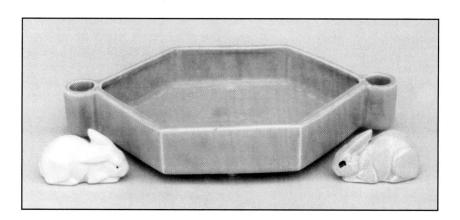

Right: Candleholder Tray. 11½". Early 1940s. NM mark. Variety of colors. Rare. $125.00 – 150.00. Rabbit. 1½" tall. Early 1940s. Variety of colors. USA mark. $250.00 – 350.00.

Vase. 5½". 1940s. This piece is most commonly found marked with the Brush name. However on a very rare occasion, it has been found with the "NM" mark. $75.00 – 100.00.

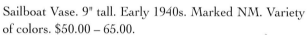

Sailboat Vase. 9" tall. Early 1940s. Marked NM. Variety of colors. $50.00 – 65.00.

Donkey Pitcher. Example with rare cold paint. 7" x 5". Early 1940s. NM mark. $200.00 – 300.00.

Flower Pot. Early 1940s. No mark. Variety of colors. 3¾", $20.00 – 25.00; 5" & 6", $35.00 – 50.00.

Pot and Saucer. Early 1940s. NM mark. Note uncommon style of the NM mark at right. Variety of pastel colors. 6", $60.00 – 75.00; 5", $45.00 – 60.00; 3¾", $35.00 – 45.00.

Dragonfly Planters. Early 1940s. No mark. Variety of pastel colors.
3½", $35.00 – 45.00.
5½", $60.00 – 75.00.
4½", $50.00 – 60.00.

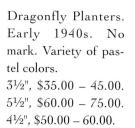

Flower Holder. 5" x 3½". Early 1940s. USA mark. Variety of colors. $40.00 – 55.00.

Hobnail with Leaf Border pattern. Vase and Pot with Saucer shown. Early 1940s. NM mark. Variety of pastel colors. Left to right: 7" Vase, $60.00 – 75.00; 6" Pot, $60.00 – 75.00; 5" Pot, $45.00 – 60.00; 3¾" Pot, $35.00 – 45.00.

Right & Below: Hobnail Round Pitcher. 6". Early 1940s. No mark. Variety of colors. $100.00 – 150.00.

Square Top Hobnail Jardiniere pictured in both sizes. Early 1940s. USA mark. Variety of pastel colors. 5½", $60.00 – 80.00; 3¾", $55.00 – 70.00.

Butterfly Ivy Vase in standard production design on left and very rare, non-production design on the right. 4½" size. USA mark. Variety of pastel colors. Standard design, $50.00 – 90.00; rare design, $200.00 – 300.00.

Commonly called the Arrowhead vase. 8" tall. 1940s. McCoy mark. Variety of pastel colors. $50.00 – 60.00.

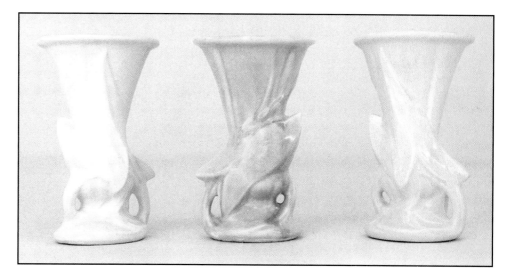

Left: Deer Fernery. 9". Right: Butterfly Fernery, also 9". Both pieces are from the 1940s and come in a variety of pastel colors. They both can be found with an NM mark and with no mark. The NM marked pieces have a braided design around the top edge. The unmarked pieces have a couple of resting legs across the bottom as opposed to the design all around the bottom on the NM marked pieces. The NM marked pieces are very rare. Deer Fernery, no mark, $40.00 – 50.00, NM mark, $70.00 – 90.00; Butterfly Fernery, no mark, $75.00 – 95.00, NM mark, $125.00 – 150.00.

The Butterfly pattern was sold in the early 1940s and remains one of the most popular lines to collect. There were 26 different shapes made. The divided planter was made only in white. All other shapes were made in six pastel glazes, blue, yellow, aqua, lavender, pink (coral), and white.

On the opposite page the complete collection available is pictured in aqua. Many collectors decide to collect just one color of the Butterfly. If you decide to do the same, we recommend you consider the following information. Of course, as we noted above, the divided dish only came in white so that would only be considered part of a color collection if you decide to collect white.

•Pink (Coral): Of the 25 potential shapes, to date, nine of them have never been found in coral. This fact makes this the most difficult if not truly impossible color choice for your collection.

•Lavender: Probably the next toughest, if not also impossible, choice. The wall pocket and the platter are not known to exist in anyone's collection to date.

•Blue: Here the challenge is the wall pocket — only two are known to exist to date, but they were found by a collector.

•White: The Castlegate vase is the rarest white piece. Only two or three are known for sure but all these found by collectors. The two square top planters are also tough in this color.

•Yellow/Aqua: These colors are about the same difficulty so likely the easiest to find, if that word can be used. In both colors, the platter is the most difficult to obtain. However a few are known to exist in both glaze colors so they are findable. Aqua as a total collection may be a little more attainable than yellow as there are a number of pieces that are much more scarce in yellow than in aqua. None of the choices obviously offer an easy road, but then maybe that's as it should be. So consider the above as you decide to go for a color and best of luck in your hunt!

Divided Planter. Only white. 7½" x 5¾". NM mark. $100.00 – 125.00.

All pieces either have an "NM" mark or USA mark. The only exception is the 9" Fernery.

Top right, opposite page (left to right)

Description	Size	Value Range
Handled Vase	10"	$125.00 – 200.00
Fernery	8¼" x 4"	$40.00 – 50.00
Fernery	5½" x 3¼"	$30.00 – 40.00
Butterfly Vase	7½" x 5½"	$75.00 – 125.00
Fernery	9" x 3½"	$75.00 – 95.00
Wall Pocket	7" x 6"	$250.00 – 400.00
Platter	14" x 8½"	$250.00 – 400.00
Hanging Basket	6½"	$150.00 – 300.00
Pitcher	10"	$125.00 – 200.00
Jardiniere	4½"	$30.00 – 50.00
Jardiniere	3½"	$25.00 – 40.00

Bottom right, opposite page (left to right)

Description	Size	Value Range
Jardiniere	7½"	$90.00 – 150.00
Jardiniere	5¼" x 5¼	$90.00 – 150.00
Jardiniere	3¾" x 3¾"	$65.00 – 90.00
Vase	9"	$80.00 – 125.00
Castlegate Vase	7" x 6"	$125.00 – 200.00
Console Bowl	11" x 7½"	$90.00 – 130.00
Vase	8¼"	$45.00 – 75.00
Vase	6¼"	$25.00 – 40.00
Console Bowl	8½" x 6"	$50.00 – 90.00
Ivy Vase	4½"	$50.00 – 90.00
Console Bowl	5" x 3¾"	$45.00 – 75.00
Flower Pot	6½"	$60.00 – 95.00
Flower Pot	5"	$35.00 – 60.00
Flower Pot	3¾"	$30.00 – 50.00

WALL POCKETS

Collecting wall pockets continues to be a very popular area of collecting McCoy pottery. If this is an area of particular interest to you, please see our Volume I book on McCoy for information and photos of over 100 additional McCoy pottery wall pockets.

Left: Leaves & Berries pattern. 7" long. 1940s. No mark. Variety of gloss colors. Shown in beautiful cobalt blue. $175.00 – 250.00.

Wall Pocket (Mexican). 7½" long. No mark. Pastel colors on standard production pieces. Sample shown is very rare piece with cold paint decoration. Standard, $50.00 – 90.00. Rare piece, $200.00 – 300.00.

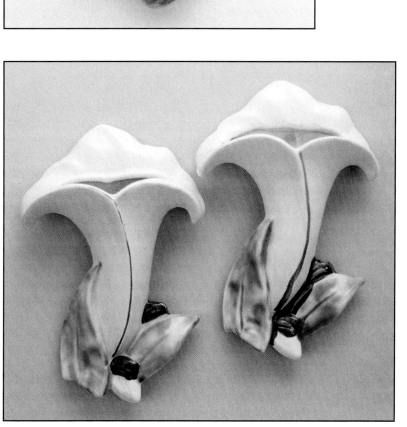

Lily Wall Pocket. 6½" long. Late 1940s. McCoy mark. Standard glazes. Yellow or white decorated as shown on right in photo. Left lily wall pocket pictured has unusual light pink glaze color. Standard, $70.00 – 100.00. Rare color, $150.00 – 200.00.

Clown Wall Pocket. 8" long. 1940s. McCoy mark. Shown with two colors of cold paint decoration. Gray is quite rare. Red decoration, $100.00 – 150.00. Gray color, $150.00 – 200.00

Lady with Bonnet. 8" long. 1940s. McCoy mark. Wall pocket pictured with red polka dot pattern was production decoration. Other pieces shown were not standard decoration. $50.00 – 125.00.

Lady with Bonnet Wall Pocket. Same as normal piece of pottery but with very special decoration. Was cold painted and signed by over 30 employees as a get-well gift on Valentine's Day. Dated 1944. $400.00 – 500.00.

Clock Wall Pocket. Mid 1950s. McCoy mark. Body of piece is about 8" long. Made in several production glaze color combinations. This example is a non-production white with black decoration under glaze. Standard glazes, $125.00–150.00; white, $200.00 – 250.00.

Violin Wall Pocket. 10¼". Mid 1950s. McCoy mark. Production glazes included brown, aqua, white, and tan. Pictured in photo is a black glaze which is rare. Brown or aqua glazes, $100.00 – 150.00; white or tan, $150.00 – 200.00; black, $200.00 – 250.00.

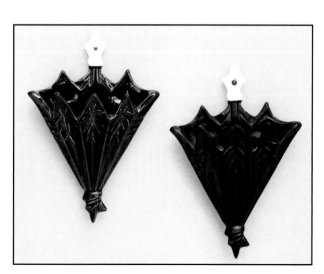

Left & above: Umbrella Wall Pockets. 8¾" x 6". Mid 1950s. McCoy mark. Production glaze colors were gloss green, yellow, and black. Later a gold color was produced as part of the Sunburst line. Pictured above is an uncommon white color with the similar drip finish as that of the Sunburst gold glaze. Left is the standard gloss black pictured with a non-production matte black finish. Gloss glazes, $60.00 – 75.00; white or gold, $75.00 – 95.00; matte black, $175.00 – 225.00.

Vases with applied bud. 5¾" tall. Late 1940s. Marked McCoy. Both styles came in white, pink, or yellow gloss decorated glazes as shown on pieces in middle of photo. Outer pieces in photo have non-production glazes. Both vase shapes are of equal value.
Production glazes, $35.00 – 45.00; Non-production glazes, $100.00 – 125.00.

Feather Vase. 8½" tall. 1954. No mark. Note photo of bottom; you will find other similar non-McCoy vases but bottom will be completely flat and glazed. Variety of glaze colors. $50.00 – 65.00.

Goose with Cart. 8" x 4¾". 1940s. Note as pictured, NM or McCoy mark. Of course the NM marked piece would be the older style. Variety of glaze colors. $35.00 – 45.00.

Popular Heart Vase with little cupid print, "What About Me?" 6" tall. No mark. Wide variety of matte and gloss glazes made. Note in the top "V" area of each vase pictured, the one on the left has a "tab" in that spot and the other does not. The style with no tab is harder to find. $50.00 – 75.00.

Rare examples of special decoration on Heart Vases. $200.00 – 300.00.

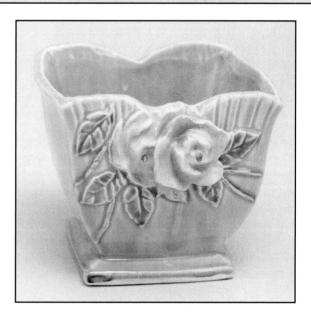

Small Wild Rose Vase in another non-production glaze color. 6½" tall. McCoy mark. $100.00 – 125.00.

Small Wild Rose Jardiniere in non-production glaze color. 4" x 4". Early 1950s. McCoy mark. See our Volume I book for complete line of six wild rose shapes and examples of the four production glazes made. $75.00 – 100.00.

Dutch Shoe Planter. 7½" long. Late 1940s. Marked McCoy. As you can see, made in a wide variety of glaze colors. $25.00 – 50.00.

Dutch Shoe Planter. 7½" long. 1953. Marked McCoy. Much harder to find than the style above. $30.00 – 60.00.

Above & right: Cope Monkey Planter. Not a catalog item. When this hard-to-find piece is found, it is with a white gloss glaze with cold paint decoration if the paint has survived (see Volume I). 5½". No mark. The above example is a very rare glaze decoration with brown highlighting. The example on the right is a standard white glaze piece which Leslie Cope personally decorated for a collector in 1994. (Note signature and date on ear.)
Brown glaze, $200.00 – 250.00.
Cope decorated, $400.00 – 500.00.

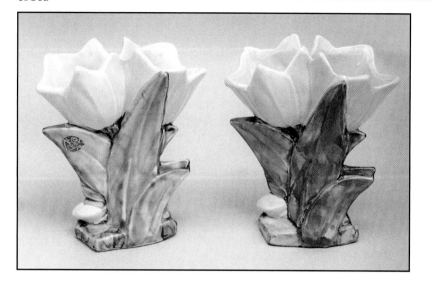

Double Tulip Vase with yellow decoration. 8" tall. Late 1940s. Marked McCoy. As pictured, this yellow decoration came in a matte (left) and gloss version (right). $85.00 – 110.00 each.

Double Tulip Vase, white with red tipping decoration. 8" tall. Late 1940s. Marked McCoy. As shown, this decoration came in a gloss finish with brilliant red decoration (left) and a matte glaze with a soft pink tipping (right). $85.00 – 110.00 each.

The original Double Tulip Vase was released for sale in the late 1940s and sold well into the 1950s. This same vase is the one pictured on the left. In 1967, when Mount Clemens Pottery Co. bought Nelson McCoy Pottery, they reissued this previously very successful vase in that year except marked the bottom with "USA 640" instead of the "McCoy" mark. (See bottom photo.) With the two vases together, you can see the 1967 issue actually has more of a cream-based color than off white. These vases are actually more scarce than the older style.
Original style, $85.00 – 110.00.
1967 issue, $85.00 – 110.00.

Hyacinth Vase. 8" tall. 1950. McCoy mark. There were three standard glazes; pink, blue, and lavender. The standard blue is pictured on the left in the photo. On the right is a beautiful non-production glaze, almost a lavender of sorts with dark highlighting.
Standard glaze, $100.00 – 125.00.
Non-production glaze, $150.00 – 200.00.

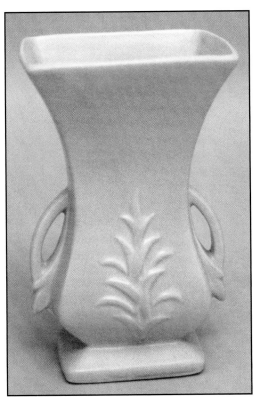

Vase. 8¼" tall. Late 1940s. McCoy mark. These two vases above were sold in a wide variety of matte & gloss glazes. NOTE: Ears on handles of bottom vase are down while those of the upper vase are up. This does not produce a difference in value, but it sure is interesting from the point of view of the collector! $30.00 – 50.00.

10" Vase. 1940s. McCoy mark. This vase was sold in a variety of matte pastel glazes. It has also been found in two examples of wonderful multiple glaze colors. The left, looking rather like a Hull Pottery glaze, is a little harder to find than the right which is similar to the Rustic glazes of the late 1940s.
Standard pastel glaze (not pictured), $95.00 – 125.00.
Rustic style glaze, $95.00 – 125.00.
Pink/green "Hull"-like glaze, $125.00 – 150.00.

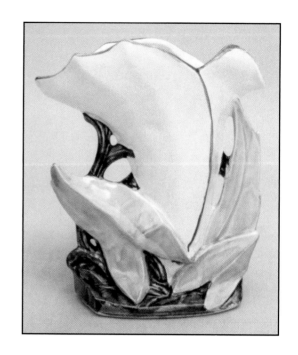

Vase with Contrasting Leaf. 9" tall. Mid 1950s. McCoy mark. The standard glazes are chartreuse or shrimp over-drip with a green leaf. (See Volume I, pg. 144.) The above example of black with an orange leaf is very rare.
Standard glaze, $100.00 – 125.00.
Rare glaze, $200.00 – 250.00.

Wide Lily Vase. 8½" tall. Mid 1950s. McCoy mark. The glazes usually found are a gloss white with green leaves in matte white with matte blue leaves. The above example is a white vase with gloss blue leaves which is very uncommon.
Standard glaze, $300.00 – 400.00.
Rare glaze, $400.00 – 500.00.

Sunflower Vase. 9" tall. Mid 1950s. No mark. The standard glazes were a variety of of solid colors. The above example is a very rare Sunflower Vase with a bright selection of colors.
Standard glaze, $40.00 – 60.00.
Rare glaze, $200.00 – 300.00.

Tall Fan Vase. 14½" tall. Mid 1950s. McCoy mark. The standard glazes are green or yellow with a decorated foot of green or brown respectively. The above uncommon example is green with brown.
Standard glaze, $150.00 – 200.00.
Odd glaze, $200.00 – 250.00.

Above right & left and below right: Planter Bookends. 6¼" x 5½" each. 1953. Marked McCoy. Green leaves with yellow flower, and gray leaves with maroon flower were the catalog glaze combinations. Also found with a bit more difficulty is the beige/brown leaves with green flower. The three photos contain combinations that are yet another degree more difficult to obtain. Catalog combinations, $90.00 – 125.00. Beige/brown leaves with green flower, $125.00 – 150.00.
Glaze color combinations pictured, $200.00 – 250.00.

Vase with Ivy. 6" size. Late 1950s. McCoy mark. Rare piece. $250.00 – 300.00

Large & Small Centerpiece Planters. Mid 1950s. McCoy mark. Large, 12" x 6". Small, 8" x 4". The glaze color combinations on the example of the large centerpiece include a very vivid red which is not a production color. The glaze on the small centerpiece is one of the standard glaze combinations.
Large Centerpiece, $65.00 – 80.00.
Small Centerpiece, $40.00 – 50.00.

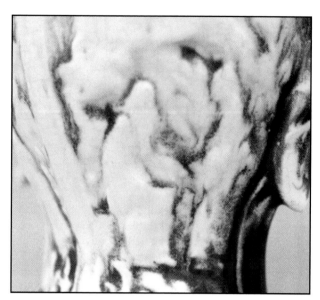

Handled Vase. 9" tall. 1945. McCoy mark. This piece was released the same year as the Rustic Line. Look closely! Can you see the image of the Oriental figures? $70.00 – 90.00.

Fish Jardiniere. 7½". 1958. McCoy mark. Standard glaze is a beige color base with brown or green spray. See "Top 100 Section" for photos and values. The example pictured is a non-cataloged turquoise/blue heavy spray. This is even more difficult to find for a collection. $300.00 – 350.00.

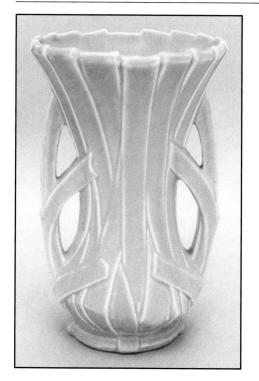

Vase. 8" tall. Late 1940s. McCoy mark. Very similar to a body design on a production pitcher of the same period, this vase was not a cataloged piece, Very rare. $200.00 – 300.00.

Large Double Handled Vase. 12" tall. 1947. McCoy mark. Made for several years in a wide variety of gloss glazes. This example is very unusual in that it is a matte aqua glaze.
Standard glaze, $85.00 – 110.00.
Aqua glaze, $150.00 – 200.00.

Wheelbarrow with Rooster Planter. 10½" x 7". 1955. Marked McCoy. Produced with three different color combinations: green wheelbarrow with yellow rooster; yellow with brown; and white with black. The example to the right is an unusual combination, not cataloged.
Standard combo, $100.00 – 125.00.
Unusual combo, $125.00 – 175.00.

Also pictured: Bear Planter, 5½" x 7". McCoy mark. Made in brown glaze as shown as well as a yellow color. $125.00 – 150.00.

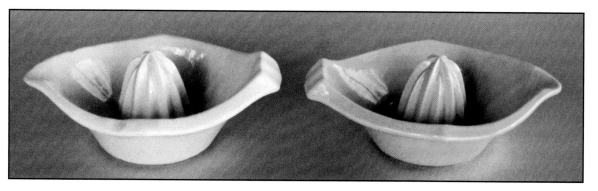

Reamer. 8" long. 1949. Yellow or white. $60.00 – 75.00.

Tall Vases

No. 316—10½ x 8½"
Fan Vase
White, Yellow, Green
Packed 1 Doz. Wt. 42 lbs.
$6.00 per Dozen

No. 324—13½ x 10" Vase
White, Green Agate, Black
Packed 1/3 Doz. Wt. 28 lbs.
$14.40 per Dozen

No. 46—12" Vase
White and Green Gloss
Packed ½ Doz. Wt. 34 lbs.
$9.60 per Dozen

No. 409P—12"
Vase—Gloss Finish
Green, Yellow, White
Packed ½ Doz. Wt. 22 lbs.
$9.00 per Dozen

No. 327—14" Cat Vase
White, Black, Gray Matt
Packed ½ Doz. Wt. 28 lbs.
$12.00 per Dozen

No. 328—14" Footed Vase
White, Green, Fawn
Packed ½ Doz. Wt. 28 lbs.
$12.00 per Dozen

No. 332—12" Vase
White, Gray, Yellow
Packed ½ Doz. Wt. 29 lbs.
$10.80 per Dozen

No. 85—Vase
Sizes 10"-12"-14"
Green, White
10"—$ 6.00 per Doz.   1 Doz. 42 lbs.
12"—$ 9.00 per Doz.   ½ Doz. 37 lbs.
14"—$13.50 per Doz.   ½ Doz. 44 lbs.

9

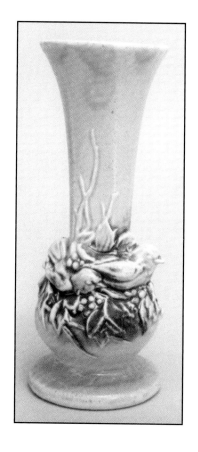

Snowman Planter. 6" x 4". 1940s. Marked McCoy. White with black or red decoration. The red is just a little harder to find. $60.00 – 75.00.

Uncle Sam Vase. 7½" tall. Early 1940s. McCoy mark. Glaze colors are white, yellow, or green. Finding an example with cold paint is a real prize. $50.00 – 75.00.

Bud Vase. 8" tall. 1950. McCoy mark. Blended green and brown spray. $35.00 – 50.00.

Shell Planter. 5" x 4". 1955. No mark. Usual glazes are yellow or green. Pink & brown shown are quite rare.
Yellow or green, $15.00 – 20.00.
Pink or brown, $50.00 – 60.00.

Rolling Pin with Boy Blue Planter. 7½". 1952. Green or yellow decorated. You can see slight variations in decoration colors have been found. $60.00 – 75.00.

Fisherman Planter. 6" x 4½". 1957. McCoy mark. Standard glaze brown spray with yellow or green interior. $150.00 – 200.00. This piece was personally decorated by designer, Leslie Cope, dated 1984. $500.00 – 600.00.

The Sports Planters Line included two styles of cars with the same brown spray glaze. 9½" x 4½". No mark. $60.00 – 80.00.

Sand Butterfly pattern in the same brown spray glaze as the Sports Planters. However, this was part of a line called Chocolate Bisque advertised in 1958 which, in addition to the sports planters and cars, had six other planter & pot shapes.

Rodeo Cowboy Planters. 7¾" x 4". 1956. McCoy mark. Both styles come in either of the two glaze combinations pictured: orange tan with brown spray, or ivory with green & brown spray. $150.00 – 200.00 The McCoy mark on the Bucking Bronco style is always backwards (above photo).

Plow Boy Planter. 8" x 7". 1955. McCoy mark. Brown blend standard glazes as shown. $100.00 – 125.00.

A very special hand decorated example of the Plow Boy Planter. $250.00 – 350.00.

The Plow Boy Planter in a non-cataloged solid green glaze. $125.00 – 150.00.

Liberty Bell Planter. 10" x 8¼". McCoy mark. Standard glaze coloring, ivory/green decorated. Planter can be found with the "4th of July" and the "8th of July" marking. The 4th marking seems to be a bit tougher to find but not enough for different values. The planter has also been found in a non-cataloged solid green.
Standard glazes, $200.00 – 250.00, Solid green, $250.00 – 300.00.

Spring Wood

A hand decorated Dogwood pattern on a group of distinctively styled Jardinieres, Vases and Planters finished in satin glazes of pink, white, and mint green.

1910 - 6½"

1912 - 8"

1915 - 10½"

1917B–10" Jardiniere with Brass Stand. overall Height 20½"

1911 - 7"

1913 - 7½"

1916 - 9¼"x6¼"

1914 - 8½"

1917 - 10"

THE NELSON McCOY POTTERY COMPANY

Factory - Office   **Roseville, Ohio**

Printed in U.S.A.

LITHOGRAPHY BY PAPPAS BROS. PARKERSBURG, W.

Original Spring Wood catalog page from the 1960 Nelson McCoy Pottery Company catalog.

Cascade

New designs decorated with iridescent colors, coordinated to harmonize with any color theme - Moderately priced.

1501 - 6¼"

1506 - 7"

1504 - 9"x7"

1503 - 7½"

1503 - 7½"

1505 - 9"

1502 - 5"

1507 - 10½"x7½"

THE NELSON McCOY POTTERY COMPANY
Factory - Office   Roseville, Ohio

Printed in U.S.A.

LITHOGRAPHY BY PAPPAS BROS., PARKERSBURG, W. VA.

Original Cascade catalog page from the 1960 Nelson McCoy Pottery Company catalog.

The two versions of the Swan Vase. The white one was produced in 1948 and the other in 1956. Both marked McCoy. The older one is more common and is valued at $40.00 – 50.00. The newer version is more rare and has a value of $50.00 – 60.00.

1940s Double Duck Planter in uncommon lavender color. $35.00 – $40.00.

Green Antelope Centerpiece. 1955. Also produced with a black base. $250.00 – 350.00.

Selection of the 1957 Cook-Serve line that was made as Yellow Ovenproof ware. There were 12 different pieces produced with red cherries, green leaves & brown stems.
Pint Covered Casserole, $60.00 – 80.00.
Six-Cup Beverage Jug, $60.00 – 80.00.
10 oz. French Casserole, $45.00 – 60.00.
Cream & Covered Sugar Set, $60.00 – 80.00.

Fawn Planters. 12½" x 8". 1954. Shown in chartreuse with the very rare black & brown colored deer. $300.00 – 350.00.
More common hand decorated natural color shown in Volume I, page 203. $250.00 – 300.00.

Bird Dog Planters. 12½" x 8½". 1954. Also shown in chartreuse with black or brown dogs. These are difficult to find in this unusual color combination. $250.00 – 300.00.
Shown on page 203, Volume I, in natural colors.

Green Spinning Wheel Planter. 7¼" x 7¼" and 6¾" x 6". 1953. Hand decorated white dog. $30.00 – 40.00. Green Wishing Well Planter. Marked McCoy. $30.00 – 40.00.

Green Twin Swans Planter. 8½". 1953. Marked McCoy. Was first made in yellow or white; the green is not a common color. $50.00 – 60.00.

Poodle Planter. 7½" x7½". 1956. Unusual pink & white color. McCoy mark. $100.00 – 150.00.

Rabbit & Stump. 5½". Pink & blue. 1951. $100.00 – 125.00 Natural color on page 154, Volume I.

Baby Crib Planter. 1954. Two colors produced with no mark, pink or blue. $60.00 – 70.00.

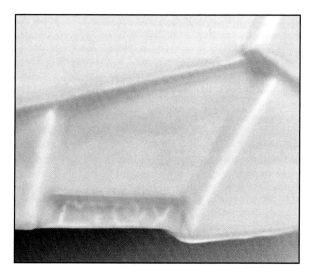

Planter. 8" x 4". 1953. Pink, yellow, green & aqua. McCoy mark as shown on the right. Note the location of the mark. $30.00 – 40.00.

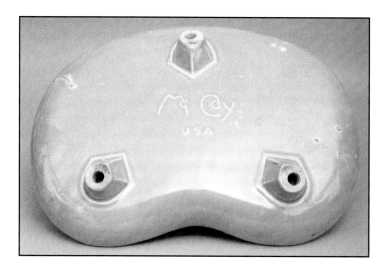

Could be the largest McCoy mark ever used, 4½"x2½".

Covered Casserole. 6½". 1953. Ivory, brown, turquoise, and chartreuse. $30.00 – 50.00.

Pedestal Planter. 9" x 4½". 1950s. McCoy mark. $20.00 – 30.00.

We have been told that the McCoy Bird Bath was produced in response to the success the Ransbottom Bird Baths had enjoyed. The McCoy Bird Bath, however, did not sell very well and was quickly discontinued. The short production time makes it rare.

Bird Bath. 1960s. Speckled white. With legs. $175.00 – 200.00

Bird Bath. 18" x 13". Blue or speckled white. $175.00 – 200.00.

Three-piece Cabbage Range Set. 1954. Consists of 7" Grease Jar and 4" Salt & Pepper Shakers with corks.
Shakers, $75.00 – 100.00.
Cabbage Grease Jar, $100.00 – 125.00.

Three-piece Set with 5½" Cucumber Salt & Bell Pepper Shakers with corks. 1954.
Shakers, $75.00 – 100.00.
Cabbage Grease Jar, $100.00 – 125.00.

1959 Antique Rose Line

Produced in white or two-tone brown with flecked blue (page 91). Decorated in an old-fashioned moss rose pattern and trimmed in bright gold.
7½" Swan. McCoy mark. $50.00 $60.00.
Low Flower Bowl. 12" x 7½". $45.00 – 55.00.
Flower Bowl. 9½" x 6½". $40.00 – 50.00.
Pitcher Vase. 9" tall. McCoy mark. $35.00 – 40.00.

Sprinkling Can Planter. 7" x 6". McCoy mark.
$50.00 – 60.00.

Brown & Flecked Blue Low Flower Bowl. $45.00 – 55.00.

Brown Antique Rose, 1959

10-Cup Coffee Pot. $40.00 – 45.00.
Low Bowl. $10.00 – 15.00.
Swan, 7½". $50.00 – 60.00.

12" Planting Dish. $30.00 – 45.00.
10" Vase. $40.00 – 45.00.
36 oz. Tea Pot. $40.00 – 50.00.

10" Low Bowl. $20.00 – 25.00.
Covered Casserole. $35.00 – 45.00.

Harmony

900 - 6"   904 - 6"   905 - 7"

Hand decorated modernistic designs. Simple lines that accent the floral arrangement. Priced for volume sales at a profit.

902 - 8½"   901 - 9¼"   907 - 7½"

908 - 12"   906 - 9¼"   903 - 12"

Original Harmony catalog page from the 1960 Nelson McCoy Pottery Company catalog.

Harmony Selection, 1960

12" Planter, $25.00 – 35.00. 8½" Planter, $25.00 – 30.00. 9¼". Planter $20.00 – 25.00.
All the Harmony is marked McCoy.

6" Planter. $15.00 – 20.00. 6" Vase. $15.00 – 20.00. 9¼" Vase. $20.00 – 25.00. 7" Vase. $20.00 – 25.00.

12" Vase. Hand decorated. McCoy mark. $30.00 – 40.00.
7½" Jardiniere. McCoy mark. $40.00 – 50.00.

Biscuit Jar. $35.00 – 40.00.
12" Centerpiece. Esmond mark. $35.00 – 40.00.

The Esmond mark on the Biscuit Jar.

Coffee Mug. $10.00 – 12.00.
5¼" Napkin Holder. $35.00 – 45.00.

Esmond by McCoy Pottery.
Beverage Server & Stand. $40.00 – 60.00.
Coffee Server. 7". Esmond mark. $30.00 – 40.00.
Covered Sugar. 2¾" x 5". $25.00 – 30.00.

Large Bowl. $20.00 – 30.00. Utility Bowl. $25.00 – 30.00. Photo above right shows Esmond marks on Bowls.

Pots & Saucers. 1953. Pictured in all seven colors & all sizes made. 3½", $12.00 – 15.00; 4½", $15.00 – 20.00; 5½", $15.00 – 25.00; 6½", $20.00 – 30.00. All marked McCoy.

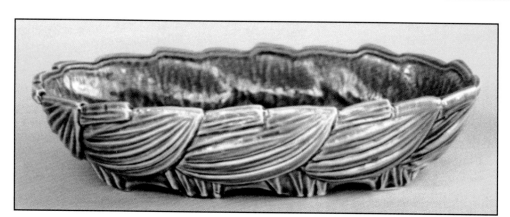

Centerpiece available in yellow or green. 10½" x 7". 1955. McCoy mark. $40.00 – 50.00.

Garden Club

Fan Vase. 7½" x 7". $60.00 – 70.00.

Planter. 5¾" x 4¾". $25.00 – 35.00.

Pillow Vase. 5½" x 4". $20.00 – 25.00.
Pitcher Vase. 8" tall. $20.00 – 30.00.
Planter. 7½" x 3½". $20.00 – 25.00.

Flower Pot. 6½". $15.00 – 20.00.
Tall Pedestal Vase. 12". $30.00 – 40.00.

Large Vase. 9½" x 11". $80.00 – 100.00.
Pot with Saucer. 7½". $20.00 – 25.00.

*All pieces on this page are dated
1958 and marked McCoy.*

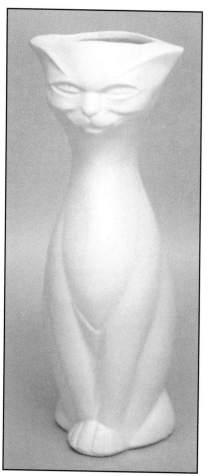

14" Cat Vase. 1960. McCoy mark. Pictured in the three available colors: black, gray matte, and white. These vases were only made for a short time, are very collectible and sought after by collectors. $200.00 – 250.00.

Chromoveil Pot & Saucer. 5" or 6". 1956. White, yellow, pink, or green. $20.00 – 40.00.

Cat Tea Pot. 1969. $95.00 – 150.00. Beware of German look-alike.

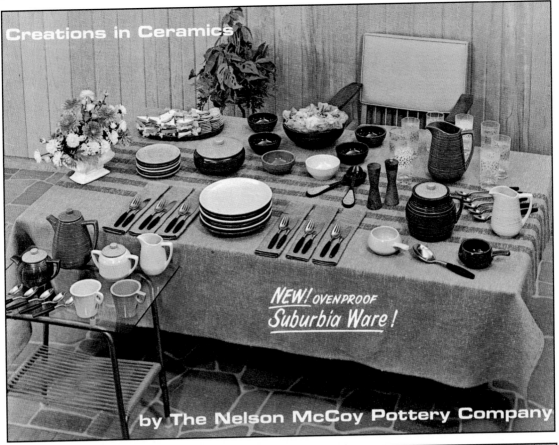

Two wonderful 1960s catalog pages from the Nelson McCoy Pottery.
Top: Suburbia Ware. Bottom: The Artisan Line.

Jardiniere. 1960. Available sizes: 8½", 10½", and 12½". Colors: white, green, and yellow. McCoy mark.
8½". $20.00 – 30.00.
10½". $30.00 – 50.00.
12½". (shown) $50.00 – 75.00.

Two pieces of the 1960 Artisan Line in green. Other colors: white, yellow, and blue.
6"x6" Arrangement Vase. Marked McCoy. $30.00 – 40.00.
6¼" Bud Vase. $25.00 – 30.00.

1962 Swirl Line Pieces. Colors: White, orchid (shown), tangerine, black satin, aqua, lemon yellow, and green. McCoy mark. From left:
7" Jardiniere. $20.00 – 25.00.
6" Jardiniere. $20.00 – 25.00.
6" Vase. $20.00 – 25.00.
8" Vase. $25.00 – 35.00.

Antique Curio Five Finger Vase. 1962. Mold has leaves on only one side, but it is more common to have leaves on both sides. McCoy mark. $60.00 – 75.00.
For the complete line, see page 266, Volume I.

Jardiniere. 10½". 1960. McCoy mark. Available in seven sizes from 4½" to 10½". White, green, and tangerine. Just the right size (10½") for 3-month-old Laine Whaley. $15.00 – 75.00 depending on size.

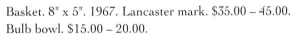

Basket. 8" x 5". 1967. Lancaster mark. $35.00 – 45.00. Bulb bowl. $15.00 – 20.00.

1954 Flower Pots in all the available colors & sizes. Green, blue, maroon, and yellow. 4½", 5½", 7½", and 8½". McCoy mark. $20.00 – 50.00.

Wonderful 6½" Hanging Basket. No mark. $45.00 – 60.00.

10" Jardiniere. $35.00 – 45.00.
13" Vase. $30.00 – $40.00.
Both pieces have a McCoy mark.

Three sizes of Jardinieres.
All three have a McCoy mark.
5". $15.00 – $20.00.
8". $25.00 – $35.00.
10". $35.00 – $45.00.

All pieces on this page are from the 1962 Vesta Line. Colors produced were white, yellow, green, black, lilac, and apricot. Decorated in gold.

Colorful Turkey Platter. 19". 1960s. $80.00 – 100.00.

Decorating with McCoy Planters can be rewarding. Planting Dish. 8¼" x 3½". 1954. McCoy mark. Yellow or gray with decorated foot. $20.00 – 25.00.

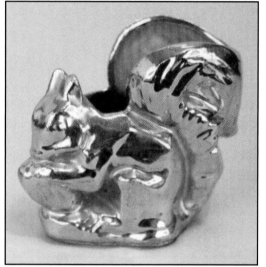

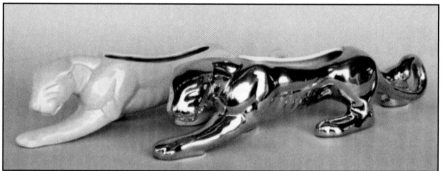

1955 Squirrel Planter. Rare gold example. $75.00 – 100.00.

Panthers. 1950. No mark. Rare gold example. $70.00 – 90.00. Chartreuse, $40.00 – 60.00.

Shell Centerpiece. 10¾" x 9½". 1955. No mark. Yellow, salmon, and chartreuse. Hard to find. $60.00 – 75.00.

6½" White Brocade Fancy Vase. Same shape as in Sunburst at left. McCoy mark. $40.00 – 50.00.

Top photo: Sunburst gold pieces. 1957. McCoy mark. 24K stamp in circle.
Left to right: 6" Pitcher Vase. $40.00 – 50.00.
5½" Flower Bowl. $30.00 – 40.00.
6" Pedestal Vase. $35.00 – 40.00.

Bottom Photo: 5¾" Vase, $35.00– $40.00.
6½" Fancy Vase. $40.00 – 50.00.

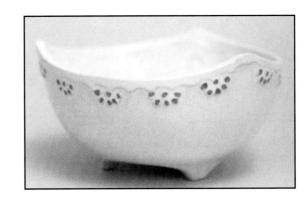

Early American Line Footed Bowl. 7" x 3½". 1967. McCoy mark. $30.00 – 40.00.

Basket Line Vase. 8". 1959. McCoy mark. $40.00 – 50.00. 10½" Basket. $50.00 – 60.00.

Early American Planter. 7½" x 4". McCoy mark. $20.00 – 25.00.
Early American Vase. 9" x 6". McCoy mark. $40.00 – 50.00.

Floral Country

9.00   0153 0829
Sconce

0148 0800
Nightstick Candle Holder

9.00   0151 0829
Matchbox Holder

0704 0800
Candlesticks

7.00   0146 0829
Wall Pocket

0150 0829
Utensil Holder

0147 0 29
Chamber Tray

Candles not included.
Utensils not included.

7531 0829
9 x 10½" Pitcher & Bowl

7533 0829
6 x 7½" Pitcher & Bowl

13

Original 1982 Nelson McCoy Floral Country catalog page.

Blue Country

0153 5300
Sconce

0148 5300
Nightstick Candle Holder

0151 5300
Matchbox Holder

0704 5300
Candlesticks

0146 5300
Wall Pocket

0150 5300
Utensil Holder

0147 5300
Chamber Tray

Candles not included.
Utensils not included.

7531 5300
9 x 10½" Pitcher & Bowl

7533 5300
6 x 7½" Pitcher & Bowl

12

Original 1982 Nelson McCoy Blue Country catalog page.

FLORALINE

Introduced in 1960 for the sole purpose of selling to the florist industry, Floraline was immediately very successful for McCoy. The simple molds and limited glazes also made the line very profitable. Marked Floraline USA.

Floraline Advertising Ashtray with old pipe & matches. $40.00 – 50.00.

Floraline Rectangular Vases. Marked Floraline.
8" tall. $20.00 – 25.00.
7" tall. $15.00 – 20.00.

Pillow Vase. $20.00 – 25.00.
5" Vase. $15.00 – 20.00.
4" Vase. $15.00 – 20.00.

Top: 4" Pedestal Vase. $18.00 – 22.00.
5" Round Vase. $15.00 – 20.00.
4" Round Vase. $15.00 – 20.00.

Bottom: Floraline Pedestal Vases.
4", 5", and 6". $10.00 – 20.00 each.

Caterpillar Planter. $30.00 – 40.00.
4" x 4" Square Baby Blocks. Pink or blue.
$20.00 – 30.00.

Green Caterpillar Planter. 13½"
long. $30.00 – 40.00.
Red Floraline Jardiniere. 9" across.
$30.00 – 40.00.

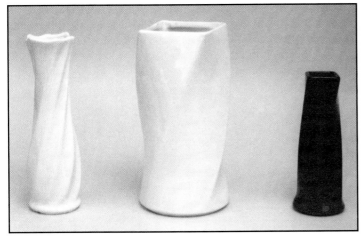

8½" Spiral Vase. $25.00 – 30.00.
9" Twist Vase. $25.00 – 30.00.
6½" Twist Vase. $20.00 – 25.00.

3½" Flower Bowl. $15.00 – 20.00.
9" Green Vase. $20.00 – 25.00.
5" Planter. $15.00 – 20.00.

6" Pillow Vase. $20.00 – 25.00.
9¼" Round Vase. $15.00 – 20.00.

11½" Jardiniere. Fergie not included. White, green, or black. $50.00 – 70.00.

8" x 4" Pebble Planter. $15.00 – 20.00.

Floraline mark on the Goblet Vase.

10¼" Green Vase. $25.00 – 35.00. Flower Basket. $35.00 – 45.00.

6½" Goblet Vase. $15.00 – 25.00.

3" Pedestal Vase. $10.00 – 15.00.
6" Mug Vase. $15.00 – 25.00.
5" Oval Planter. $15.00 – 20.00.

9¼" Round Vase. White, green, or
black. $15.00 – 20.00.

7½" Pedestal Urn. $15.00 – 25.00.
6" Round Vase. $10.00 – 15.00.
9" Pedestal Urn. $20.00 – 25.00.

8½" Vase. $20.00 – 30.00.
8" Round Vase. $20.00 – 25.00.
9" Green Diamond Design Vase. $25.00 –
30.00.

Floraline Auto Planter. 8" x 3½". $25.00 – 35.00

Floraline Madonna Planter. 7" x 6". Rare find. $175.00 – 225.00.

Double Mum Pot. 13½" x 5½". $25.00 – 30.00. Pinched Pot. 4". $15.00 – 20.00.

Bird on Flower Branch Shoe Planter. 8". $30.00 – 40.00.

Oval Candleholder Centerpiece. 15". $35.00 – 40.00.

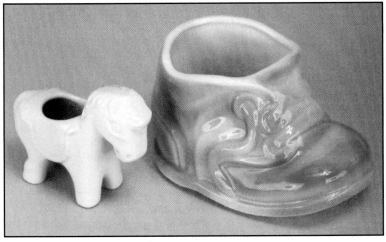

Horse Planter. 5" x 3¾". $15.00 – 20.00.
Baby Shoe Planter. 8". $40.00 – 50.00.
(Horse planter shown for size comparison.)

3" x 5" Baby Planter. $25.00 – 30.00.

Floraline Animal Planters
Dog. 4½" x 3". $10.00 – 15.00.
Horse. 5" x 3¾". $15.00 – 20.00.
Turtle. 5¼" x 3¼". $12.00 – 18.00.
Bear. 5" x 3½". $10.00 – 15.00.

Large 10¼" Vase. $25.00 – $35.00.
7" Hourglass Vase. $20.00 – $25.00.

Over 70 Years of Craftsmanship

Even in today's highly mechanized world some things must be done by hand. At Nelson McCoy Pottery there are many talented workers using skills that have been handed down through the ages to bring you a truly hand crafted work of art.

Photo of company flyer showing production of the Floraline Turtle.

8" White Jardiniere. $25.00 – 35.00.
10" Centerpiece. $20.00 – 25.00.

10¼" x 8" Donkey Planter. Brown, black, and white. $50.00 – 60.00.
8" Vase with Tassels. $20.00 – 25.00.

Vase. 7". $15.00 – 20.00.
Goblet Vase. 4". $10.00 – 15.00.
Boat Bowl. 10". $15.00 – 20.00.

Square Vase. 4". $8.00 – 12.00.
Centerpiece. 5". $15.00 – 25.00.
Jardiniere. 4". $8.00 – 10.00.

Pedestal Vase. 4". $8.00 – 10.00.
Square Vase. 4". $8.00 – 10.00.
Goblet Vase. 6". $18.00 – 25.00.

Horticulture

0290 0873
14 oz. Happy Face Mug

0290 2073
14 oz. Happy Face Mug

0386 2073
Smile Pot and Saucer

0373 0100
5½" Pot and Saucer

0372 0100
4½" Pot and Saucer

0374 0100
6½" Pot and Saucer

0375 0100
7½" Pot and Saucer

3001 7900
6½ x 4½" Planter

22

Original early 1980s Nelson McCoy Horticulture catalog page.

GOLD TRIM

Gold Trim pieces were most likely trimmed in gold by someone other than McCoy as discussed in our Volume I, page 180. There are many collectors of Gold Trim McCoy pottery, hence the values have risen sharply during the past couple of years. The pieces can be beautiful and great fun to collect. The trim is done in 23K gold by hand, so there are no two pieces exactly alike.

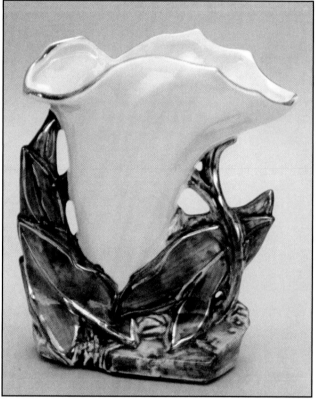

Above is a very beautiful 1955 Yellow Poppy Vase with Gold Trim. It has the McCoy mark and was trimmed by the Shafer Company of Zanesville, Ohio. 8½". $1,000.00 – 1,400.00.

Wide Lily Vase. 8½". 1956. McCoy mark. $600.00 – 800.00

Page 115

Top photo: Ivy Vase. 9" tall. 1955. Hand decorated. McCoy mark. $200.00 – 300.00.
Ivy 6 cup. Teapot. 1950s. Hand decorated. McCoy mark. $125.00 – 175.00.
Ivy 8 oz. Creamer. 1950s. Hand decorated. McCoy mark. $40.00 – 50.00.
Ivy 8 oz. Sugar. 1950s. Hand decorated. McCoy mark. $40.00 – 50.00.

Middle photo: 1955. Triple Lily Vase. 8½". White & yellow. McCoy mark. $100.00 – 125.00.

Bottom photo: Wagon Wheel Planter. 12¼" x 4". 1956. McCoy mark. $100.00 – 125.00.
Log Planter. 8½" x 4". 1954. Yellow. McCoy mark. $80.00 – 110.00.

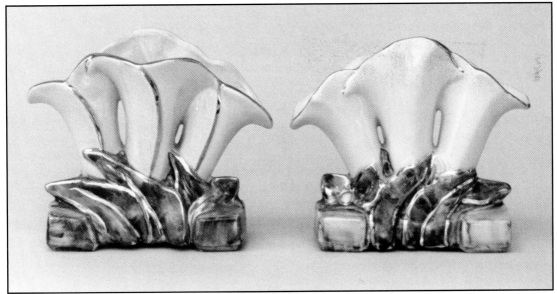

 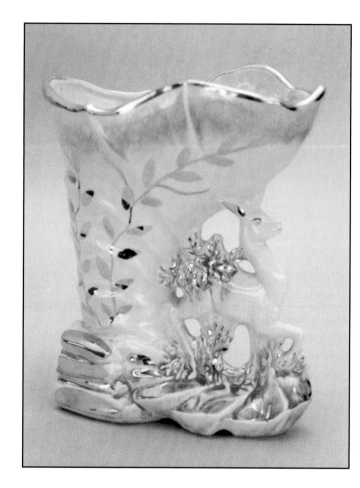

Above are two wonderful examples of the 1954 Fawn Planters with different Gold Trim painting.
9" tall. McCoy mark. $150.00 – 200.00.

Page 117
    Top photo: Burgundy Ball Planter. 3½". 1940s. NM mark. $60.00 – 75.00.
          Lamb Planter. 8½". 1954. McCoy mark. $95.00 – 120.00.

   Middle photo: Yellow Ball Planter. 3½". 1940s. NM mark. $60.00 – 75.00.
          Yellow Log Planter. 7½" x 3½". 1954. McCoy mark. $80.00 – 110.00.

  Bottom photo: Kitten Planter. 7" x 4½". 1953. McCoy mark. $60.00 – 70.00.
          3½" Pot with Saucer. 1953. McCoy mark. $25.00 – 40.00.
          Duck Planter. 8" x 5". 1952. White or yellow. McCoy mark. $50.00 – 65.00.

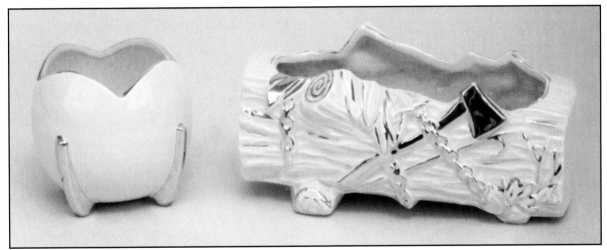

Bird Dog Planter. 12½" x 8½". 1954. McCoy mark. $250.00 – 350.00.

Below: Quail Planter. 7½" x 6". 1955. McCoy mark. $150.00 – 200.00. Twin Shell Planter. 8½". 1956. McCoy mark. $35.00 – 45.00.

Page 119

Top photo: Baby Carriage Planter. 7¾" x 6". 1955. McCoy mark. $100.00 – 120.00.
Hobby Horse Planter. 8" x 6½". 1955. McCoy mark. $100.00 – 125.00.

Middle photo: Low Handle Vase. 9" tall. 1950s. McCoy mark. $85.00 – 120.00.
Cradle Planter. 8½". 1950s. McCoy mark. $100.00 – 125.00.

Bottom photo: Cat Planter. 7" x 4". 1953. McCoy mark. $75.00 – 100.00.
Cowboy Hat Planter. 8" x 3". 1956. McCoy mark. $65.00 – 90.00.

Two fine examples of Gold Trim. Note the different floral decals. 32 oz. Pitcher. 6".
1940s. McCoy mark. $100.00 – 125.00.

Another 1940s Gold Trim Pitcher. 6½" tall, 32 oz.
McCoy mark. Lovely flowers. $150.00 – 200.00.

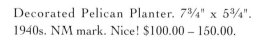
Decorated Pelican Planter. 7¾" x 5¾".
1940s. NM mark. Nice! $100.00 – 150.00.

Swan Vase. 9" high. 1956. McCoy mark. $75.00 – 100.00.
Modern Vase. 9" high. 1951. McCoy mark. $80.00 – 100.00.

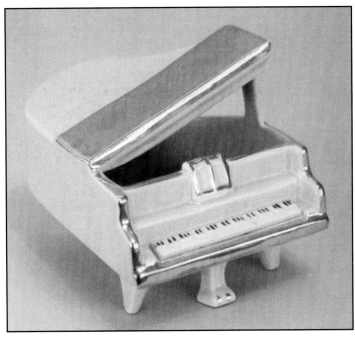

Basket Planter. 9" x 5¼". 1957. McCoy mark. $65.00 – 80.00.

Piano Planter. 5" x 6". 1959. McCoy mark. Exquisite. $150.00 – 200.00

Gondola Candy Boat. 1955. McCoy mark. $60.00 – 75.00.

Wonderful Wheelbarrow with Rooster Planter with Gold Trim. 10½" x 7". 1955. McCoy mark.
$125.00 – 175.00.

Promotional Republican Ashtray. $50.00 – 75.00.

Fancy Lotus Leaf Pot. 4½". 1950. McCoy mark. $40.00 – 50.00.

Wishing Well Planter. 6¾" x 6". 1950. McCoy mark. Gold Trim is hard to see in this photo. $30.00 – 40.00.

Urn Wall Pocket. 6½" x 4½". 1955. McCoy mark. 50.00 – 75.00. Brocade Planter Bowl. 5½" x 4". 1956. McCoy mark. $30.00 – 40.00.

Grape Vase. 9" tall. 1951. Solid gold grapes. McCoy mark. $100.00 – 150.00.

Pear Wall Pocket. 7" x 6". Early 1950s. No mark.
$155.00 – 200.00.

Umbrella Wall Pocket. 8¾" x 6". 1955. No mark.
Great find with Gold Trim. $150.00 – 200.00.

Urn Wall Pocket. 6½" x 4½". 1955.
McCoy mark. $50.00 – 75.00.

Rare Bananas Wall Pocket. 7" x 6".
No mark. $200.00 – 250.00.

Grape Wall Pocket. 7" x 6". Early 1950s. No mark. With great Gold Trim. $200.00 – 250.00.
Red Apple Wall Pocket. 7" x 6". Early 1950s. No mark. Nice addition to any collection! $150.00 – 200.00.

On the following pages, we show what we, Hanson, Nissen, and Hanson (HNH), feel are the top 100 findable pieces of Nelson McCoy Pottery (not including Cookie Jars). The key word in making these selections is FINDABLE. If we did not feel a new collector would have the opportunity to purchase an item within a couple of years, we did not include it in our selection. This rule excludes many wonderful pieces that most collectors are seeking, but we wanted to make the Top 100 a group of great pieces that a new collector could realistically hope to acquire in a reasonable amount of time.

A second criterion of this selection is that a collector is collecting all eras of Nelson McCoy Pottery and not focusing on just one, such as only Wall Pockets, Butterfly, NM, Hobnail, Grecian, etc. We elected to combine some categories into one selection in the photographs. For example, the photo of the Flower Bowl Ornaments carries one number, but shows several pieces. Any one of the pieces within the group photo satisfies that selection for the Top 100.

With these thoughts in mind, have fun going over the HNH Top 100. See how your collection stacks up to the list. The sequence of numbering the Top 100 is based on approximate chronological order.

1. Early Oil Jars with Handles. No mark. Blended & matte glazes. Beautiful. 18", $300.00 – 400.00. 15", $250.00 – 300.00.

2. Jardiniere & Pedestal Set, pictured in all the glazes known to be produced. Brown & green onyx, white, matte green, and brown & green matte. No marks. Jardiniere, 8½". Pedestal, 12½". $250.00 – 350.00.

3. Sand Butterfly 20" Sand Jar. No mark. Pictured in matte green (with Fergie). Also aqua, white, and brown matte. $450.00 – 600.00.

4. Double Handle Vase. 12" high. 1940s. Variety of colors. $100.00 – 150.00.

5. Vase with Leaves. 12" high. 1930s. Matte colors. $200.00 – 300.00.

6. Lizard Handle Vase. 9" & 10" high. Matte colors. $300.00 – 400.00. (No marks on these vases.)

Page 129:
7. Floor Vase. 1930s & 40s. Also known as the "Sand Dollar Vase." 14" high. In addition to the glazes pictured, this vase was also made in medium blue, dark blue, and early matte green. Don't try this at home! $250.00 – 350.00.

8. Jardiniere & Pedestal Sets with 7" Jardiniere & 6½" Pedestal. Also known as the Stubby or Berries & Leaves Stubby sets. 1930s & 1940s. No mark. $200.00 – 250.00.

9. 1940s Umbrella Stand. 19" high. Available in natural, matte & gloss glazes. Muffy really likes these Umbrella Stands. No mark. $250.00 – 350.00.

10. Low Sand Butterfly Porch Jar. 11" size. No mark. $175.00 – 225.00. The older pieces are not marked, but the newer ones have the McCoy mark.

 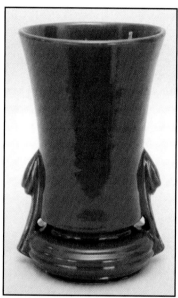

11. Floor Vase. 12" high. 1940s. No mark $90.00 – 125.00.

12. Porch Jar. 11" x 9½". 1940s. Marked NM. White & green. Nice! $150.00 – 200.00.

13. Basketweave pattern Jardiniere & Pedestal. 8½" Jardiniere with 12½" Pedestal and 10½" Jardiniere with 18½" Pedestal. Great display. Small size, $250.00 – 350.00. Large size, $450.00 – 550.00.

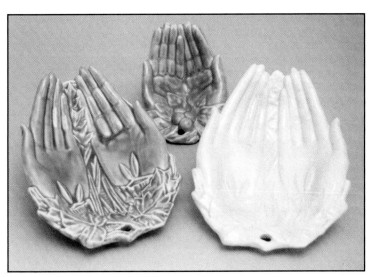

14. Novelty Hands Tray. 8½". NM mark. $100.00 – 125.00. (5¾", $35.00 – 50.00, shown for size comparison, not part of Top 100.)

15. Backwards Bird Planter. NM mark. $50.00 – 60.00.

16. Oil Jars. 12". 1930s. NM mark. Various glazes. $125.00 – 200.00.

17. Lion Planter. 8¾" x 4". 1940s. NM mark. Pastel colors. $80.00 – 110.00.

18. Horse with Holder. 7" x 5". 1940s. NM mark. Pastel colors. $75.00 – 90.00.

19. Dogs with Holder. 7" x 5". 1940s. NM mark. Pastel colors. $60.00 – 75.00.

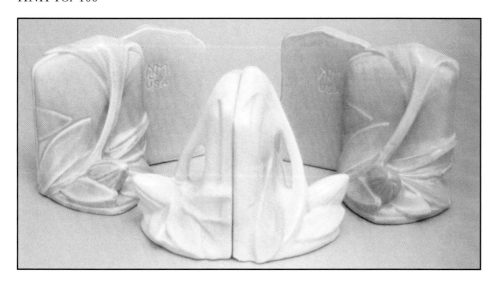

20. Lily Bud Bookends. 5¾". 1940s. NM mark. Pastel colors. $150.00 – 200.00.

21. Bird Bookends. 6". 1940s. NM mark. Pastel colors. $175.00 – 225.00.

22. Candleholder Bookends. 6". 1940s. NM mark. Pastel colors & mustard rust. $125.00 – 150.00.

23. NM Flower Holders.
Fish, $75.00 – 150.00.
Swan, $50.00 – 90.00.
Pigeon, $40.00 – 100.00.
Turtle, $50.00 – 100.00.
Hands, $50.00 – 100.00.

See Volume I, page 86 for more details.

24. Flower Bowl Ornaments.
Duck, $75.00 – 90.00.
*Fawn, $80.00 – 100.00.
Peacock, $100.00 – 125.00.
Fawn, $75.00 – 90.00.
Wren, $60.00 – 80.00.
Fawn, $85.00 – 100.00.
*Fawn has NM mark.
All the others have no mark.

25. 1940s Stretch Animals.
Dachshund, $175.00 – 225.00.
Ramming Goat, $200.00 – 250.00.
Dog, $200.00 – 250.00.

26. Hand Vase. 7½" high. 1943. NM mark. $150.00 – 200.00.

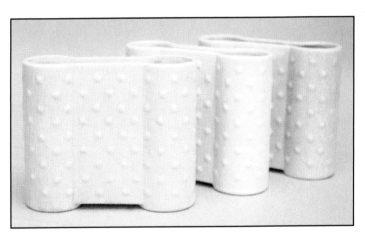

28. Hobnail Castle Gate. 6" Vase. No mark. Pastel colors. $150.00 – 200.00.

27. Hobnail Pitchers. 6" round. 1940s. $90.00 – 125.00; 10" tall. $100.00 – 150.00.

29. Lily Bud Line Vase. 10". 1940s. NM mark. 8" shown for comparison. 10", $80.00 – 100.00; 8", $50.00 – 65.00.

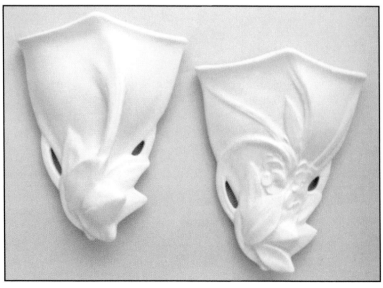

30. 9" Hobnail V Vase. NM mark. $125.00 – 150.00.

31. Vase. 7½" high. 1940s. No mark. Pastel colors. $85.00 – 110.00.

32. 1940s Lily Bud Line Wall Pockets. Left: NM mark. $200.00 – 250.00. Right: McCoy mark. $250.00 – 300.00.

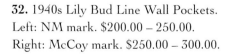

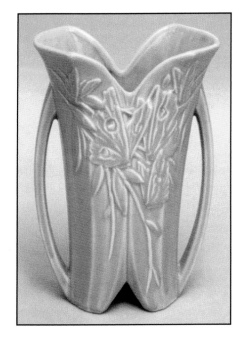

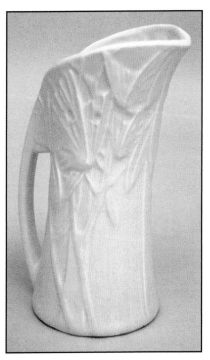

34. Butterfly Pitcher. 10". NM mark. $150.00 – 225.00.

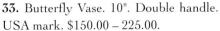

33. Butterfly Vase. 10". Double handle. USA mark. $150.00 – 225.00.

35. Butterfly Platter. 14". NM mark. Nice! $250.00 – 400.00 depending on color.

36. Butterfly Castle Gate Vase. 7" x 6". USA mark. $150.00 – 200.00.

37. Butterfly Wall Pocket. 7" x 6". NM mark. $250.00 – 350.00.

39. Rustic 6" x 6" Jardiniere (faces). 1945. McCoy mark. $50.00 – 75.00.

38. Vase. 10". 1940s. McCoy mark. Matte glazes. $95.00 – 110.00.

40. Blossomtime Wall Pocket. 8". 1946. McCoy mark. White or Yellow. $95.00 – 130.00.

41. Blossomtime Vase Selection.
1946. McCoy mark.
7", Divided Handle, $50.00 – 60.00.
6¼", Handled, $40.00 – 50.00.
6½", Urn Vase, $50.00 – 60.00.

42. Wild Rose Selection. 1952.
Jardiniere, $75.00 – 90.00.
8" Vase, $75.00 – 90.00.
Jardiniere, $75.00 – 90.00.

All marked McCoy. Produced in
four pastel colors.

43. Clown Wall Pocket. 8".
1940s. McCoy mark.
$100.00 – 150.00.

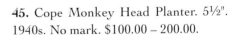

44. Clock Wall Pocket. 8". 1950s. McCoy
mark. $125.00 – 150.00.

45. Cope Monkey Head Planter. 5½".
1940s. No mark. $100.00 – 200.00.

46. Early 1950s Fruit Wall Pockets make a wonderful collection! Pear, $65.00 – 80.00; Grapes, $80.00 – 100.00; Apple, $50.00 – 60.00; Banana, $125.00 – 150.00; Orange, $65.00 – 80.00.

47. Fruit Planters make perfect additions to your Fruit Wall Pocket collection. Orange, $40.00 – 60.00; Pear, $35.00 – 50.00; Apple, $35.00 – 50.00; Lemon, $75.00 – 100.00; Bananas, $100.00 – 125.00.

48. 1950s Flower Forms.
Pink Poppy, $600.00 – 700.00.
Yellow Poppy, $700.00 –
800.00.

All marked McCoy. Interesting
to note the variations in color
definition; some collectors consider these to be four colors.

49. Magnolia Vase. 8½". 1953.
McCoy mark. $150.00 – 175.00.

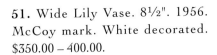

50. Petal Vase. 9". 1955. McCoy
mark. $150.00 – 175.00.

51. Wide Lily Vase. 8½". 1956.
McCoy mark. White decorated.
$350.00 – 400.00.

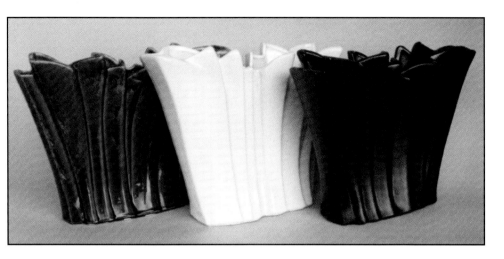

52. Large Fan Vase. 13½" x 10". McCoy mark. Green, black, and white. $250.00 – 350.00. Also known as Blades of Grass.

53. Ivy Vase. 9". 1953. McCoy mark. Hand decorated. $100.00 – 150.00.

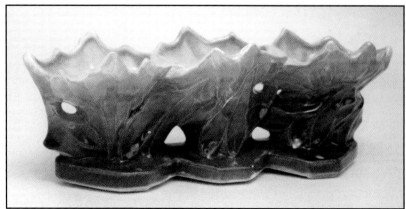

54. Triple Pot Planter. 12½" x 4½". 1956. McCoy mark. $90.00 – 120.00. Brown color, $95.00 – 125.00.

55. Tall Fan Vase. 14½". 1954. McCoy mark. $150.00 – 200.00

56. Ram's Head Vase. 9½" high. 1950s. $125.00 – 175.00.

57. Violin Wall Pocket. 10½". Mid 1950s. McCoy mark. $100.00 – 150.00.

58. Lily Wall Pockets. 6½". Late 1940s. Hand decorated. McCoy mark. $85.00 – 100.00.

60. Piano Planter. 5" x 6". 1959. McCoy mark. White, yellow, and black. $100.00 – 150.00.

59. Grecian Tall Urn Vase. 9½" tall. 1956. McCoy mark. $100.00 – 150.00.

61. Basket Vase. 9" x 5½". 1954. McCoy mark. Ruby & green on ivory. $90.00 – 110.00.

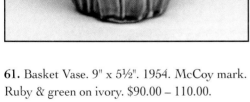

62. Mermaid Lamp. 9¾" x 6. No mark. $200.00 – 300.00.

63. Fish Planters. 12" x 7". 1955. Pink and green, pink, or green. $700.00 – 1,000.00. Very desirable.

64. Fish Jardiniere. 7½". 1958. McCoy mark. Brown or green spray. $350.00 – 400.00.

65. Large Turtle Planter. 12½" x 9". 1955. McCoy mark. $150.00 – 200.00. Green or chartreuse drip.

66. Liberty Bell Planter. 10" x 8¼". 1954. McCoy mark. $200.00 – 300.00.
Sessions Clock shown for similarity.

67. Bear with Ball Planter. 5½" x 7". 1950s. McCoy mark. $100.00 – 125.00.
Vintage plastic pin along for the ride.

68. Wheelbarrow with Rooster Planter. 1955. McCoy mark. $100.00 – 125.00. Fresh eggs not included.

69. Fisherman Sports Planter. 6" x 4½". 1957. McCoy mark. $150.00 – 200.00.
Golf Planter. 6" x 4". McCoy mark. $150.00 – 200.00.
The Sports Planters are very hard to find with good cold paint and the paint's condition can really affect the value.

70. Flying Ducks Planter. 10¾" x 8½". 1955. McCoy mark. $125.00 – 175.00.
Very hard to find in mint condition. Check the wings and beaks for damage.

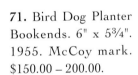

71. Bird Dog Planter Bookends. 6" x 5¾". 1955. McCoy mark. $150.00 – 200.00.

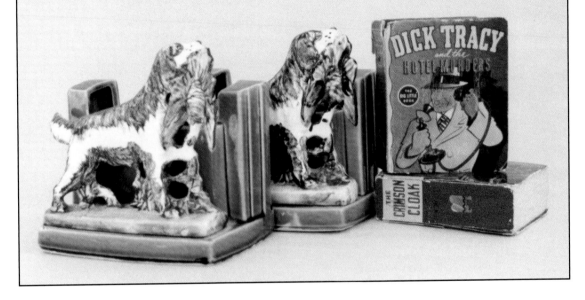

72. Plow Boy Planter. 8" x 7". 1955. McCoy mark. $100.00 – 125.00.

73. Fawn Planter. 12" x 8". 1954. McCoy mark. $250.00 – 300.00.

74. Bird Dog Planter 12½" x 8½". 1954. McCoy mark. $200.00 – 250.00.

Below: **75.** Bird Dog Planter. 7¾". 1959. McCoy mark. Brown or white with decorated spray. $125.00 – 175.00.

76. Calypso Planter. 1959. Banana Boat Planter. 11". McCoy mark. $125.00 – 175.00. Barrel Planter. 7½" x 5". 1959. McCoy mark. $100.00 – 140.00.

77. Scoop with Mammy. 7½". 1953. McCoy mark. Desirable planter. $150.00 – 200.00.

78. Butterfly Spoon Rest. 7½" x 4". 1953. McCoy mark. Gloss green or yellow. $100.00 – 150.00.

79. Zebra Planter. 8½" x 6½". 1956. McCoy mark. $550.00 – 700.00.

Note the Cope design style on the back side of the Zebra Planter.

80. Jardiniere & Pedestal Set. 1955. Jardiniere is marked McCoy. 9½" Jardiniere, 14½" Pedestal. $300.00 – 350.00 set.

82. Jardiniere & Pedestal Set. 1955. Both pieces are marked McCoy. 8½" Jardiniere, 12½" Pedestal. $200.00 – 250.00 set.

81. Sand Jars. 14" x 10". 1955. Marked McCoy. $200.00 – 250.00.

83. Lily Bookends. 5½" x 5". 1948. Fragile flower. Green with decorated lily. $125.00 – 150.00.

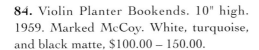

84. Violin Planter Bookends. 10" high. 1959. Marked McCoy. White, turquoise, and black matte, $100.00 – 150.00.

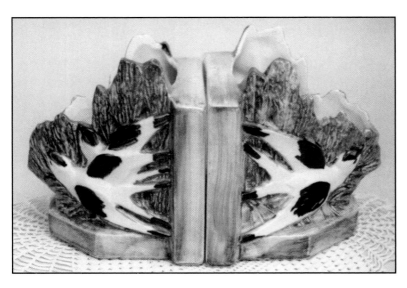

85. Swallow Bookends. 6" x 5½". 1956. Marked McCoy. Ivory with hand decoration. $200.00 – 250.00.

86. Carriage Planter. 8" x 9". 1955. Umbrella is removable. Be aware of reproductions. Marked McCoy. Green or black with yellow trim. Shown with vintage carriage pin. $150.00 – 200.00.

87. Duck with Umbrella Planter. 7½" x 7¼". 1954. Marked McCoy. Yellow or white. $100.00 – 150.00.

88. Frog with Umbrella Planter. 6½" x 7½". 1954. Marked McCoy. Two-tone green or black. $125.00 – 175.00.

89. Jeweled Planter. All marked McCoy. $85.00 – 125.00.

90. Jardiniere. *7½".* 1955. Marked McCoy. Pink, ivory, or chartreuse. $100.00 – 125.00.

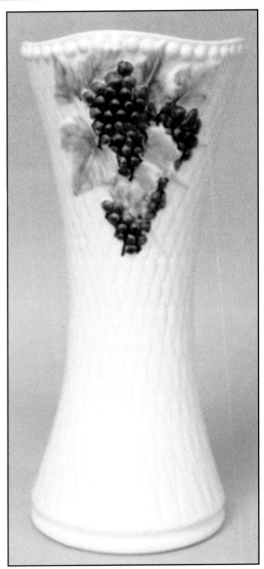

91. Antique Curio Vase. 14" tall. 1962. Marked McCoy. Matte white, gloss green, or gloss brown, with hand-decorated grape pattern. $75.00 – 100.00.

92. Pussy at the Well Planter. 7" x 7". 1957. Marked McCoy. Green or brown & green. $125.00 – 175.00. Note verbiage on planter: "Stung by the splendor of a sudden thought."

93. Parrot Pitcher Vase. *7".* 1952. McCoy mark. Green or brown spray. $150.00 – 200.00. Vintage plastic parrot pin added for fun.

94. Rodeo Cowboy Planter. *7¾"* for both pieces. 1956. Marked McCoy. Same value for Bucking Bronco and Calf Roping motifs. Pictured with 1950s child's cowboy belt. $150.00 – 200.00.

95. Fawn Vase. *9".* 1954. Marked McCoy. All colors shown. $100.00 – 120.00.

96. Kitten with Ball of Yarn Planter. 7" x 5½". McCoy mark & model number 3026, $80.00 – 100.00. Looks as if our kitten has found its way to the yarn department.

97. El Rancho Chuck Wagon Food Warmer. 1960. No mark. Brass wagon wheels and candleholder came with piece. $225.00 – 250.00.
The Chuck Wagon was part of the El Rancho Barbecue Service. Once you have one piece, chances are you will want to collect them all. See page 308 in Volume 1.

98. Sombrero Serve All Five-quart Bowl. 12" x 13". 1960. Sombrero used for chips & bowl used for ice or chips. $350.00 – 400.00.
Important part of the McCoy El Rancho Barbecue Service. The western theme clock pictured for size comparison.

99. 1969 "Jupiter 60" Iron Horse McCormick Train Decanter Set. Consists of Locomotive, Wood Tender Car, Mail Car, and Passenger Car. $250.00 – 350.00.

100. The Pottery Shop Sign. 4" x 5". Produced by McCoy. See page 292 of Volume I. $350.00 – 500.00.

We hope you have enjoyed going through the HNH Top 100 section. Making the selections was a great deal of fun for us. So how did you do? Check your results on the following chart and see where you fall. Collecting is fun!

Number of pieces from the HNH TOP 100

 0–10 – Off to a good start
11–30 – A collection is developing here
31–50 – You're well on your way to a fine collection
51–60 – You have turned the corner and are past
　　　　the halfway mark.

61–80 – A serious collection is in the making
81–90 – Very impressive
91–100 – Congratulations! An enviable collection resides
　　　　here!

As in Volume I, we were able to obtain a significant number of lamps to include for this reference. McCoy lamps are generally not marked McCoy and for the most part were produced for lamp manufacturers. Many of the lamps are easy to identify because their shape is similar to the production vase or planter. The early lamps are easy to spot because of their glazes.

Round Shaped Lamps. 1930s. Onyx glaze & medium green glaze. $100.00 – 125.00 each.

Matte Brown & Green Lamp. 1930s. Flower design base with great handles. $125.00 – 175.00.

Berries & Leaves Design Lamp. 1930s. Matte brown & green with tassels. $125.00 – $175.00.

Berries & Leaves Ball Lamps. 1930s. Brown onyx, rose, and medium green. Nice collection! $100.00 – 150.00.

Brown Onyx Double Handle Lamp. 1930s. $120.00 – 150.00.

V2 Medium Blue Lamp. 9" tall. 1926. V2 mark. $100.00 – 125.00. Blue Onyx Berries & Leaves Ball Lamp. 1930s. $100.00 – 150.00.

Brown Onyx Double Handle Lamp. 1930s. $120.00 – 150.00.

 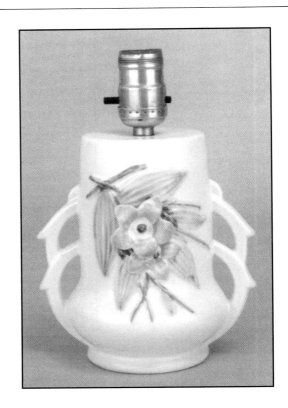

Blossomtime Lamps. 1946. Both with standard colors.
Left: 6¼" Double Handle, $150.00 – 200.00. Right: 7" Divided Handle, $175.00 – 200.00.

Floral Design Lamp. 1940s. Not common to find great cold paint! Note leaves & berries in handle design. $100.00 – 150.00.

Wild Rose Design Lamp. 1952. Great find! $300.00 – 350.00.

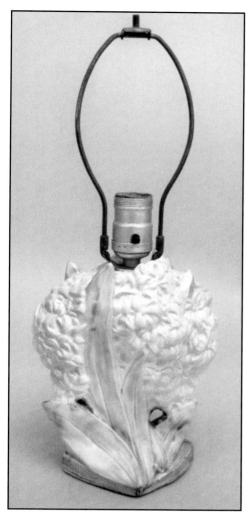

Close-up of the hardware connection to show factory finish. Homemade Hyacinth lamps have been found made from production vases filled with plaster.

Hyacinth Lamp. 8". 1950. McCoy mark. Wonderful flower form design. $400.00 – 500.00.

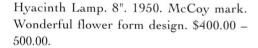

Sunflower Shape Lamp. 9". 1954. No mark. Unusual color. $300.00 – 350.00.

Late McCoy Cherub Design Lamp Base. Ivory with brown spray. $75.00 – 100.00.

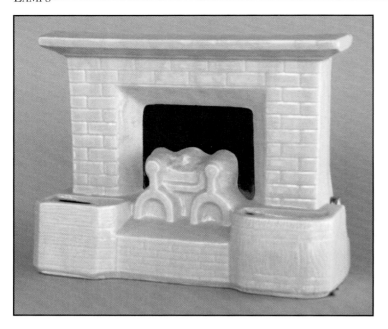

Fireplace Lamp. 6" x 9". 1950s. No mark. Unusual pink color. $75.00 – 100.00.

Rocking Chair Planter Lamp. 8½" x 5½". 1954. McCoy mark. $50.00 – 75.00. Note the hardware holder.

Antique Curio Finger Lamp. 8" x 10". 1962. $100.00 – 125.00.

Wagon Wheel Lamp. 8" high. 1954. Original shade. No mark. $75.00 – 100.00.

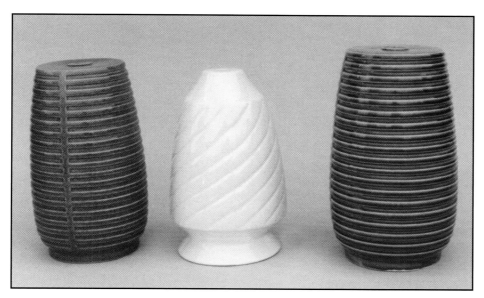

Exceptional collection of McCoy-produced Lamp Bases from the 1970s. These pottery bases were used by lamp factories that did not make their own bases. There are no marks. $40.00 – 60.00 each.

McCoy Ashtrays were, for the most part, produced in the 1960s and 1970s. As stated in Volume I, ashtrays can be a collection all by themselves. We hope you enjoy the spoof collection below.

"Some things are for the birds. This is for ashes." Marked McCoy. $35.00 – 50.00.

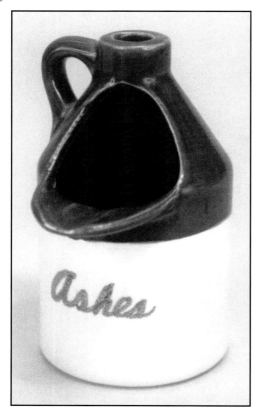

"There's one in every Bar…" Marked McCoy. $35.00 – 50.00.

"I should have danced all night." Marked McCoy. $35.00 – 50.00.

Promotional Jug Ashtray. McCoy mark. $20.00 – 30.00.

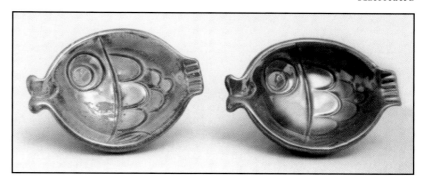

Zane's Truce Commemorative Historic Ashtray by Al Kubert. McCoy mark. $50.00 – 60.00.

Novelty Fish Ashtray. 4". Taupe or honey glazed brown. $10.00 – 15.00. Note the two different glaze colors & marks from two different eras of McCoy Pottery, Mt. Clemens and Lancaster Colony.

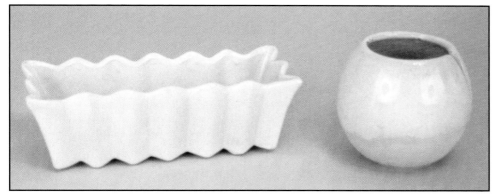

1960 Planting Dish, 9". $15.00 – 20.00.
Ball-shaped Ashtray. McCoy mark. $20.00 – 25.00.

Oval Designer Ashtray. 8". McCoy mark. $25.00 – 35.00.
Cornucopia Vase. 7" x 6". 1957. McCoy mark. $30.00 – 40.00.

Banks are becoming a serious McCoy collectible. There are many bank collectors that McCoy collectors must compete with for new finds, but that hasn't stopped the category from gaining popularity among McCoy Pottery collectors.

The Cats at the Barrel Banks. MCP mark. Red, white, blue & yellow. Also found in light brown. See Volume I, page 317. $65.00 – 80.00.

The Covered Bridge Bank. MCP mark. Shown in red & hand decorated. The glaze of both banks is chalk like, much like the Sports Planters. $75.00 – 95.00.

Safe Bank. McCoy mark. $55.00 – 65.00.

Save at Dollar Federal Bank. 9" high. No mark. $50.00 – 60.00.
Have Fun with My Beer Bank. 8¼" high. No mark. $50.00 – 60.00.

Immigrant Industrial Savings. 7½".
No mark. $50.00 – 75.00.
1932 Pierce Arrow Decanter. 11".
McCoy mark. $75.00 – 125.00.
The white & gold colors were likely
not produced.

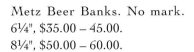

Metz Beer Banks. No mark.
6¼", $35.00 – 45.00.
8¼", $50.00 – 60.00.

Lucky Penny Puppy Bank.* $50.00 – 60.00.
National Bank of Dayton Wise Owl. $55.00 – 65.00.
*Lucky Penny Puppy Bank has not been verified as McCoy, but several
collectors believe it was produced by the Nelson McCoy Pottery.

"Give a Hoot…Don't Pollute." 1974. Woodsy Owl
Bank. $100.00 – 125.00.

Hung-over Dog Banks. 6" x 8". Both colors shown. $35.00 – 45.00.

Hamm's Bear Bank. Same size as the Cookie Jar of same name. 1972. No mark. $100.00 – 150.00. The Hamm's Bear Bank is attached to a board because it won't stand up without support. It was never produced, probably because of this fault.

Winking Pig Bank. Same size as the Cookie Jar of same name. 1972. No mark. $100.00 – 150.00.
Note: The back of Pig Bank shows the slot for the coins.

Football Banks. 1948. Brown & white. Hard to find. $125.00 – 175.00. Megaphone (rare). $250.00 – 300.00.

Tea Pot Bank. 1940s. $60.00 – 85.00. This is also a very hard piece to find.

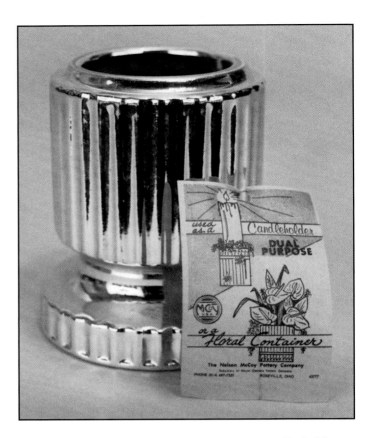

Reds & Oranges Line with green interior. 1973. All marked McCoy.
7" x 9" Basket, $35.00 – 45.00.
9" Pitcher Vase, $30.00 – 40.00.
12" Strap Vase, $75.00 –$100.00.

Dual Purpose Vase/Holder. 1974. Use as candle holder or vase. $15.00 – 20.00.

Large Pitcher & Bowl Set. 11½" x 14". 1974. Antique. MCP mark. $100.00 – 150.00.

Suburbia Ware 5-cup Coffee Server. 1964. Pictured without lid. $35.00 – 45.00 with lid.

Pitcher and Bowl Set. 1973. McCoy mark. Ship motif. Bowl 11½" x 9½". Pitcher 8" tall. $60.00 – 80.00.

Tudor Rose Violet Pot. 2½". 1965. McCoy mark. $10.00 – 15.00.
Tudor Rose Vase. 7½". 1965. McCoy mark. Cascade Line shape (see page 212 of Volume 1). $30.00 – 40.00.

Functional and Decorative Gifts
Hanging Pot. 5¼" x 6¼". 1974. MCP mark. $25.00 – 30.00.
Pitcher without Bowl. 8". 1973. MCP mark. $20.00 – 25.00.

Crestwood Line Pieces. 1964. Colors: Sunset Orange, Chrome Yellow & Mellow White with a 22K gold treatment. Marked McCoy.
7½" Pedestal Bowl, $30.00 – 40.00.
4½" Footed Planter, $35.00 – 40.00.

Flower Bowl. $25.00 – 35.00.

Centerpiece Planter. 10" x 10". $30.00 – 40.00.
Garden Club Vase. 5" x 5". 1966. McCoy mark. $15.00 – 20.00.

8½" Jardiniere. Mellow White with label. $40.00 – 45.00.

Early 1970s Deer Planters. Pictured in non cataloged white & standard natural color. Very desirable collectibles! Marked #3028. $70.00 – 90.00.

Soup & Sandwich Sets. 1963. Turquoise, yellow, beige or oatmeal. $35.00 – 45.00.

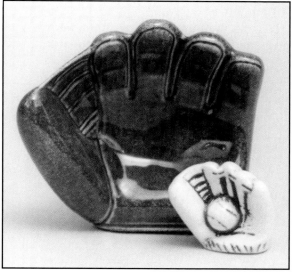

Baseball Glove Paperweights. 5". $75.00 – 100.00. Miniature, $125.00 – 150.00. (Miniature glove was not produced.)

0432 4000
10½" Jardiniere

0431 7900
8½" Jardiniere

3021 2000
9 x 7" Strawberry Jar

3027 8571
Dog Planter

3028 1771
Deer Planter

3026 3671
Kitten Planter

Plants not included.

Original catalog page from the 1970s Nelson McCoy Pottery Company.

Oral Roberts Association Easter Plate. 7" diameter. 1972. Marked Frankoma, but made by McCoy for the association. Apparently there were more given away than Frankoma was able to produce, so McCoy made some.

McCoy piece is marked O.R.A. 1972. Frankoma has red clay and is marked J.F., 1972. $25.00 – 35.00.

Oval Flower Bowl. 6½". 1954. McCoy mark. $18.00 – 25.00. Strawberry Jar. 9" x 7". 1974. Marked McCoy. Exotic green, gloss white, and red clay. $35.00 – 40.00.

Horticulture Line Pot & Saucers. 1974. 7½", $15.00 – 25.00. 6½", $10.00 – 20.00. 5½", $10.00 – 15.00. As also produced in a 4½" size. Brown, green, white, and teal.

Corinthian Garden Line Vases. 11" tall. 1969. Marked McCoy. $30.00 – 40.00.

Vinegar & Oil Cruets. 1970s. $15.00 – 25.00 set.

Hammered Design Coffee Mug. 1970s. $10.00 – 15.00.
Hammered Design Butter Crock. $15.00 – 20.00.

Ye Old Kettle Planter. 5½" x 5½". 1955. McCoy mark. Black, green, and yellow. Brass or black bail with tripod. $35.00 – 45.00.
Coal Bucket Planter. 8" x 10". 1974. McCoy mark. $35.00 – 75.00.

New Starburst Line Centerpiece with Candle Holders. 1972. Marked MCP. Green, white, and yellow. $80.00 – 100.00 set.

Safe & Decorative Ashtray with the original MCP sticker. 1971. $20.00 – 35.00. Pretty enough to be a centerpiece.

Golden Brocade Line, pictured in their original boxes. 10½" x 6½". 1970. Fruit & Nut Platter. $25.00 – 35.00.
8" Pedestal Candy Dish. $25.00 – 35.00.

No. 712 Coffee Serving Set. 1965. 18-cup Coffee Pot, 48 oz. Coffee Mugs. $100.00 – 120.00 set.

PAC Man Paperweight. 1980s. Advertising piece for Burroughs Corporation (see bottom sticker). $50.00 – 75.00.

Decorative Stein. 70 oz. 1973. White, honey brown, birchwood, and harvest gold. $20.00 – 30.00.
Burlap Bag Hanging Basket. 1977. Designed to hang by a rope. $15.00 – 20.00.

Pitcher with possible glaze test formula. 1969. This shape pitcher was produced for many years in three sizes, 6 oz., 16 oz., and 32 oz. There were a large number of 32 oz. Advertising Pitchers produced, as shown above right, using this mold.
Test Pitcher, all sizes. $35.00 – 50.00.
Advertising Pitchers, 32 oz. $20.00 – 40.00.

Soup Bowl with Rose Decal. Large coffee cup-shaped. Sold originally with saucer. $8.00 – 10.00. 10" Round Planting Dish. 1970s. $25.00 – 30.00.

Spoon Rests. 1975. Produced for the tableware lines of the era with decals to match the line. All are marked McCoy #232. $15.00 – 25.00.

Top photo: Lorena Bicentennial Project Planters (see page 314 of Volume 1). 1976. Produced in white & black decorated. Gold, brown & green are rare colors. Standard color, $50.00 – 75.00. Rare color, $100.00 – 125.00.

Middle photo: McCormick Iron Horse "Jupiter 60" Locomotive & Coal Car Decanters (see page 320 of Volume 1 for details). The silver glaze is really rare! Locomotive. $100.00 – 150.00.
Coal Car. $80.00 – 120.00.

Bird Feeder Hanging Basket. 1975.
No mark. $40.00 – 60.00.

Advertising Tequila Cuervo Service. 8¾" x 6". 1970s. $75.00 – 100.00 set.

1970s. Econo-Line Jardiniere. Marked 502 USA Econo-Line. Same model number as similarly shaped Floraline Jardiniere. $20.00 – 25.00.

Futura Stoneware. Four-piece Place Setting. 1975. Cataloged as Brown Drip. Original box. $30.00 – 40.00.

Daisy Delight

7129 3216
2 cup Teapot

1421 3216
2 qt. Casserole

7010 3216
6 oz. Custard Cup

0658 3216
Bread/Relish Tray

0135 3216
Utensil Holder

0131 3216
9 x 6½" Cookie Jar

1725 3216
Center of Table Set

1418 3216
6 cup Teapot

Utensils not included.

1429 3216
32 oz. Pitcher

1415 3216
Salt & Pepper Shakers

7013 3216
Butter Dish

1414 3216
Sugar & Creamer

6

Original Daisy Delight catalog page from the 1970s Nelson McCoy Pottery Company catalog.

7108 3216
12 oz. Soup Mug

7120 3216
Soup'N Sandwich Set

1717 3216
Margarine Container

0286 3216
6 oz. Tea/Coffee Cups

0134 3216
4 pc. Canister Set

7515 3216
8½ x 10½" Pitcher & Bowl

1460 3216
4 pc. Place Setting

1443 3216
16 pc. Starter Set

7528 3216
5½ x 8" Pitcher & Bowl

1413 3216
16 oz. Bowl

7003 3216
7¼" Plate

7002 3216
10" Plate

1412 3216
10 oz. Mug

7

Original Daisy Delight catalog page from the 1970s Nelson McCoy Pottery Company catalog.

Welch's Advertising Pieces, Pitcher & Mugs. Welch's Way Promotion. Marked USA. Pitcher, $35.00 – 50.00. Mugs, $15.00 – 20.00 each.

Child's Drawer Pulls. 1970s. Hard to find! $50.00 – 75.00 each.

Floral Design Dinnerware. 1970s. Covered Butter, $18.00 – 24.00; Covered Sugar, $15.00 – 20.00; Covered Creamer, $15.00 – 20.00.

Schlitz Beer Advertising Promotional
Pieces. 1970s.
Mugs, $15.00 – 25.00 each.
Vase, $25.00 – 30.00.

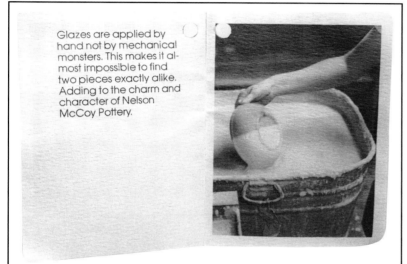

Glazes are applied by hand not by mechanical monsters. This makes it almost impossible to find two pieces exactly alike. Adding to the charm and character of Nelson McCoy Pottery.

Interesting page from the hang tag attached
to the Ladle shown below, explaining and
promoting the handwork done.

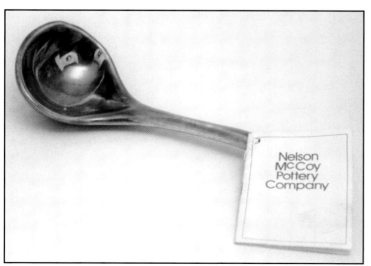

Ladle from Punch Bowl Set with original hang tag. 1970s.
$15.00 – 20.00.

Pickling Crocks. 9-quart. 1979. From McCoy's Nostalgia Buyers Guide. Lancaster mark. $40.00 – 50.00 each.

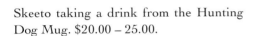

Skeeto taking a drink from the Hunting Dog Mug. $20.00 – 25.00.

Advertising Mug. $20.00 – 25.00.

Johnnie Walker Promotional Pitcher. $30.00 – 40.00.

Inhaler. 9" high. 1970s. Printed on piece, EARTHENWARE INHALER. Manufactured for S. Maw Son A. Thompson. $75.00 – 100.00.

Hand-formed Roman Pot. 7" x 5¼". 1974. Marked McCoy. $20.00 – 30.00. 1970s Tea Pot with Bamboo Handle. McCoy mark. $30.00 – 40.00.

Sports Mugs. 1988. No mark. Baseball, Basketball, Football, Golf, Tennis, and Soccer. $20.00 – 30.00 each. Collect them all.

1970s Turtle Planter. 8" x 5". Unusual matte yellow color. $35.00 – 50.00. Pictured with the more common green color, $20.00 – 25.00.

Model KC-500 Kitchen Clock. 1972. Sun-Rise Den & Kitchen Clock collection. Pitcher, 7½" x 7¼". Pocket Planter, 7" x 4¾". Marked USA on Planter. Clock & Planter, $50.00 – 75.00 set.

Strawberry Country

0134 3239
4 pc. Canister Set

0131 3239
9" x 6½" Cookie Jar

0658 3239
Bread/Relish Tray

1421 3239
2 qt. Casserole

7129 3239
2 cup Teapot

0286 3239
6 oz. Tea/Coffee Cups

0135 3239
Utensil Holder

1415 3239
Salt & Pepper Shakers

1432 3239
4 qt. Soup Tureen w/Ladle

0657 3239
Bread Stick Holder

1418 3239
6 cup Teapot

8

1970s Strawberry Country catalog page.

1429 3239
32 oz. Pitcher

7108 3239
12 oz. Soup Mug

1414 3239
Sugar & Creamer

1725 3239
Center of Table Set

7528 3239
5½ x 8" Pitcher & Bowl

7013 3239
Butter Dish

7527 3239
10 x 11" Pitcher & Bowl

7515 3239
8½ x 10½" Pitcher & Bowl

7010 3239
6 oz. Custard Cup

1717 3239
Margarine Container

9

1970s Strawberry Country catalog page.

Strawberry Country Kitchenware selection. 1970s. Marked McCoy and very colorful.
Sugar & Creamer, $30.00 – 40.00.
6-cup Tea Pot, $35.00 – 45.00.
Coffee Mugs, $10.00 – 15.00 ea.

32 oz. Strawberry Country Pitcher. $35.00 – 50.00.

Indoor/Outdoor Hanging Planters. 1976. Lancaster mark.
Bird, $30.00 – 40.00.
Owl, $35.00 – 45.00.

Turtle & Snail Planters. 1977. Can be used as hanging baskets. Lancaster mark.
Turtle, $30.00 – 40.00.
Snail, $35.00 – 45.00.

Wabbit Collection Child's Service. 1970s. Lancaster mark. Pink, blue & white.
Wabbit Handle Cup, $30.00 – 40.00.
Wabbit Face Plate, $20.00 – 30.00.
Wabbit Handle Bowl, $30.00 – 40.00.

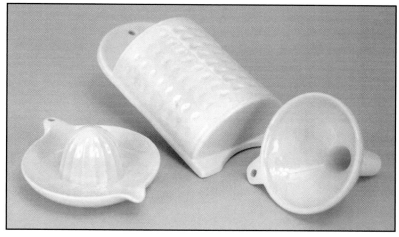

Islander Collection Kitchenware. 1979.
Reamer, $20.00 – 30.00.
Utensil Holder, $15.00 – 25.00.
Funnel, $15.00 – 20.00.

Islander Collection Kitchenware. 1979.
Serving Bowl, $20.00 – 25.00.
Creamer, $15.00 – 25.00.
Covered Sugar, $20.00 – 25.00.
Small Dish, $10.00 – 12.00.

Pasta Corner

7072 1240
12½" Lasagne Platto

0661 1240
Vino Set

7099 1240
Parmigiano Shaker

7070 1240
9½" Antipasto Platto

0655 1240
Insalata Set

0127 1240
Sale and Pepe Shakers

0131 1240
96 oz. Zuppa

0658 1240
Pane (Bread/Relish Tray)

0118 1240
12½" Pasta Bowl

Nelson McCoy

A Lancaster Colony Company
Nelson McCoy Pottery Company
Roseville, Ohio 43777

24

25M1P1582

Late 1970s Pasta Corner catalog page.

Canyon Dinnerware. 1977. McCoy produced a line similar to Canyon named Mesa. Mesa has a higher gloss finish than Canyon.
Sugar, $20.00 – 25.00.
Creamer, $15.00 – 20.00.
Handled Bowl, $10.00 – 15.00.
Salt & Pepper, $20.00 – 25.00.
Coffee Pot, $30.00 – 40.00.

Canyon Canister Set.
Sold as four-piece set.
Small, $20.00 – 30.00.
Medium, $25.00 – 35.00.
Large, $30.00 – 40.00.

Canyon Dinner Plates.
Square Salad, $8.00 – 12.00. Square Dinner, $15.00 – 20.00. Round Dinner, $10.00 – 15.00.

PINK & BLUE

0118 3700
12½" Spaghetti Bowl

0134 3700
4 pc. Canister Set

0109 3700
3 pc. Bowl Set

0114 3700
10 qt. Mixing Bowl

0108 3700
1½ qt. Mixing Bowl

0107 3700
1 qt. Mixing Bowl

0106 3700
1.4 pt. Mixing Bowl

1717 3700
Margarine Container

0112 3700
6 qt. Mixing Bowl

0110 3700
3½ qt. Mixing Bowl

0168 3700
2 qt. Mix'N Pour Bowl

Utensils not included.

10

0135 3700
Utensil Holder

7050 3700
12 oz. Individual French Casserole

Late 1970s Pink & Blue Kitchenware catalog page.

Three exquisite Vases with floral designs from the late 1940s.

1940s North Pole Planters. Aqua & burgundy & pink Noel Planter from the same era.

Large Mama Duck with Scarf Planter. 10" across. Late 1940s. McCoy mark.

Frog with Baby. 3½".
NM mark. Matte yellow.
Blue Rhinoceros
Planter. NM mark.
Cope Original.

Natural color Frog Planter. 3¼"
high. NM mark.
Bird-in-Flight Flower Holder.
NM mark.

Kitten Planter. 1953. McCoy mark.
Baseball Boy Paperweight. 1978. No
mark. Both have an unproduced
white glaze finish. The Baseball Boy
is the same as on the top of the Baseball Boy Cookie Jar.

Harry S. Truman, 33rd President, 1884 – 1972, Commemorative Plates.

4" Pink Compote. McCoy mark.

4" Flower Pot. Marked McCoy.

Richard Nixon Mug made for Rumph. Blue is decorated; white is bisque.

Colorful 1950s Floral Theme Vases. The vase on the left is the same as the vase on the right, showing the reverse side and different colors.

Berries & Leaves Jardiniere. 8". 1930s. NM mark. Matte glazed art pottery. Collectors would love to find one of these.

Woodpecker Wall Pocket. Extraordinary detail.

Clown & Pig Planter. 8½" long. 1951. McCoy mark. Looks like the Clown & Pig Planter referenced on page 149 in Volume I, but if you look closely, the ears of the pig are different and the pig body is slimmer.

Davy Crockett Planter. Another one of those great finds! Found in July of 1998 by a serious collector. Sometimes it really pays to go antique shopping.

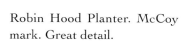

Robin Hood Planter. McCoy mark. Great detail.

Robin Hood Mug. McCoy mark. Spinning Wheel with Kitten Planter. McCoy collectors would love to have one of these.

Colorful unproduced Bookends.

Large stand-up Clemson Tiger Paw Sign.

WWII Land Mine in mint condition.

1961 Pot & Saucer with glaze test formula printed on bottom. (Fawn Brown & Har. Yellow #111).

Crouching Cat Planter from the 1940s with an NM mark. Recently found by an avid McCoy collector. What a find! We have never seen one of these and have no catalog reference. It is approximately the same size as the NM Lion or Horse Planters.

Sitting Elephant Paperweight & Miniature Flag Holder. Designed to hold a small flag such as on the Lorena Bicentennial Planter, page 315, Volume I.
1949 Fish Pitcher in a rare blue glaze. See page 200 of Volume I for more standard colors.

Extraordinary 1980 Nelson McCoy Sales Award Cup. As a salesman, you could dream of winning this award. As a collector, you could dream of finding this award.

Velma & Leslie Cope. Velma is holding her favorite planter.

The Cope Gallery opened on October 6, 1968, on the second wedding anniversary of Leslie & Velma Cope, as a place to live, work and display their pottery & paintings. Since then it has become the place to visit for McCoy collectors while in Ohio. Leslie, 85 years old, still works seven hours a day in his studio. He told us that he likes to paint two pictures at a time, so when he gets tired of one, he can work on the other for awhile.

The gallery, in Roseville, Ohio, is a virtual museum of Sidney & Leslie Cope McCoy Pottery designs. It's a real treat for McCoy Pottery collectors to be able to view all of these outstanding pieces in one place. It made us wonder why some of these wonderful designs never got produced.

Leslie worked with his father, Sidney, as his assistant for 30 years. Sidney Cope played a very important role as the head designer for McCoy Pottery and most of the more sought after pieces of McCoy were designed by Sidney Cope. Leslie Cope is a very accomplished artist in his own right. His works are in the permanent collection of the Metropolitan Museum of Art in New York, Carnegie Institute in Pittsburgh, the Library of Congress and Capital University.

Here is a great example of a Cope design, the Ram's Head Vase.

There are no values shown for the pieces in the Cope Gallery Collection. Most are one-of-a-kind examples.

We would like to thank Velma & Leslie Cope for graciously allowing us to take the following priceless pieces of Cope designed pottery out of their cases for photography. It has enabled us to show the Cope designs in a way that they deserve.

Tiles designed & painted by Sidney Cope when he worked for the Mosaic Tile Company.

Velma Cope's favorite planters. They are beautiful!

Unproduced line of double & triple vases with a pretty and decorative leaf motif.

A wonderful V-design Vase & an intricate Swan Vase that looks similar to the Swans produced in the late 1940s and again the mid 1950s.

Pair of matte blue Candle Holders. They would look good on any table.

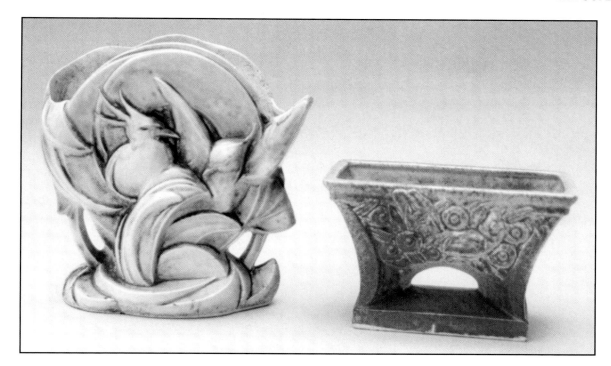

The rustic glaze on two unproduced planters.

Green Leaf planter and a hand-painted planter with blue Swimming Fish.

Great display of Flower Bowl Ornaments. You can see the McCoy mark on the Angel Fish; it was not produced in this glaze. The Mermaid & Fish Ornaments were not produced.

Display of unproduced floral motif vases. There is some resemblance to the Blossomtime & Wild Rose lines.

Hand-decorated Cobblers Bench Planter with embossed slogan: "Never do today what you can put off till tomorrow." Rustic Line shape Soap Dish in unproduced blue glaze. See Volume I, page 214 for more information on the Rustic Line.

Unproduced Flying Ducks Planter with similar duck design as on the 1955 production Flying Ducks Planter referenced on page 202 of Volume I.

Cope Figural Ornaments. Iguanas in three glazes, Lark & Seal in the same glaze, and a Stork-like Bird.

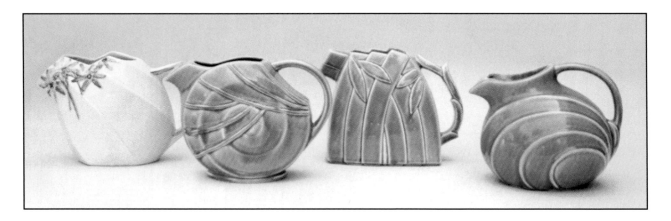

An array of Cope designed Pitchers. The Pitcher at the far right was produced and was very popular.

Two unproduced Pitchers with the same leaf design as the produced vase to the right.

Matte glazed Butterfly & Berries Flower Trough & Duck in Flight Ashtray.

Impressive hand-decorated Panther Planter & Double Giraffe Planter in a rustic glaze.

Colorful assortment of Flower Bud Wall Plaques.

Highly detailed Dancing Gypsy Troupe Figural Ornaments.

Hand-decorated Aquatic Bird Bookends. Wonderful!

Trained Elephant Planter & Flower Bowl with attached leaves.

Deco Bird Planter & matte glazed Flower Bowl with attached Bird Flower Ornament.

Hand-decorated Flower Bowl with an attached Bird Flower Frog.

Flower Bowl with attached bud. Tall matte white Lily Vase. Miniature Spinning Wheel Planter. Full size version produced in 1953.

Cope decorated Butterfly Spoon Rest & Penguin Spoon Rest. Both produced in 1953, but not with this intricate decoration.

Large early vases with mysterious and exotic design.

Miniature Vase alongside a flock of strange little birds. Cope decorated Old Mill Planter alongside a miniature Pelican & Vase in the same unproduced glaze.

Cope decorated Arcature Vases from 1951. These glazes were not produced. Modern 8" multicolor Vase.

Rustic glaze leaf motif Table Set.
Washer Women & an Elegant Lady.

Humorous Hiding Frog Vase
with Bird Ornaments.

Metallic glaze on unusual Monkey
Pitcher and Large Billed Bird
(ashtray?).

1953 Mammy on Scoop Planter
and realistic setting Chipmunk
Planter.

Cookie Boy (Bare Headed) Cookie Jar showing bottom with NM mark.
Please see page 222.

Cookie jars were an important component of the success of the Nelson McCoy Pottery throughout most of their production years. The first jars were made in the late 1930s and were followed by literally a few hundred cookie jars through to the mid-1980s when the Nelson McCoy Pottery was sold by Lancaster Colony and merged into Designer Accents. As you will see in the upcoming pages, the variety of color, design, size, functionality, character, etc. of the McCoy cookie jars is really wonderful and enjoyed by many collectors. Collecting McCoy cookie jars has been a popular activity for a number of years and had established itself in the collecting world far before the collecting of non-cookie jar pottery of the Nelson McCoy Pottery Co. became so popular.

We have organized the presentation of the cookie jars in approximate chronological order. Where known, we have listed the year a jar was introduced. We have not included sizes for most of the jars as they are all pretty similar. However, it will be noted if there is something unusual related to the size. We have purposely left out the catalog numbers for the jars as they are confusing and seem not really to provide any meaningful information for the collector. When first introduced, a cookie jar was assigned a specific catalog number and sold with that number. However, if that cookie jar was discontinued a few years later when a new jar was introduced, McCoy would frequently reassign that same catalog number of the discontinued jar. In other cases, there were production jars

that were never given a catalog number. The point here is that the catalog number does not consistently help in defining a period in time a specific jar was produced or in establishing a sequence of the jars' introduction. We have indicated if the jar is found marked with the McCoy name. If we indicate a USA mark, there is no McCoy name with it. Of course, "No mark" means just that.

As with the non-cookie jar values, the price values indicated throughout the book are based on pieces without any damage. This means no hairlines, chips, cracks, crazing, or flakes. The price range shown accounts for variation in prices throughout the country. It also considers that one particular piece may have a sharper look than a different sample of the same piece, due to the color of the same glaze or the crispness of the piece out of the mold.

Throughout the jar section, you will discover outstanding examples of special decoration or color of a particular jar that are likely one-of-a-kind jars or certainly rare. On several of these jars, you will see a dollar value with a plus (+) sign. We are simply indicating a bare minimum but the (+) sign tells you the jar could possibly sell for a much higher value. This point is to inform the collector that this is indeed a rare jar of significant value but it is not possible to accurately value with a specific range.

Reproductions: What an unpleasant topic that unfortunately needs to be noted. Cookie jars have not escaped the greed of the reproduction makers. In the McCoy Pottery cookie jar arena, there are actually quite a few of the jars that have been reproduced. Many times the glaze colors, the size, or even the weight of the reproduction jar will give itself away. However, some are certainly better than others and it's important for collectors to educate themselves on this topic. In the photos below, you can see an original jar pictured on the right with the reproduction jar on the left. The photos make it pretty obvious which one is the "Real" McCoy but for some of these reproductions, having them by themselves can make a collector ponder for quite awhile. At this time, we are aware of the following

McCoy jars that have been reproduced in some form:

Betsy Baker	Gleep
Cauliflower Mammy	Hamm's Bear
Chairman of the Board	Hillbilly Bear
Chef Bust	Hobby Horse
Clown Bust	Indian
Cookstove	Leprechaun
Dalmatians (in the Rocking Chair)	Mammy
Davy Crockett	Tepee
Boy on Football	

Ball shape Jar. Honeycomb design. 1930s. No mark. Green & brown glaze pictured. Also came in maroon. $30.00 – 40.00.

Concave shape. Floral decoration on Black only. 1930s. Marked USA. $35.00 – 45.00

OPPOSITE PAGE:

Row 1

Old Milk Can. Molded handles with hand decoration. 1939. No mark. Glaze colors were black, ivory, yellow, green & blue. $45.00 – 60.00.
Tilt Pitcher Jar. Hand decorated. 1939. No mark. Glaze colors included black, green (both pictured), blue or yellow. $45.00 – 60.00.

Row 2

Bean Pot with Handles in 3-quart & 4-quart size. Hand decorated. 1939. No mark. Glaze colors were black or ivory. $35.00 – 45.00 for either size.
Round Ball shape. Molded handles with hand decoration. Angled Finial style. 1939. Also made same jar with a squared off finial shape (not shown). 1948. No mark. Glaze colors were yellow, blue & green. Angle finial, $35.00 – 45.00. Square finial $40.00 – 50.00.

Row 3

Concave shape. All three examples shown on this row are the same jar. Hand decorated. Note: The difference between this jar and the concave one above is that the floral pattern on this jar is partially embossed into the jar. 1942. No mark. Variety of glaze colors. $35.00 – 45.00.

Hobnail Heart Shape Jar. 1940. No mark. Made in the five pastel glaze colors shown above. $400.00 – 500.00.

Mammy with Cauliflowers Jar. Basic white glaze with hand decoration. Limited Edition made. 1939. McCoy mark. Beware of reproductions. $1,000.00 – 1,200.00.

OPPOSITE PAGE:
Row 1
Cookie Boy (Bare Headed). Early 1940s. NM mark. Glaze colors were aqua, white, and yellow. This jar is very rare. $800.00 – 1,000.00.
Cookie Boy (With Hat). Mid 1940s. McCoy mark. Glaze colors were aqua, white, and yellow. $175.00 – 250.00.

Row 2 & Row 3
Hobnail Round. Molded handles with angled or square top finial. 1940. No mark. Standard glaze colors were yellow, blue, and green, but jar has actually been found in many different wonderful colors. Standard glaze, $100.00 – 125.00. Non-standard glaze, $150.00 – 200.00.

Extremely rare Mammy Jar. 1942. McCoy mark. Has the words "Dem Cookies Sho Got Dat Vitamin A." Has been found in solid yellow and aqua. Was likely also made in solid white. This would be consistent with the Cookie Boy and the Penguin Jar made in the same three colors during the same era. No facts to prove this jar was actually ever in production. $4,000.00 – 5,000.00.

Below: Mammy Jar. A re-issue of the earlier jar but simply with the word "Cookies." 1948. McCoy mark. Also made in aqua, white, and yellow.
White, $100.00 – 150.00.
Aqua or yellow, $400.00 – 500.00.

Penguin. 1940. Marked McCoy. Made in yellow, white, and aqua. Frequently hand decorated. Right is special Cope decoration example.
White, $125.00 – 175.00.
Yellow or aqua, $175.00 – 250.00.
Cope, $1,000.00+.

Clown Bust. 1943. McCoy mark. Hand decorated. $50.00 – 75.00.

Split Trunk Elephant. 1943. Hand decorated. Pink ears. McCoy mark. $250.00 – 300.00.

Bear (Cookie in Vest). McCoy mark. First made in 1945 without "Cookies" at bottom. In 1953, it was re-issued with "Cookies" added. Without "Cookies", $65.00 – 75.00.
With "Cookies", $75.00 – 85.00.

Apple Jar. 1950. McCoy mark. Came in yellow or aqua. $40.00 – 50.00.

All three marked McCoy. Apple with Green Leaf. 1957. $75.00 – 85.00.
Larger Apple with Green Leaf. 1967. $60.00 – 70.00.
Apple with Gold Leaf. 1956. $90.00 – 100.00.

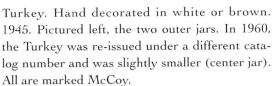

Turkey. Hand decorated in white or brown. 1945. Pictured left, the two outer jars. In 1960, the Turkey was re-issued under a different catalog number and was slightly smaller (center jar). All are marked McCoy.
Older jar, $300.00 – 350.00.
Newer jar, $200.00 – 250.00.

The beautiful decoration on the back of the older Turkey jar (left) and the 1960 model (right).

Dutch Boy. 1945. Marked McCoy. Hand decorated. $30.00 – 45.00.

Dutch Boy/Dutch Girl. 1946. Marked McCoy. Hand decorated. Very rare. Similar shape as the Dutch Boy Jar only slightly taller. Other difference is the boy image is on one side and the girl image from the Dutch Girl Jar is on the other. $200.00 – 300.00.

Dutch Girl. 1946. Marked McCoy. Hand decorated. $60.00 – 80.00.

Decorated Clown. McCoy mark. 1945.
Left: Cope decorated.
Right: More of a production decoration. Production decorated, $50.00 – 75.00.
Cope decorated, $200.00 – 300.00.

The Cylinder shapes were made with numerous styles of decoration, glaze colors, and patterns from the mid 1940s into the 1960s. There are actually two sizes. All the early jars from the mid 1940s to mid 1950s are of the taller variety; about 8½" tall. In the early 1960s, the smaller, about 7½" tall, style went into production.

Left: You can see an Apple design in both sizes. $45.00 – 60.00 for either size.

Two older style Poppy designs. $45.00 – 60.00.

Chef Mixing a Dish design. 1946. $55.00 – 70.00.

Additional Cylinder styles.
Mustard, $40.00 – 50.00.
Amber, $45.00 – 60.00.
Yellow with green bands, $95.00 – 110.00.

More Cylinders.
Black with pink lid, $50.00 – 60.00.
Brown Drip, $45.00 – 55.00.
Yellow with black lid, $40.00 – 50.00.

Action Cylinders. All 7½" tall. Cookie Express. "Honest Mom, I didn't snitch the cookies." and "Anytime is Cookie Time." $60.00 – 80.00

Pastel glazes. 7½" tall.
$50.00 – 60.00.

Square Jar. Hand decorated with V finial shape. 1947. Marked McCoy. $40.00 – 50.00.

Hexagon Jar with square handles. The finial has a W shape. Hand decorated. 1947. Marked McCoy. $45.00 – 55.00.

Same Hexagon Jar with special decoration. $200.00 – 300.00.

Oval Plain Jar in blue glaze. Marked McCoy. Actually, quite rare. Likely early 1960s. $100.00 – 150.00.

Love Birds (Kissing Penguins). 1946. Marked McCoy. Production Jar was white with hand decoration as shown in picture below right. The white example below left is unusual color decoration. Green/brown glaze in bottom photo is rare as is the coloring of the beautiful jar in upper right photo.

White decorated. $100.00 – 125.00.

Special glazing. $300.00 – 400.00.

Left: Green/brown. $200.00 – 250.00. Right: Standard decoration. $65.00 – 80.00.

Left: Pear. Has been found in a few solid colors. $100.00 – 125.00.
Right: Flat Leaf Apple. $90.00 – 110.00.

Flat Leaf Apple. $90.00 – 110.00.

Flat Leaf Apple. $90.00 – 110.00.

Bunch of Bananas. Yellow with green & brown tinting. Note the wide variation available in the yellow color. 1948. McCoy mark. $125.00 – 150.00.

Hobby Horse. 1948. Marked McCoy. Production glazes were white (not shown) or brown and green under glaze shown in right photo. Left is a Cope decorated example. Production glazes, $100.00 – 150.00.
Cope decorated, $500.00+.

Pear. Yellow, spray decorated with red. 1952. Marked McCoy. $75.00 – 95.00.

Pear with the little cat from the Pussy at the Well McCoy planter attached as a handle. Likely one-of-a-kind. $500.00+.

Mr & Mrs. Owl. 1952. Marked McCoy. Hand decorated. Also found with pine cone lid. $75.00 – 95.00.

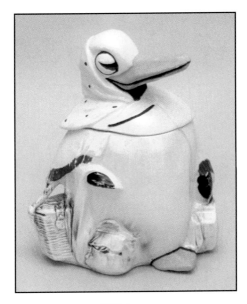

Mother Goose. 1948. Marked McCoy. Hand decorated white or brown under glaze. $150.00 – 175.00.

Kittens on Ball of Yarn. 1954. Marked McCoy. Hand decorated. Base glaze colors were maroon, yellow, and green. $80.00 – 95.00.

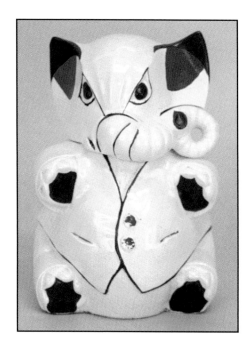

Elephant with Trunk on lid. 1953. No mark. $175.00 – 200.00.

Flower Pot with Plastic Flowers. 1950s. McCoy mark. $450.00 – 550.00.

Honey Bear (on the side of the tree). 1953. Marked McCoy. Rustic looking glaze. Jar on right in photo is the most common glaze found. Others are quite difficult to find.
Rustic, $65.00 – 80.00.
Yellow, $125.00 – 150.00.
White, $200.00 – 250.00.

Animals on Cylinders. 1950s. Marked McCoy. Pink ears.
Lamb, $175.00 – 200.00.
Cat, $200.00 – 225.00.
Dog, $175.00 – 200.00.

Clown in Barrel. 1953. Marked McCoy. As you can see above, they were produced in a wide range of colors. The pink and white examples are the more difficult of that group to obtain. The solid green example is very rare (top right).
Yellow, blue or green, $75.00 – 85.00.
Pink or white, $125.00 – 150.00.
Solid green, $200.00 – 250.00.

Indian. 1954. Marked McCoy. The story goes that an original design of this jar was prototyped and submitted to Pontiac Motors. The project was not accepted, so the design was changed and McCoy released it as their own product. Produced in two glaze colors: majolica on left and birchwood on right.
Majolica, $375.00 – 425.00.
Birchwood, $325.00 – 375.00.

Stagecoach. No mark. Hand decorated in various shades of brown or white. $800.00 – 1,000.00.

Pineapple. 1955. Marked McCoy. Most commonly found in natural colors as shown. Gold tint is somewhat rare.
Natural, $65.00 – 80.00.
Gold tint, $125.00 – 150.00.

Pumpkin (Jack-o-Lantern). 1955. Marked McCoy. Orange with matching cover or green cover. $500.00 – 600.00.

Two Kittens in a Basket. 1950s. Marked McCoy. $600.00 – 700.00.

Rooster. Marked McCoy. First introduced in 1956 in the brown blend glaze as shown. The following year they added the white with black spray. $60.00 – 95.00.

Lollipops. White with hand-painted lollipops. McCoy mark. 1958. $65.00 – 80.00.

Strawberry. Red with white drip glaze and green cover. McCoy mark. 1955. $65.00 – 80.00.

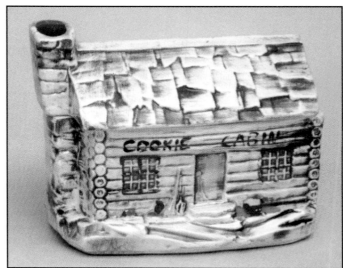

Modern. White with red decoration. Angled lid. McCoy mark. 1958. $65.00 – 75.00.

Cookie Cabin. 1956. Marked McCoy. Ivory with brown decoration. Much less common, white with black decoration.
Brown, $65.00 – 80.00.
Black, $150.00 – 175.00.

Animals on Basketweave Bottoms. 1956. Marked McCoy. All hand decorated. All four styles $75.00 – 90.00.

Pine Cones, Apples, and Pears on Basketweave Bottoms. 1957. Marked McCoy. Hand decorated under glaze. All three styles $70.00 – 85.00.

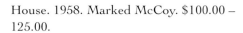

House. 1958. Marked McCoy. $100.00 – 125.00.

Floral Cookie Jar. 1956. Marked McCoy. Hand decorated. White with red flowers or yellow with blue flowers. $50.00 – 60.00.

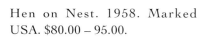

Hen on Nest. 1958. Marked USA. $80.00 – 95.00.

Davy Crockett. 1957. Marked USA. Hand decorated. $575.00 – 650.00.

Teepee Cookie Jars. 1956. Marked McCoy.
Top photo: Straight-top Style, $250.00 – 300.00.
Bottom photo: Slant-top Style, $300.00 – 350.00.

Jug (Cookie Jug). 1958. Marked McCoy. Two sizes: 9½" & 8½" tall. $35.00 – 45.00 each.

Covered Wagon. Production glaze is ivory with brown spray. 1960. Marked McCoy. Gold example is very rare.
Production glaze, $80.00 – 95.00.
Gold, $400.00+.

Gingerbread Boy. 1961. Marked USA. $75.00 – 85.00.

Fruit in Basket. 1961. Natural colors. Hand decorated as shown by left jar. This jar is marked McCoy. Right jar is marked with #157 which was the catalog number of the production run of jar on left. Right jar is slightly taller than the left one. $65.00 – 80.00 each.

Corn (Ear of Corn). 1958. Marked McCoy. Shown in production yellow with original sticker and unusual white glaze color.
Yellow, $150.00 – 175.00.
White, $300.00 +.

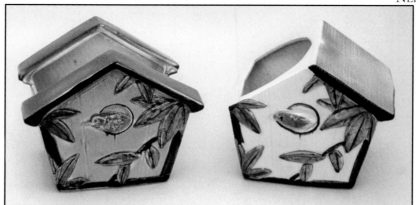

Wren House. 1959. Marked McCoy. Came with black or green trim. The roof also was produced in two styles. See top photo.

Middle photo shows the style with a center portion of the entire roof as the lid.

Bottom photo: Style is pictured with one entire side of the roof as the lid.

Center lid, $400.00 – 500.00.

Side lid, $150.00 – 200.00.

Tulip. Flower pot shape. White with red or yellow tulip decoration. 1958. McCoy mark. $225.00 – 275.00.

Drum. White with red decoration. Brown decoration is very unusual. 1960. McCoy mark.
Red, $75.00 – 90.00.
Brown, $200.00 +.

Old Churn. 1961. No mark. Three bands around churn. $225.00 – 250.00.

Barrel Cookie Jar. 8¾" & 10" tall. 1958. No mark.
Small, $30.00 – 35.00.
Large, $35.00 – 40.00.

Animal Crackers. 1960. Marked McCoy. Made with & without small raised dots. $85.00 – 100.00.

Squirrel. 1961. Marked McCoy. Production glaze coloring as pictured on left. Very rare jar. On right is the same jar from the Cope collection.
Standard, $3,000.00 – 4,000.00. Cope Jar, $5,000.00+.

Leprechaun. Possibly only 100 made. No mark. Made in solid red or green. $1,800.00 – 2,500.00.

Globe. Hand decorated countries. 1960. Marked McCoy. $300.00 – 375.00.

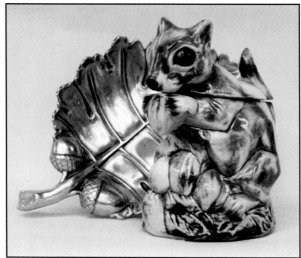

Kookie Kettle. Black matte with gold decoration. 1960. Marked McCoy. $35.00 – 40.00.

Chipmunk. Ivory with brown spray. 1960. Marked McCoy. $100.00 – 125.00.

Left: Same Kookie Kettle as above only in Antique Rose design. $200.00 – 250.00.
Right: Cylinder with same Antique Rose design. $55.00 – 65.00.

Wishing Well. "Wish I Had A Cookie". 1961. McCoy mark. $40.00 – 50.00.

Wedding Jar. White with 22K gold trim and finial. 1961. McCoy mark. $75.00 – 90.00.

Floral Cookie Jar. McCoy mark. Black with floral decoration. $35.00 – 40.00.

Nibble Kettle. 1960. McCoy mark. Black or white. White, $80.00 – 100.00. Black, $50.00 – 60.00.

Caboose. 1961. Marked McCoy. Hand decorated. $200.00 – 225.00.

Christmas Tree. Hand decorated. 1959. Marked McCoy. Far left example has exceptional amount of silver highlight decoration. $800.00 – 1,000.00.

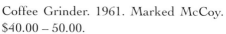

Kettle. 1961. Antique bronze finish. Marked McCoy. $30.00 – 40.00.

Coffee Grinder. 1961. Marked McCoy. $40.00 – 50.00.

Pitcher (Gay Time) Jar. Blue with white cover and decal decoration. Marked McCoy. 1961. Note the two different decal designs available. $65.00 – 80.00.

Oaken Bucket. 1961. No mark. Left example of brown spray decoration is most commonly found. Gray color is less common. Silver overtone is very rare.
Brown, $25.00 – 35.00.
Gray, $35.00 – 40.00.
Silver, $75.00 – 100.00.

Windmill. Blue spray with hand decoration. 1961. McCoy mark. $85.00 – 100.00.

Rocking Chair (Dalmatians). 1961. Marked McCoy. $325.00 – 375.00.

Lamp. 1963. Marked McCoy. Most commonly found in black with gold trim accents. White jar with the gold trim accents is difficult to find.
Black, $60.00 – 70.00.
White, $100.00 – 125.00.

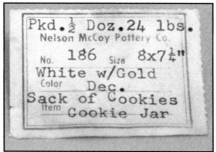

Original tag from the Sack of Cookies Jar.

Sack of Cookies. 1961. Marked McCoy. White with gold decoration. $85.00 – 100.00.

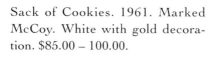

Puppy (holding sign). 1961. Marked McCoy. $50.00 – 60.00.

Kettle. 1963. Marked McCoy. Antique bronze finish. $40.00 – 50.00.

Cookie Jars

No. 170—9½ x 7"
Drum Cookie Jar
White w/Red Decoration
Packed ½ Doz. Wt. 29 lbs.
$11.40 per Dozen

No. 171—9½ x 8"
Kettle Cookie Jar
Black Matt w/Gold Decoration
and Brass Handle
Packed ½ Doz. Wt. 26 lbs.
$11.40 per Dozen

No. 172—10½ x 7"
Chipmunk Cookie Jar
Ivory w/Brown Spray
Packed ½ Doz. Wt. 24 lbs.
$11.40 per Dozen

No. 173—9½ x 7½"
Globe Cookie Jar
Aqua w/Decorated Countries
Silver Airplane & Gold Trim
Packed ½ Doz. Wt. 28 lbs.
$11.40 per Dozen

No. 153—9½ x 8"
Wren House Cookie Jar
Pink w/Black Trim
Brown w/Green Trim
Packed ½ Doz. Wt. 30 lbs.
$11.40 per Dozen

No. 175—10 x 8"
Animal Cracker Cookie Jar
White w/Decorated Crackers
Packed ½ Doz. Wt. 28 lbs.
$11.40 per Dozen

No. 148—9½ x 7½"
Covered Wagon Cookie Jar
Ivory w/Brown Spray
Packed ½ Doz. Wt. 32 lbs.
$11.40 per Dozen

No. 176—11 x 8"
Turkey Cookie Jar
Natural Decoration
Packed ½ Doz. Wt. 36 lbs.
$11.40 per Dozen

No. 147—10 x 7½"
Barrel Cookie Jar
Brown Decorated
Packed ½ Doz. Wt. 31 lbs.
$11.40 per Dozen

No. 147S
8¾ x 6½"
Barrel Cookie Jar
Brown w/Yellow Decoration
Packed 1 Doz. Wt. 42 lbs.
$7.80 per Dozen

No. 144—9½ x 7"
Jug Cookie Jar
White w/Brown Cover
Packed ½ Doz. Wt. 31 lbs.
$11.40 per Dozen

No. 144S
8½ x 6½"
Jug Cookie Jar
White w/Brown Decoration
Packed 1 Doz. Wt. 42 lbs.
$7.80 per Dozen

No. 20—7¾ x 7½"
Apple Cookie Jar
Yellow w/Sprayed Decoration
Packed ½ Doz. Wt. 26 lbs.
$11.40 per Dozen
Also available in solid Red w/Green
Leaves specified as No. 20R
Same Price

No. 151—9 x 8" House Cookie Jar
Green and Brown Spray Decorated
Packed ½ Doz. Wt. 35 lbs.
$11.40 per Dozen

No. 28SA
9½ x 6½"
Cookie Jar
White w/Red Apple Decoration
Packed 1 Doz. Wt. 42 lbs.
$7.80 per Dozen

No. 143—9 x 8½"
Lollipop Cookie Jar
White w/Hand Painted Lollipops
Packed ½ Doz. Wt. 26 lbs.
$11.40 per Dozen

No. 136—8½ x 6¾"
Cabin Cookie Jar
Ivory w/Brown Spray
Decorated
Packed ½ Doz. Wt. 29 lbs.
$11.40 per Dozen

Note: All Cookie Jars Individually Boxed except nos. 144S, 147S and 28S. In addition, you may make up your own Assortment of any THREE jars illustrated above which will be packed 2 each in a ½ Dozen Master Carton.

11

Hand
Decorated
Ceramic
Cookie
Jars

HAND DECORATED
Cookie
Jar

180 - Wishing Well

181 - Wedding Jar

182 - Caboose

187 - Wind Mill

179 - Coffee Grinder

184 - Pitcher

186 - Sack of Cookies

178 - Oaken Bucket

McCOY
U.S.A.

185 - Puppy

THE NELSON McCOY POTTERY COMPANY
Factory - Office   Roseville, Ohio

183 - Floral

Printed in U.S.A.

LITHOGRAPHY BY PAPPAS BROS. PARKERSBURG, W. VA.

Stove (Cook Stove). Black or white with hand-decorated trim. 1962. Marked McCoy. $30.00 – 40.00.

Below: Cookie Bank. 1961. Marked McCoy. $150.00 – 175.00.

Picnic Basket. 1961. No mark. Ivory with hand-decorated fruit. $60.00 – 75.00.

Circus Horse. Marked McCoy. 1961. Production glaze black with hand decoration with cold paint as shown. White horse was not production glaze and all hand decoration is under glaze; missing lid. Black, $200.00 – 250.00. White, $1,000.00+.

Grandfather Clock. 1962. No mark. Black/brown spray decoration as pictured in far left example is most common glaze found. Green and silver are tough to find. Has also been found in solid yellow.
Black/brown, $80.00 – 100.00.
Green, silver, or yellow, $125.00 – 150.00.

Cookie Safe. 1962. Marked McCoy on legs. $60.00 – 70.00.

Cookie Mug. 1965. Birchwood with brown decoration. $40.00 – 45.00.

Cookie Bell. Hand decorated. 1963. No mark. $40.00 – 50.00.

Engine. 1962. Marked McCoy. The first production color was the black with red and gold decoration as shown above. The yellow color pictured above with black and red decoration was the second production color combination made. The other glaze colors shown below, orange and silver, are quite rare. This Engine Jar has also been found in a solid matte gold coloring.
Black, $125.00 – 175.00.
Yellow, $175.00 – 225.00.
Orange, $225.00 – 250.00.
Silver or gold, $250.00 – 300.00.

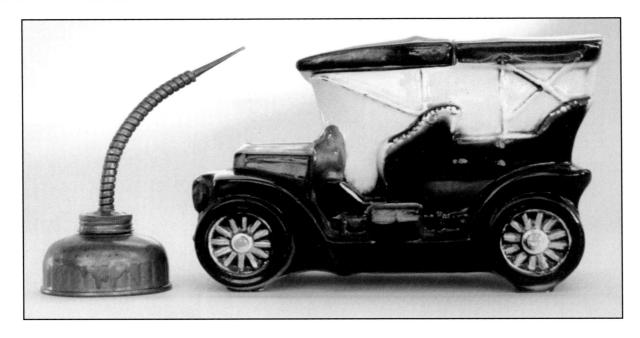

Old Fashioned Auto (Touring Car). 1962. Marked McCoy. Black with hand-painted trim.
$85.00 – 100.00.

Chef (Bust). 1962. No mark. $90.00 – 110.00.

Spaceship (Friendship 7). Black with white trim.
1962. No mark. $150.00 – 200.00.

Early American (Frontier Family). 1964. No mark. $50.00 – 60.00.

Round Plain. White with gold decoration. 1964. No mark. $40.00 – 50.00.

Tomato. Red with green stem. 1964. McCoy mark. $60.00 – 70.00.

Duck. 1964. No mark. Green leaf in bill and red decoration. $75.00 – 90.00.

Snow Bear. 1965. Marked McCoy. Hand decorated. $60.00 – 65.00.

Country Stove. First issue in 1963. Re-issued in 1978 and again in 1983. McCoy mark. Made in black and white. $25.00 – 35.00.

Cookie Pot. 1964. McCoy mark. Came in blue or white with decal. $35.00 – 50.00.

Jewel Box (Cookie Box). Basic white with green trim. 1963. Marked USA. $125.00 – 150.00.

Cookie Log with Squirrel finial. 1971. $35.00 – 45.00.

Cookie Jug. 1965. Marked McCoy. $35.00 – 45.00.

Barn (red barn, cow in door.) 1963. Marked McCoy. $350.00 – 400.00.

Astronauts. Cover has astronauts sitting on space capsule. 1963. Marked USA. $700.00 – 900.00.

Kangaroo. 1965. Marked McCoy. Birchwood color. $375.00 – 450.00.

Kangaroo. Was released after the birchwood color Kangaroo Jar. No mark. $275.00 – 300.00.

Round Canister. Shown with original box. 1969. Marked McCoy Brown drip glaze example pictured. Also came in almond with a dark brown cover and in an all-yellow glaze coloring. $40.00 – 50.00.

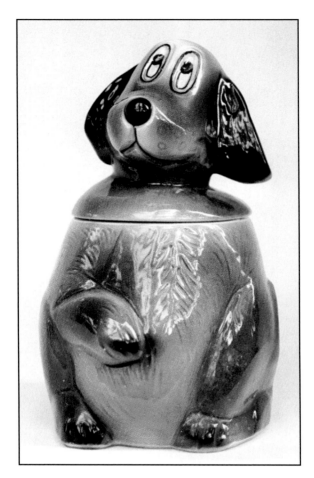

"Mac" Dog. 1967. Marked USA. Sprayed decoration in browns with black facial features. $80.00 – 95.00.

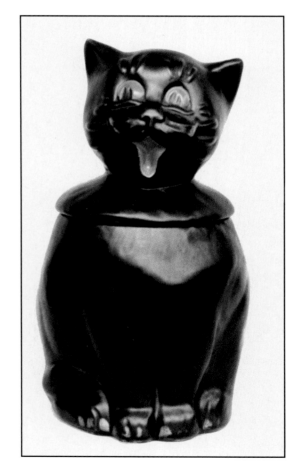

Coalby Cat. Black with decorated facial features. 1967. Marked USA. $325.00 – 375.00.

Soup Tureen. 1965. McCoy mark. $55.00 – 70.00.

Colonial Fireplace. 1967. Marked USA.
Hand decorated. $75.00 – 90.00.

Cookie Kettle. 1965. No mark. Gold lettering
(Gypsy Pot). $35.00 – 50.00.

Forbidden Fruit. 1967. Marked McCoy. Most
common glaze coloring pictured on left. Green tone
glaze on right jar is quite rare.
Standard glaze, $65.00 – 80.00.
Rare glaze, $125.00 –150.00.

Fortune Cookie (Chinese Lantern). 1965. McCoy mark.
Black top. Rings can be found in a variety of colors. Sample in photo is a red one with only a little of the color
remaining. $55.00 – 75.00.

Aladdin Teapot. Made for only one year, 1965 –
1966. McCoy mark. $50.00 – 70.00.

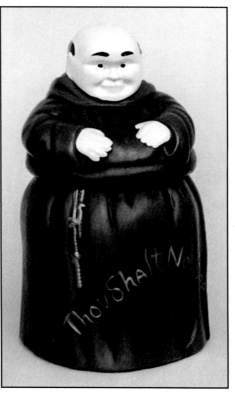

Dutch Treat Barn (Girl in Door). 1968. No mark. $40.00 – 50.00.

Monk (Thou Shall Not Steal). 1970. No mark. $40.00 – 50.00.

Early American Chest (chiffonier). Spray decorated brown. 1965. McCoy mark. $80.00 – 90.00.

Barrel. "Cookies" sign on finial. Marked McCoy. 1969. Black or brown. $125.00 – 150.00.

Cylinder: Nursery Characters. Six designs: Mary, Mary Quite Contrary; Humpty Dumpty; Little Miss Muffet; Little Bo Peep; Little Boy Blue; Baa Baa Black Sheep. 1970. No mark. $65.00 – 80.00.

Modern Pineapple. 1967. Marked USA. $75.00 – 90.00.

Cylinder (Mediterranean). Stained glass diamond shape decoration. 1967. Marked McCoy. $70.00 – 80.00.

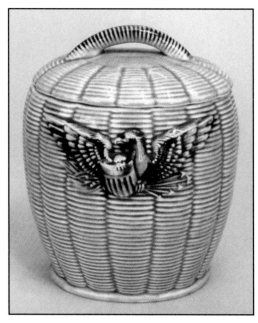

Cylinder (Honeycomb). Marked McCoy. 1969. Yellow or red glaze. $75.00 – 85.00.

American Eagle. 1968. Came in dark and light brown glaze colors. Example shown is light color. No mark. $40.00 – 50.00.

White Rooster. White with red comb and wattle. 1970. Marked McCoy. $50.00 – 60.00.

Time for Cookies (Mouse on Clock). 1968. No mark. Browntone glaze on left was production style. Silver glaze on right is difficult to find. Brown, $40.00 – 50.00. Silver, $200.00 – 225.00.

Quaker Oats. 1970. Made for the Quaker Oats Co. Marked USA. $500.00 – 600.00.

Apollo. Silver with hand decoration. Marked McCoy. 1970. $900.00 – 1,100.00.

Stump (Monkey on Stump). 1970. Marked McCoy. $60.00 – 75.00.

Snoopy (on dog house). 1970. Made for Sears, Roebuck & Co. Marked "United Features Syndicate." $175.00 – 200.00.

Cylinder. Popeye (1971), Bugs Bunny (1971), and Yosemite Sam (1972). No marks. Pictured below is the same jar with a two-tone glaze. Difficult to find. Any of the "Decal" Jars, $150.00 – 200.00. Two-tone, $60.00 – 75.00.

Sad Clown. 1970. Hand decorated. Marked McCoy. $75.00 – 85.00.

Pirate's Chest. 1970. Marked McCoy. Silver spray. $125.00 – 150.00.

Stump (Rabbit with a Cookie). 1971. McCoy mark. $65.00 – 75.00.

Stump (with Mushroom). 1972. McCoy mark. $55.00 – 65.00.

Stump (with Frog). 1972. McCoy mark. $75.00 – 85.00.

Cylinder shape. Floral decals in panels. 1970. Marked McCoy. Wide variety of colors. $35.00 – 45.00.

Orange and Apple Jars. Both big jars. 1970. Marked McCoy. $50.00 – 60.00 for each.

Little Red Bean Pot. 1971.
Marked McCoy. $35.00 – 45.00.

Barnum's Animals. 1972. USA
mark. $300.00 – 350.00.

Teapot. Made in white, green, and
metallic black. 1972. Marked
McCoy. $50.00 – 70.00.

New Strawberry. Red or
white with green cover.
1972. Marked McCoy.
$35.00 – 45.00.

Happy Face (Have A Happy Day). Shown with original box. 1972. Marked McCoy. $60.00 – 80.00.

Same Happy Face jar as at left only in black with gold decoration. Very rare. $200.00 – 300.00.

Photo from booklet on Nelson McCoy Pottery showing the hand decorating of the Happy Face jar. Booklets were shipped along with many pieces from the same era.

Cookie Jug. Ceramic Cork. 1971. No mark. $30.00 – 40.00.

Lemon. 1972. Marked McCoy. Shown with original box. $50.00 – 60.00.

Bear (Hamm's Bear). 1972. Marked USA. $225.00 – 250.00.

Rag Doll (Raggedy Ann). 1972. Marked USA. $100.00 – 125.00.

Pig (Winking Pig). 1972. Marked USA. $275.00 – 325.00.

Red Apple. 1972. Cover similar to one on Lemon. Marked McCoy. $40.00 – 50.00.

Early American Milk Can. 1972. Jar on left made in bronze and silver as shown. Marked Mc-Coy. $50.00 – 60.00.

W.C. Fields Snack Jar. 1972. Marked USA. $175.00 – 200.00.

Right: Milk Can. 1972. Marked McCoy. Several colors available for these jars and Jar on right in above photo. $35.00 – 45.00.

Same jar as above with very special hand decoration under glaze. $1,000.00+.

Burlap Bag. Similar base with two different covers. Red Bird. (1972). Marked USA. $55.00 – 70.00. Half circle finial. (1973). Marked McCoy. $40.00 – 50.00.

Cookie Jars

7.45   0131 3700
9 x 6½" Canister

0131 3239
9 x 6½" Canister

1123 3642
7¾" x 6½" Panel

0157 0500
11 x 7" Green Pepper

✓ 0183 0873
10 x 7" Bobby Baker
12.20

✓ 0201 3273
8 x 9" Pig
12.20

✓ *10.80* 0204 4000
10 x 8" Owl

✓ *15.60* 0206 8573
9 x 6¾ x 8" Dog House

12.50 0210 0873
11 x 10" Panda Bear

✓ 0216 3573
10.00 12 x 7" Koala Bear

0214 3699
8 x 5½" Round w/assorted Floral decals

18

Catalog page with Green Pepper, etc.

24.85 0219 8071
7¾ x 7" Kitten on Coal Bucket

18.75 0222 4673
11½ x 11" Football

18.75 0221 3673
13 x 8" Baseball

0223 7271
8 x 7 x 7" Strawberry Basket

0235 2073
11½" Happy Face

10.30 0253 7542
10" Fruit Festival Milk Can

0263 0825
10 x 8½" Strawberry

0266 3500
11½ x 7½" Cookie Churn

0271 4073
4 x 9½" Timmy Tortoise

9.90 0272 3573
11 x 6½" Hound Dog

1109 0800
9 x 6¼" Basket Weave

1109 7900
9 x 6¼" Basket Weave

7024 1600
8½ x 7½" Round

19

Catalog page.

Pepper. 1972. Marked McCoy. Production glaze colors were green and yellow. Brown and "mango" are very unusual glaze colors for this jar.
Standard glaze colors, $40.00 – 50.00.
Brown glaze, $125.00 – 150.00.
Mango glaze, $250.00 – 300.00.

Milk Jug (Spirit of '76). 1973. Marked McCoy. $35.00 – 45.00.

Milk Can (Spirit of '76). 1973. Marked McCoy. Pictured with original box. $60.00 – 75.00

Grandma (Granny). 1974. Marked McCoy. White with hand decoration. $125.00 – 150.00.

Grandma (Granny). 1972. Marked USA. Full color. $90.00 – 110.00.

Woodsy Owl. 1973. USA mark. $225.00 – 275.00.

Uncle Sam's Hat. 1973. USA mark. $700.00 – 900.00.

Pitcher. Examples shown are Yorkville and Blue Willow decal patterns. These pitchers were also made with Spice Delight and Fruit Festival decals. 1973 – 1977. Marked McCoy. $35.00 – 50.00.

Clyde. 1974. Marked McCoy. $225.00 – 275.00.

Canister. 1974. Made in a wide variety of decals and patterns. Marked McCoy. $45.00 – 60.00.

A very unusual decoration of the jar below. $1,000.00+.

Bobby the Baker. 1974. Marked McCoy. Note different hat styles.
Left Jar, $50.00 – 65.00.
Right Jar, $40.00 – 50.00.

Freddy the Gleep. Shown with original box. 1974. Marked McCoy. Also has been found in solid chartreuse green. $450.00 – 500.00.

Tea Kettle. 1974. Marked McCoy. Pictured left in photo. Other Kettle shown is from 1963; previously listed. Newer one is 12" in length in comparison to 11" on the older style. $35.00 – 45.00.

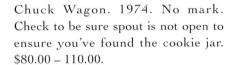

Chuck Wagon. 1974. No mark. Check to be sure spout is not open to ensure you've found the cookie jar. $80.00 – 110.00.

Milk Can. Made in a wide range of decals and patterns. Issued through the mid 1970s. Some have McCoy mark, others are marked USA. $50.00 – 75.00.

Betsy Baker. Basic white with red decoration. 1975. Marked McCoy. This jar was made with three different hat styles known. The two shown above have about the same value. $275.00 – 325.00.
The third style (not pictured) looks a bit like a sun hat with a brim all the way around and slightly turned down. $600.00 – 800.00.

Cork Lid. 1975. Marked McCoy. Jar came with lids with two different shapes to their bottom; cannot tell when lid is on jar. $150.00 – 200.00.

Pagoda. 1974. Brown or yellow top. Plain or floral decal. Marked McCoy. $40.00 – 50.00.

Bamboo. Spray painted in brown and tan. 1974. Marked McCoy. $50.00 – 60.00.

Owl Cookie Jars. Left and right Owl Jars in picture. 1978. Marked McCoy. $35.00 – 45.00.
Center Owl Jar. 1976. Marked McCoy. $50.00 – 60.00.

Cylinder. 1975. Marked McCoy. Made with a variety of decals and patterns. $25.00 – 35.00.

Cylinder (Madrid). 1974. Marked McCoy. $65.00 – 80.00.

Cylinder (Nostalgia). 1974. Marked McCoy. $45.00 – 60.00.

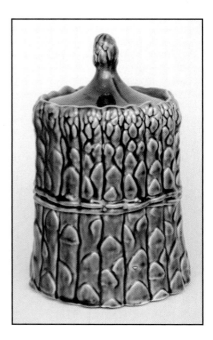

Milk Can. Made with several decorations. See page 275 for others. $50.00 – 75.00.

Pitcher. Spice Delight. For other examples of this same jar, see page 273. $35.00 – 50.00.

Asparagus. 1977. No mark. $40.00 – 50.00.

Cookie Churn. Light brown; two bands. 1977. No mark. $30.00 – 40.00.

Liberty Bell. 1975. Bronze finish. Marked McCoy. $60.00 – 75.00.

Tan and Brown. Random brush strokes. 1975. Marked McCoy. $65.00 – 75.00.

Milk Can. 1975. Marked McCoy. Made with a wide variety of decals and patterns. $40.00 – 50.00.

Peanut. 1976. Marked McCoy. Yellow or brown. $40.00 – 50.00.

Duck. 1976. $150.00 – 200.00.

Gypsy Pot. 1975. No mark. Hammered effect to finish. Bronze or white. $35.00 – 45.00.

Left to Right: Basket of Eggs, Basket of Strawberries (both 1977), Basket of Tomatoes, Basket of Potatoes (both 1978). All marked McCoy.

Basket of Strawberries, $55.00 – 65.00.

All other styles, $40.00 – 50.00.

Round (Canyon). 1979. Marked McCoy. $35.00 – 45.00.

Country Kitchen. 1978. Marked USA. White; flower impressed. $85.00 – 95.00.

OPPOSITE PAGE

Top Row

Left to right: Timmy Tortoise. Brown with butterfly finial. 1977. McCoy Mark. $35.00 – 45.00.

Timmy Tortoise. Non-production glaze colors. McCoy mark. $300.00+.

Hound Dog. Brown or rattan. 1977. USA mark. $25.00 – 35.00.

Center Row

Tilt Cookie/Candy Jar. Made with different decals. 1977. McCoy mark. $30.00 – 40.00.

Corn. 1977. Marked McCoy. Yellow or white. $80.00 – 90.00.

Panda Bear. 1978. Marked McCoy. The red Avon heart was on jars for Avon representatives. $45.00 – 55.00. With Avon heart, $80.00 – 90.00.

Bear and Barrel. Marked USA. 1978. $85.00 – 95.00.

Soccer Ball. 1978. Has whistle for finial. No mark. $1,800.00 – 2,000.00.

Soccer Ball. 1978. Rare yellow glaze. No mark. $2,000.00+.

Yellow Mouse. 1978. Facial features hand decorated. McCoy mark. $35.00 – 45.00

Pig. 1978. White with markings in black. McCoy mark. $40.00 – 50.00.

Ice Cream Cone. Hand decoration. 1978. McCoy mark. $40.00 – 50.00.

Panda Bear. 1978. USA mark. Hand decoration. $150.00 – 200.00.

Round-Brown Drip
█████████ #7024 1600
Pack 4
Wt. 21, Cube 1.69

School Bus
#0352 1P73
Pack 4
Wt. 18, Cube 1.46

Pink & Blue Stripe
#0131 3700
Pack 4
Wt. 23, Cube 1.69

House
#0161 8800
Pack 4
Wt. 25, Cube 2.17

Panda Bear
███████████
Pack 4
Wt. 19, Cube 1.69
#0210 0873

Garbage Can
#0356 4900
Pack 4
Wt. 18, Cube 1.69

Bobby The Baker
#0183 0873
Pack 4
Wt. 27, Cube 1.69

Traffic Light
#0351 1P73
Pack 4
Wt. 20, Cube 1.69

Pig
#0201 3273
Pack 4
Wt. 24, Cube 2.17

Lunch Box
#0357 8800
Pack 4
Wt. 20, Cube 1.46

Strawberry
#0263 0825
Pack 4
Wt. 22, Cube 2.17

Catalog page with Pig, etc.

Hocus Rabbit. 1978. Marked McCoy. Center and right photos show standard colors with hand decoration. Left photo is non-production glaze. Standard colors, $40.00 – 50.00. Special colors, $100.00 – 150.00.

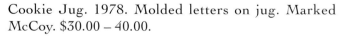

Old Fashioned Milk Can. Re-issue of similar older jar. 1978. No mark. $50.00 – 60.00.

Cookie Jug. 1978. Molded letters on jug. Marked McCoy. $30.00 – 40.00.

OPPOSITE PAGE — (Left to right)

Top Row: Round Canister. 1978. McCoy mark. Several glaze colors made. $25.00 – 35.00.

Lunch Bucket. 1978. USA mark. Contrasting top/bottom colors. $35.00 – 45.00.

Round (Blue Field). 1979. McCoy mark. $35.00 – 45.00.

Center Row: Basketweave. 1978. USA mark. All white or ivory with brown top. $35.00 – 45.00.

Traffic Light. 1978. USA mark. Solid yellow base color. $40.00 – 50.00.

Garbage Can. 1978. USA mark. Ivory color. $30.00 – 40.00.

Boy on Baseball. White baseball, red seams. Marked McCoy. 1978. $275.00 – 325.00. This jar has also been found in a lamp form.

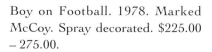

Boy on Football. 1978. Marked McCoy. Spray decorated. $225.00 – 275.00.

Catalog page.

OPPOSITE PAGE – (Left to right)

Top Row: Koala Bear. 1983. McCoy mark. Spray decorated brown. $85.00 – 100.00.

Koala Bear. 1983. McCoy mark. Rare white under glaze. $300.00+.

Strawberry Basket. 1978. McCoy mark. Dark (pictured) or light basket. $90.00 – 100.00.

Center Row (Both photos): Kitten on Coal Bucket. 1983. Several color combinations made. McCoy mark. Brown Kitten on black coal bucket, $200.00 – 250.00. All other glaze combinations, $250.00 – 300.00.

Dog House. 1983. Marked McCoy. Hand decorated. $200.00 – 250.00.

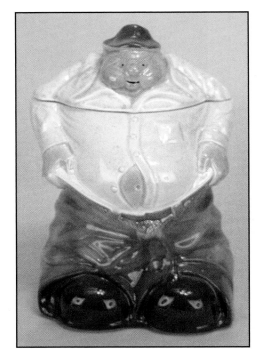

Chairman of the Board. 1985. USA mark. $450.00 – 550.00.

Pig. 1985. USA mark. $125.00 – 150.00.

Nabisco. 1974. McCoy mark. $60.00 – 80.00.

OPPOSITE PAGE (Left to right)

Top Row: Panel. 1985.USA mark. Various decal decorations. $30.00 – 35.00.
Grub Box. 1979. McCoy mark. Light or dark brown. $150.00 – 200.00.

Center Row: Hot Air Balloon. 1985. USA mark. Hand decorated. $35.00 – 45.00.
Burlap Sack. 1985. McCoy mark. Loop finial. $30.00 – 40.00.
School Bus. 1985. USA mark. Yellow, black, and white. $50.00 – 60.00.

Bottom Row: Christmas Teddy Bear. 1986. USA mark. Non-production. Rare. $400.00+.
Teddy Bear & Friend. 1986. USA mark. Bird on top of his head. $45.00 – 55.00. (Shown with original box).

Tug Boat. 1985. USA mark. $35.00 – 45.00.

Bear & Beehive. 1983. USA mark. $40.00 – 50.00.

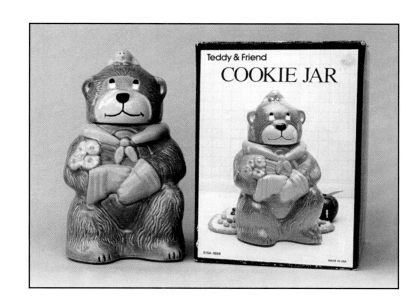

Chilly Willy. 1986. Marked USA. Shown on right with original box. White hat with a variety of colors of the scarf and gloves is standard production decoration. Left photo with red hat is very unusual.
Standard decoration, $40.00 – 50.00.
Unusual as left example, $100.00 – 200.00.

House. 1986. McCoy mark.
$300.00 – 350.00.

Cow. 1980s. Rare. $400.00+.

Goodie Goose. 1986. USA mark. $35.00 – 40.00.

Keebler Cookie Jar. Shaped like Keebler tree. 1986. USA mark. $50.00 – 70.00.

Coke Can. Red with white trim. 1986. USA mark. $90.00 – 110.00.

Coke Jug. Decal on jug. 1986. USA mark. $80.00 – 100.00.

Nelson McCoy

Cookie Jars

A. Coke Can
#1003 081D
Pack 4
Wt. 18, Cube 2.17

B. Coke Jug
#1004 361D
Pack 4
Wt. 21, Cube 2.17

C. Goodie Goose
#0166 0873
Pack 4
Wt. 22, Cube 2.17

Nelson McCoy
A Lancaster Colony Company

On the following pages, you will find a presentation of an absolutely wonderful selection of McCoy Cookie Jars. These jars were never put into production. There may be more than one in existence because whenever McCoy considered a new design, they would make several prototypes and more than one may have found its way out of the plant. We have not priced any of these jars. Their value can only be determined by what a given collector may pay for one of these one-of-a-kind jars on a given day. Where we are aware of a recent sale of any of the following, we have included that information for reference.

The Negro Chef jar. The only one known to exist. It may just be the most outstanding example of hand decoration on a jar by McCoy. Wonderful!

Here is a pair of the two styles of Grapes Jars that were considered but never produced. Simply beautiful! The dark style glaze jar is the only one known to exist and the pink/green jar with the bird on the lid is one of two known. Its twin was sold at auction in Roseville, Ohio, in July, 1998 for almost $7,000.00.

The Hillbilly Bear. Designed in the early 1940s.

The Fox. What an outstanding jar!

"Tony Veller." Marked NM. An example of this same jar with Cope decorations sold in 1998 for close to $10,000.

The Pillsbury Lady.

Grapes Press Cookie Jar.

Another glaze color example of the Grapes Press Cookie Jar.

Two examples of the Books Jar, only ones known to exist.

The Majorette Cookie Jar. Only one known. 1940s.

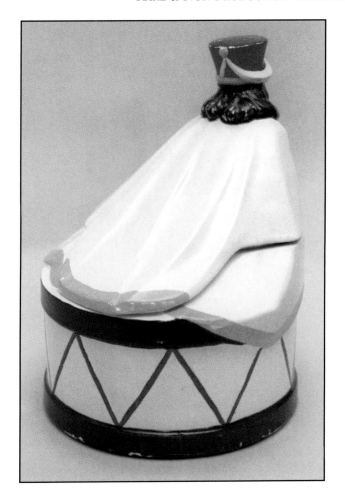

Back view of The Majorette.

White Round with Gold Rooster Finial. 1964.

Basketball.

Reclining Cow (Cookies & Milk). One of only two known to exist. The other is a white cow with black spots. The Reclining Cow shown was sold at auction in Roseville, Ohio, in July, 1998 for $10,000.00!

Vase shape with flowers. Jar color is a very dark green. Late 1950s.

Tug Boat. Only one known to exist.

Choo Choo with Smoke Jar in red glaze. Has also been found in gray and blue glazes. This red one pictured sold at auction in Roseville, Ohio, in July, 1998 for $4,600.00.

School Bus.

Sniffing Dog (with fly on nose).

Lion. This is a larger than normal jar.

Cookie Box.

White Cylinder Jar with unusual decoration.

Plate with same decoration as Christmas Jar at left. $50.00 – 60.00.

Christmas Cylinder Jar.

Turtle Cookie Jar. Only two known to exist at this time. Dated 1931 in design and has a USA mark. Likely made in the late 1930s. Collectors believe this jar may be McCoy. No confirmation of such at this time. The other example known has multiple gloss color glazes and sold at auction in July, 1998, in Roseville, Ohio for over $3,000.00.

Carrousel Cookie Jar. This jar was listed in the 1965 catalog along with the Cookie Mug and Cookie Bell. Only a few are known to exist.

These two jars are both pictured on a 1964 catalog page of a company called Great Northern Products Co. There are four other jars on that page that are proven McCoy jars. Many collectors believe these two jars to be McCoy but to date there is no documented proof. The left jar is the Corner Chest and the right the Oak Leaf. The ad notes that all the jars will be shipped from Roseville, Ohio, so that limits the possibilities of producers.

COOKIE JAR INDEX

Hanson, Bob, Craig Nissen and Margaret Hanson. *McCoy Pottery, Collector's Reference And Value Guide, Volume I.* 1996. Collector Books.

Huxford, Sharon & Bob. *The Collector's Encyclopedia of McCoy Pottery.* 1978. Collector Books.

Nichols, Harold. *McCoy Cookie Jars, From the First to the Latest.* 1987. Nichols Enterprises.

Sanford, Steve & Martha. *Guide to McCoy Pottery.* 1997. Adelmore Press.

NM Express, monthly McCoy newsletter. 1994 to present.

Our McCoy Matters, McCoy newsletter. 1988 – 1994.

McCoy Plaque. 4" x 5". Limited quantity made in 1991. This was, of course, not a Nelson McCoy Pottery piece but would be a great addition to the shelf of any collector. It duplicates the size and design of "The Pottery Shop," McCoy plaque made for J.C. Penney Co. in early 1980s but was never shipped. This plaque is only marked with the date made, 1991. It is pictured with the original pattern used to make the mold. Came with green or blue border. $200.00 – 250.00.

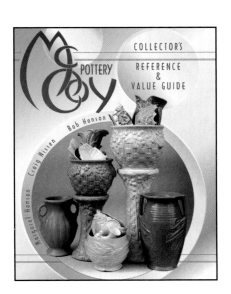

The cover of our Volume I book on Nelson McCoy Pottery. Over 2,000 pieces pictured in over 700 photos. To order, call Collector Books in Paducah, Kentucky, 1-800-626-5420.

The Collector's Cabinet

The Collector's Cabinet

Ruth Berges

San Diego • New York
A. S. Barnes & Company, Inc.
In London:
The Tantivy Press

The Collector's Cabinet text copyright ©1980 by Ruth Berges
A. S. Barnes and Co., Inc.

The Tantivy Press
Magdalen House
136-148 Tooley Street
London, SE1 2TT, England

First Edition
Manufactured in the United States of America
For information write to A. S. Barnes and Company, Inc.,
P.O. Box 3051, San Diego, CA 92038

Library of Congress Cataloging in Publication Data

Berges, Ruth.
   The collector's cabinet.

   Bibliography: p. 149
   Includes index.
   1. Porcelain—Collectors and collecting.
2. Faience—Collectors and collecting. 3. Majolica—
Collectors and Collecting. I. Title.
NK4230.B38   738'.075   77-84560
ISBN 0-498-02117-3

for my mother
for Marisol and Miranda

Contents

Preface

From Gold to Porcelain—The Art of Porcelain and Faïence was an introduction to the art of ceramics in the Orient. It briefly traced the history of faïence, and the discovery and development of porcelain manufacture in Western Europe. Individual manufactures, artists, and various categories of objects made were discussed in self-contained chapters. *Collector's Choice* of Porcelain and Faïence, the companion volume, followed a similar course, stressing Oriental influences on European factories and their interaction through itinerant workers. It was a somewhat more specialized book perhaps, less of a teaching volume, and was addressed particularly to the actual collector.

The present book, *The Collector's Cabinet*, again has the collector in mind. He may be a beginner who is looking for a starting point, or someone more advanced who seeks new ideas or stimulation. In no way does this volume intend to be patronizing. It merely chats casually with the collector, offering some insights and views gained from the author's own research and experience.

It should be pointed out that the carefully selected illustrations purposely range from modest to costly examples to show a wide choice. Many are published here for the first time. Some are of extremely rare objects; others are of more readily available specimens. As in the preceding volumes, photographs have been placed with those chapters where they are quite obviously applicable. However, some examples are of equally illustrative value to other chapters. Consultation of the comprehensive index will readily yield this information, avoiding innumerable tedious and distracting references in the text. Thus every collector referring to this book should be able to find something to appeal to his taste and in accordance with his means.

It is hoped that *The Collector's Cabinet* will find a useful place in the library of the collector as well as the art enthusiast, who simply enjoys reading about ceramics and the pleasures of collecting porcelain and faïence.

Acknowledgments

Acknowledgment is made to the following museums and collectors for their graciousness and cooperation in supplying photographs as enumerated below:

Bayerisches Nationalmuseum, Munich
Kestner-Museum, Hanover
Museum für Kunsthandwerk, Frankfurt/Main
Museum of Doccia Sesto Fiorentino
Residenzmuseum, Munich
Staatliche Museen, Kunstgewerbemuseum, Berlin
Staatliches Museum, Schwerin

Städtische Kunstsammlung, Augsburg
Mrs. S. Berges
Mr. and Mrs. Myron S. Falk, Jr.
Mrs. Harvey S. Firestone, Jr.
Mr. William H. Lautz
Mr. and Mrs. Frits Markus
Several Anonymous Collections

Any errors or omissions in the acknowledgments are unintentional, since ownership of objects may have changed while this volume was in the process of publication.

Introduction: The Collector's Decision

How does the collector begin to collect? Perhaps on impulse, by chance, after a careful personal decision, as a diversion, by following another's example, or through an inheritance. The causes and reasons for collecting are many and varied. Sometimes they overlap, but the symptoms and progress of collecting are the same consisting of the continuous desire to own and the actual acquisition of specific objects of beauty and, in most cases, of value.

The basis or nucleus of a collection is formed, continues to grow, and may eventually become diversified. Sometimes the collector feels he has reached his goal, his collection is complete, but usually that is not his last word: he will surely find another object that he must have.

While the collector's aim may be grand or modest, he is equally possessed by the irresistable urge to go out and seek new acquisitions, to pursue a known specimen or to chance upon the unexpected. The challenge of searching, the thrill of discovering, and the satisfaction of acquiring remain ever fresh and vital.

Most new collectors have an idea of what they want to collect. Some start out in different directions before they ultimately make the choice with which they will stay and feel happiest. One collector will rely totally on his dealer and be satisfied with the full documentation and description a knowledgable antiquarian will provide. Another will take a more scholarly view of his hobby and further investigate his subject through library research and museum study. Finding comparable objects pictured or described, learning more about their place in history and their significance in the life of their particular period, or discovering similar specimens in museum collections can be as gratifying and pleasurable as acquiring the object itself. Such peripheral activity, gauged to one's personal curiosity and perseverance, will certainly enhance the mere purchase of an art object. Additionally it will further one's education; the thorough study of a single art object will help one in a realistic way to relate to another era. Suddenly the distance into the past is diminished and the gap created by time, technological progress, and predictable changes in custom is bridged.

This is not intended to fault the collector who is content merely to acquire and enjoy his collection. It is sufficient for him if his aesthetic sensibility is satisfied; an object gained uplifts him from the commonplace of his daily life, from the endless rote of eating, sleeping, and working, even from the momentarily fashionable entertainments and mass-prescribed popular sports. He has found something that is entirely personal, that he can call his own, and attend to in his own time. His predilection and purpose will be reflected by his collection. It is a mirror of his personality.

His dealer's call excites him. The anticipation of

A pair of goblets of polished brown Böttger stoneware with gilt ornamentation; Meissen, ca. 1715.

A miniature vase decorated in the famille verte *manner with a floral design featuring a butterfly; porcelain of Meissen, ca. 1730.*

A small tureen and underdish painted in colors and gold with harbor scenes surrounded by lacework ornamentation; porcelain of Meissen, ca. 1730.

A sugar bowl decorated in colors and gold over underglaze blue with birds, fruit, and flowers; porcelain of Meissen, ca. 1730; Hausmalerei by Ferner, ca. 1750.

An octagonal bowl decorated on iron-red ground panels with white Chinese ornaments, the alternating white panels painted with Oriental emblems in colors; porcelain of Chelsea, raised-anchor period, ca. 1750.

An octagonal bowl decorated on iron-red ground panels with white Chinese ornaments, the alternating white panels painted with polychrome flowers; porcelain of Meissen, ca. 1730.

A dish decorated in the Imari style in shades of underglaze blue, iron red, and gold with peonies, birds in flight, and ornaments; porcelain of Arita, Japan, ca. 1700; with the Johanneum inventory mark of the Royal Saxon Collection, Dresden.

A large plate painted in colors with East Indian flowers and insects; porcelain of Meissen, ca. 1725.

A large teapot with a modeled mascaron spout, painted in polychrome and gold with Chinese playing cards in an outdoor setting, surrounded by lacework borders enclosing mother-of-pearl luster; on the reverse a merchant scene; porcelain of Meissen, ca. 1725; painted by Höroldt.

A plate decorated in underglaze blue, iron red, and gold in the Imari style; porcelain of Meissen, 1730-1735.

A tea caddy decorated in polychrome with hunting scenes and elaborate gilt ornamentation; porcelain of Meissen, ca. 1740.

A covered shell-shaped dish with a shell finial from the "swan" service, decorated in colors; in the center the coat of arms of Brühl-Kolowrat; porcelain of Meissen, ca. 1740.

A saucer painted in colors in the Watteau manner with a couple in a landscape; the border decorated with gilt lacework; porcelain of Meissen, ca. 1735; Hausmalerei by Mayer of Pressnitz, ca. 1750.

A pitcher painted in colors with botanical flowers and insects; porcelain of Meissen, ca. 1740; metal mounting.

Two plates painted in colors with groups of horsemen; porcelain of Meissen, ca. 1735; Hausmalerei in the manner of Mayer of Pressnitz, ca. 1750.

A large plate with a notched rim, painted in black monochrome with a figure in a landscape after an engraving by Pillement; porcelain of Meissen, ca. 1740.

A plate painted in polychrome with an Italian comedy scene, surrounded by a border of bird, fruit, and scrollwork ornaments; porcelain of Meissen, ca. 1735; Hausmalerei by Mayer of Pressnitz, ca. 1750.

A figure of a Turk, holding a basket, decorated in colors; porcelain of Meissen, ca. 1750; model by Kaendler.

A group of figures of a Chinese lady and her servant, decorated in polychrome; porcelain of Höchst, ca. 1765.

A fountain with a spout shaped as an eagle's head, painted with a landscape in purple monochrome; porcelain of Doccia, 1737-1757.

A figure of Pulcinella from the Italian comedy, decorated in colors; porcelain of Frankenthal, ca. 1760; model by Lanz.

17

A pair of seated figures, holding baskets of fruit; white-glazed French soft-paste porcelain, ca. 1760.

A large plate painted in polychrome with bouquets of flowers; faïence of Strasbourg, ca. 1865.

A tea caddy decorated in colors with a Chinese hunting rabbits; faïence of Durlach, ca. 1770; pewter lid. Strasbourg, ca. 1765.

*A large plate decorated in colors with roosters, birds, and a
flowering tree; faïence of Sinceny, ca. 1750.*

A sugar caster decorated in blue in the style Bérain; *faïence of Moustiers, ca. 1720.*

in this way; often they are notable for grandeur and monetary value, rather than personal warmth and expression. Frequently these collections justifiably become major museum acquisitions at which the average museum visitor gazes with awe. However, it is the smaller, specialized study collections that are carefully and thoughtfully selected and purchased, reflecting an individual person's taste and growing connoisseurship over a period of years, with which most art lovers and prospective collectors can find rapport. Such collections are the most numerous, varied, interesting, and stimulating. An admirer viewing someone's prized possessions may find that they form an intellectual and aesthetic link connecting him with the owner, most likely a stranger to him. The collector's achievement resembles that of an author or artist.

Another type of collector may suddenly tire of his treasures, dispose of them at a favorable time—usually at a profit, and start collecting again in an entirely different field. Finally, there is the collector who is excited about his art objects during the process of acquisition. Once he owns and installs them he barely acknowledges them with another glance, for his pleasure consists of searching, finding, and buying. In contrast to the romantic, who becomes attached to each object and its story, he has no use for contemplation and further study. He may on occasion be reminded of his treasures and be pleased if they are noticed by his friends or studied by a visiting scholar or museum curator. He will also feel flattered if one or another of his specimens is used for publication.

There are some collectors who prefer to buy at auction sales rather than from dealers; at auctions the factors of haste and being momentarily carried away by emotion and competitive bidding pose potential dangers. The more cautious, serious collector eschews the pressure of the salesroom atmosphere preferring the quiet, personal intercourse with a reputable dealer, at whose premises he can leisurely examine the object and make his decision.

What does the collector of ceramics collect? Ceramics of the eighteenth century and earlier periods probably offer the greatest diversification in collecting within a specific area. Choices abound in material, shape, style, size, and color. Whether one decides on sugar casters, saucers, snuffboxes, figural pieces, drug jars, tankards, tea caddies, cane handles, or decorative tablewares, to mention just a few categories, every taste and whim can be satisfied

possibly obtaining another extraordinary object will brighten his hours and days until he sees it, can handle it, and make the momentous decision of whether to call it his own. Or he may decide on the spur of the moment to make the rounds of several shops, expecting nothing and everything, then stumbling upon the unexpected. It is the unknown, the surprise element that absorbs him and really drives him relentlessly on.

Some collectors, barely concerned with artistic beauty, buy mainly for investment purposes, relying on the judgment of advisers and leaving the selection to them. Such collections rarely bear the owner's stamp and may leave an inaccurate impression of him. Many important collections have been built for a few years or a lifetime. It is never too late to start. Paradoxically, some large collections have been built within a relatively short time, while small ones grew throughout a collector's life. In this sense, collecting is like creating art. Some masterpieces were created within days, others over many years.

Collectors should not be discouraged by uncertainty or by mistakes. Knowledge is gained with each new acquisition and an error in judgment will teach a memorable lesson. Experts are not born overnight. Study and experience are equal partners. Effective collecting requires long-term dedication and patience. Taste, intuition, and common sense will help. Above all, there must be some feeling, a certain attraction to, or love for the object. In this all collectors will agree, no matter how divergent their reasons for collecting.

The Collector's Cabinet

PART I

Perennial Favorites

1

A World of Porcelain Children

Porcelain, the new European plastic medium of the eighteenth century, was particularly well-suited for the creation of small sculptures. The subject matter was widely diversified, but mostly idealized.

Individual figures and groups of figures depicted stock comedy characters and court jesters, gallants and their ladies, shepherds and gardeners, miners and soldiers, and a variety of mythological, religious, and allegorical personages. White-glazed or colorfully painted, they formed a dazzling array of the most attractive and unusual models. True, there were some caricatures like dwarfs after Callot etchings, fashionable at the time, but as a rule, in the course of the eighteenth century, people from real life were depicted.

Though they varied in subject matter, size, and coloring, the figures shared one trait: they were beautified, exemplifying the picturesque and pleasant aspects of life. The appearance of miners and other workmen, country girls, and ladies' maids was impeccable, their clothes were always intact and never looked soiled, but rather beautifully designed and colored. These small sculptures were intended for the pleasure and amusement of the nobility and idle rich: above all, they had to charm and please. The folds of a beggar's ragged garment should arouse admiration for the artist rather than sym-

A plate decorated in vivid colors and gold, depicting three putti *at play within a framework of elaborate* Laub und Bandelwerk; *the border consisting of polychrome fruit and flower vignettes alternating with gilt ornaments; porcelain of Meissen, ca. 1735;* Hausmalerei *by Bressler.*

A figure of a boy as Le Porteur de falot; *soft-paste biscuit of Sèvres, 1767; model by Le Riche.*

A pair of figures of children holding vases, decorated in colors; porcelain of Meissen, ca. 1750.

A figure of a boy feeding chickens, decorated in polychrome; porcelain of Frankenthal, ca. 1765.

A figure of a boy as a fishmonger, decorated in colors; porcelain of Meissen, ca. 1750.

Two figures of children as Italian comedy characters, decorated in polychrome; porcelain of Meissen, ca. 1760.

A group of figures of children, On ne s'avise jamais de tout, *inspired by an* opéra comique; *soft-paste biscuit of Sèvres, 1765; model by Falconet and Leclerc.*

A group of figures of playing children, La Lanterne magique; *soft-paste biscuit of Sèvres, 1757; model by Falconet after Boucher.*

A figure of a girl as a gardener, decorated in colors; porcelain of Limbach, Thuringia, ca. 1770.

A group of figures representing La Maîtresse d'école; *soft-paste biscuit of Sèvres, 1762; model by Falconet.*

A group of figures of children representing La Bohémienne; *soft-paste biscuit of Sèvres, 1765; model by Falconet and Leclerc.*

A pair of groups of children at play; Terre de Lorraine, Lunéville, ca. 1770; models by Cyfflé.

pathy for the subject's condition. This was an age of frivolity, not of social consciousness.

It comes as no surprise then that porcelain modelers with great frequency chose children as subject matter. What better pretense of innocence of which the rococo era was so fond? More often than not it became difficult to distinguish between children and cherubs. Who could resist the round, pretty faces and pleasantly plump bodies, partially undressed or entirely exposed, posing as various allegorical and mythological figures? The great Johann Joachim Kaendler at Meissen introduced children in porcelain. About mid-century, after his visit to Paris, where he was strongly influenced by the prevailing French rococo masters, in particular Boucher, his models were gradually transformed from his originally sturdy, expressive baroque children into the softer, daintier, and sweeter rococo cherubs.

Other important German factories followed Kaendler's example. Children portrayed the sea sons, gods and goddesses, and the arts; they were dressed up as gardeners, flower girls, vendors, and musicians displaying the appropriate attributes.

In France at the soft-paste factory of Vincennes, removed to Sèvres in the mid-fifties, the production of white biscuit figures predominated. Promoted by the most influential personage at the court of Louis XV, the Marquise de Pompadour, who was enchanted by these compositions, they became a factory specialty. Executed by gifted modelers after drawings by Boucher, these soft creamy-white sculptures with an unglazed mat surface depicted children in every conceivable situation and pose. They played games or at romance, they represented scenes from various contemporary comedies and pantomimes, they languished or wept over major and minor tragedies, they posed as shepherdesses, butter churners, and harvesters.

Though still under Boucher's influence, the sculptor Falconet gradually introduced a classical note. The figures of his children became more graceful and under his hand outgrew their childish chubbiness. As their bodies and limbs grew long and slender, their faces lost that wholesome roundness. Plump infants turned into adolescent-like classical nymphs and youths. Yet the enchanting sweetness and human warmth of their expressions remained.

The back-to-nature movement, preached by Rousseau in France, found a fervent follower in Johann Peter Melchior at Höchst in the 1770's. Strongly influenced by the modelers at Vincennes and Sèvres, his specialty became children. But in contrast to the white unglazed biscuit, he painted his models with delicate pastel colors. Children were dressed as Near Eastern potentates or portrayed mythological subjects; they were pictured making music, feeding birds and chickens, playing games, accidentally breaking a jug, smiling, sleeping, grieving, and weeping. Prettily presented their sorrows seemed light, their joys even lighter.

One might mention several other factories that excelled at porcelain sculptures of children such as Frankenthal, Berlin, Vienna, Nymphenburg, Chelsea, and Capodimonte. Their productions differed somewhat from one another in concept, mood, and temperament. Some appeared to be *putti*, only missing the wings; others were distinctly earthbound though with angelic expressions. All were children, tender or mischievous, with an innocence real or assumed. All reflected the incredible fantasy and originality of the eighteenth century modelers. These artists created in porcelain a world of children who could do no wrong, who would never cause a frown. They could only be loved and adored.

2

In Barnyard and Forest

Again and again we are confronted with and astonished by the extraordinary achievements of the eighteenth century modelers and painters of ceramics. The animal world in particular, so exhaustively portrayed, merits our attention. Each species, in itself, encompasses an infinite variety. To name only two popular examples, birds and dogs, is to envisage the most diverse and colorful array of household pets and other unfettered, feathered friends in porcelain and faïence, ranging in style from primitive and amusing to elegant and refined representations.

The innovative modeler responsible for a whole era of incomparable animal sculpture, who inspired numerous other artists at Meissen and factories elsewhere, was of course Kaendler. Though preceded briefly by Johann Gottlob Kirchner, another able porcelain animal modeler, it was Kaendler who intuitively understood and truly mastered the new medium. Of forty-four years spent at Meissen, Kaendler's first five years were devoted almost exclusively to the modeling of animals for Augustus the Strong's Japanese Palace. An order list for the palace specified 214 diverse large and small animals and 218 various birds of different sizes, most of which were eventually modeled and delivered.

Kaendler's powerful baroque modeling became

immediately apparent from his first large animals, including the famed recumbent goats, crowing cock, and Bolognese dog. Here was a superbly gifted sculptor who created balanced compositions accentuating strong, boldly curved lines in a way that enhanced spacious surfaces of the prized white-glazed porcelain with a dazzling play of light. Later, on smaller models, the addition of brilliant colors stressed other highlights of the modeler's craft. Any two identical models, differently decorated, surprise and delight with their effective variations.

Kaendler approached his subjects scientifically as well as artistically. It was customary, if not obligatory, for eighteenth century monarchs to cultivate an interest in zoology, and its study was enthusiastically encouraged at the Dresden court. The King supported an expedition to Africa from 1730 to 1733. He kept a fish preserve, bird sanctuary, and menagerie. A great variety of stuffed birds could also be admired in the King's art chambers. The menagerie was installed near the hunting lodge in Dresden-Neustadt, indicating that not only boar, stag, and deer were hunted, but such beasts as lions and tigers as well.

For weeks before Kaendler began to model animals, he studied them live and stuffed in Dresden

*A vase, richly decorated in colors with an elaborate
pavilion, groups of figures on islands amidst waves and
clouds, and cranes and bats in flight; porcelain of China,
K'ang Hsi period, 1662-1722.*

A barrel-shaped flask, decorated with ornamental yellow
bands and in the center with a bouquet of flowers in colors;
inscribed at each end: A ma bonne, eau de vie, 1779;
faïence of Nevers, eighteenth century.

*A large gadrooned bowl, decorated in blue and manganese
purple with* Chinoiseries; *faïence of Frankfurt, seventeenth century.*

A pair of figures of putti *as musicians, standing on rococo pedestals; decorated in colors, the bases enhanced with gilding; porcelain of Ludwigsburg, ca. 1765.*

A pair of groups of figures: "Children with a Bird Nest" and "The Flute Lesson," decorated in colors; porcelain of Höchst, ca. 1775; models by Melchior.

A pair of figures of pigeons decorated in manganese
purple, yellow, and green, and a pair of figures of canaries
decorated in yellow and green; faïence of Mosbach,
eighteenth century.

A covered dish in the shape of a lettuce, naturalistically
painted in shades of green and purplish pink; porcelain of
Meissen, ca. 1745.

A covered dish shaped as a lemon, naturalistically colored, with a finial of polychrome blossoms and leaves; resting on three leaves encrusted with colorful flowers; porcelain of Meissen, ca. 1750.

A covered dish shaped as a bunch of purplish blue grapes, the finial a yellowish green stem terminating in molded leaves; porcelain of Meissen, ca. 1760

A small, double-handled urn, painted with polychrome sprigs of flowers; filled with a strawberry plant, bearing blossoms and fruit, naturalistically colored; porcelain of Meissen, ca. 1750. An openwork basket, its intersections decorated with molded blue forget-me-nots; filled with a profusion of polychrome garden flowers; porcelain of Meissen, ca. 1765.

A covered dish in the shape of a large yellow rose attached to a white-glazed dish; German faïence, middle of the eighteenth century.

*A pair of figures of a cock and hen, white-glazed with
touches of iron red, standing on brown rockwork bases;
porcelain of Arita, Japan, early eighteenth century.*

*A pair of water droppers, in the shape of ducks, decorated
in colors; porcelain of Japan, eighteenth century.*

A figure of a rabbit, white-glazed with touches of color; porcelain of Arita, Japan, eighteenth century.

A large vase with a yellow ground, embellished with colorful floral borders; the reserve panels decorated in polychrome in the Löwenfinck manner with fantastic animals in East Indian floral settings; porcelain of Meissen, 1730-1735.

A hexagonal tea caddy painted in iron red with birds and enhanced with silver ornamentation; porcelain of Meissen, ca. 1720; Augsburg Hausmalerei.

A plate decorated in colors with a fantastic animal, butterfly, and East Indian flowers; porcelain of Meissen, ca. 1730.

A handleless cup and saucer decorated in colors with chinoiseries *surrounded by ornaments; on the reverse of the cup, a bear diving into a beehive; porcelain of Meissen, ca. 1725.*

A plate painted in purple monochrome and gold with a fantastic animal and the coat of arms of the Münchhausen family; porcelain of Meissen, 1735-1740.

A sugar bowl with the figure of a hare as a finial; painted with polychrome harbor scenes in reserves on a dark blue ground; porcelain of Meissen, ca. 1725.

A large figure of a bustard perched on a trunk with modeled oak leaves; white-glazed porcelain of Meissen, ca. 1730; model by Kirchner.

A figure of a pug, with a puppy, seated on a base encrusted with polychrome modeled flowers; naturalistically decorated in colors; porcelain of Meissen, ca. 1745; model by Kaendler and Reinicke.

A figure of a Bolognese terrier, naturalistically modeled and painted with brown patches; porcelain of Meissen, ca. 1745; model by Kaendler.

35

A pair of figures of nesting chickens, naturalistically painted in colors; porcelain of Meissen, ca. 1740; models by Kaendler.

A figure of a parrot decorated in bright colors; porcelain of Meissen, ca. 1745; model by Kaendler.

A figure of a sea gull, naturalistically modeled and decorated in colors; porcelain of Meissen, ca. 1750; model by Kaendler.

A group of figures of fighting animals; white-glazed porcelain of Vienna, ca. 1755.

A figure of a seated wolf, his tail swept forward to form part of the base; painted in naturalistic colors; soft-paste porcelain of Chantilly, middle of the eighteenth century.

A figure of a recumbent lion, painted with a yellow mane and with touches of black; faïence of Nevers, ca. 1700.

A covered dish in the shape of a fish attached to an underdish; the dish elaborately modeled with fine reeding and openwork; the fish naturalistically decorated in colors; dotted with molded green sprigs of parsley; porcelain of Volkstedt, Thuringia, ca. 1765.

A teapot in the shape of a hen, the cover finial shaped as a chick, with others peeking out from her feathers; decorated in yellow, manganese purple, and blue; North German faïence, eighteenth century; after a Meissen model by Kaendler.

and Moritzburg. Some of his best creations, including the lion, lynx, aurochs, and a rare pelican, could be compared to the King's live collection. The elephant and rhinoceros, for which no live models were available, were copied from old props formerly used for carousels, fashioned for court processions and festive occasions that took place in 1709 and 1714.

Kaendler's variety of animal sculpture abounded and included many exotic examples such as the numerous colorful parrots. But his creations, except for teapots in animal shapes modeled after Chinese examples, diverged distinctly from Oriental specimens, fascinating because of their air of fantasy. Kaendler strove for naturalistic representation,

with painstakingly detailed strokes imitating plumage and fur in clear luminous colors. The animal compositions were naturalistic too, placed in languid repose or arranged deceptively poised and casual, but throbbing with the strain and tension anticipating a sudden leap or flight. A bird's swift, darting, upward thrust, a cat's prickling awareness, a dog's moment of lazy restfulness, a chicken squatting sleepily yet warily on its nest—all actions and moods were realistically caught and portrayed. The movements and expressions were not of humans but truly those of animals and birds, accurately observed and successfully rendered.

Except for the atypical, specifically commissioned, whimsical monkey band, whose members were depicted as humans, there was nothing playful about Kaendler's animal world. However, his scientific observations did not distract him from his artistic and aesthetic principles. He was not produc-

A pair of figures of lions decorated predominantly in shades of yellow and purplish brown; seated on mottled green, yellow, and brown bases; faïence of Angoulême, eighteenth century.

ing specimens for the laboratory; he was creating works of art for the King's palace and for the castles of other wealthy noblemen.

Models of barnyard animals, as well as deer, rabbits, and songbirds were immensely popular. Horses and cats were rare, but dogs were plentiful, notably the pug which was the favorite of the period and particularly of Count Brühl. Numerous variations of pug models attest to its popularity. Surprisingly few hunting groups were created, especially in comparison to those produced so elaborately later on at Höchst and Nymphenburg.

The earliest large animal sculptures were of course frequently marred by extensive fire-cracks. As materials and firing methods improved, the specimens emerged immaculately white-glazed. About the mid-1730's Kaendler settled on smaller and moderately sized models of animals and birds as the most appropriate, manageable and attractive in porcelain. While many models were left white, at about this time the finest polychrome decoration was achieved, stressing the minutest details of each animal's appearance.

Though most models of hundreds of animals are ascribed to Kaendler, it is well known that several different modelers would form heads, bodies, and bases that were then put together under the watchful eye of the diligent master modeler.

Kaendler's unsurpassed artistry served as inspiration and was quickly imitated at ceramic centers soon flourishing elsewhere in Germany and in other European countries. Many adventurous and restless modelers, who had worked with him, eventually defected from Meissen and became attached to newly established factories, where sometimes their talents and tastes developed in novel directions.

A great deal of ingenuity flowered even at the minor factories such as those clustered in Thuringia, where a provincial rococo charm replaced the refinement and elegance associated with Meissen. Here as elsewhere spurts of inspiration resulted in fantastic tureens and *trompe-l'oeil*, as well as delightful flacons and other so-called toys, all in animal, bird, and rare fish shapes.

Soon faïence and porcelain factories were competing in producing animals. A blend of rustic robustness and blurry softness, typical of pottery modeling, characterized faïence animals and birds at such famed centers as Höchst and Strasbourg but also at lesser known, yet equally fine, workshops in Germany and France. The elements of fantasy and whimsey were usually more pervasive in the faïence models than in those fashioned out of the cool, hard

39

porcelain paste, whose sharper contours and clearer colors favored the realism Kaendler had initiated and stressed.

Some of the faïence models of course predated the achievements in porcelain such as the various animals made at Delft and Nevers. The success of Meissen porcelain manufacture and the versatility and high productivity of its chief modeler stimulated renewed activity at the older faïence centers and spurred the establishment of new ones in all of Western Europe. Dogs, lions, and numerous birds counted among favorite models.

Thus enthusiasm for animal sculpture in porcelain was quickly extended to faïence. Each is a distinguished art, highly individualistic, with its own strength and aesthetic appeal.

3
Fruits and Vegetables

Those incredible rococo inspirations, the eye-filling ceramic fruits and vegetables of the eighteenth century, are constant favorites among collectors. Interest in these marvelous creations never lags, but their desirability at times is so great and competition for their acquisition so keen, that in spite of high prices specimens virtually disappear off the market.

Taste, demand, availability, and price, four commonly interdependent factors, will subject art objects to occasional fluctuations in value, but the connoisseur knows that the genuine article endures.

From time to time fruits and vegetables are available through the liquidation of major collections and estates, and a new generation of collectors can develop an appreciation of these unique objects, their sculptural excellence and dazzling colors. Because so many examples become inaccessible through incorporation into permanent museum collections, those specimens being offered to the public are quickly acquired by avid newcomers. Usually the numerous enthusiasts who formerly favored figures, groups of figures, and animals among sculptured ceramics suddenly discover the extraordinary aesthetic appeal of fruits and vegetables.

The master modeler of the fertile imagination and indefatigable zeal and energy who was respon-

sible for the first fruits, vegetables, and flowers in imitation of nature was Kaendler at Meissen. His luscious yellow-glazed lemons, or melons tinged with green highlights, divided into two parts to form small and larger covered dishes, amusingly and cleverly enhanced with intertwining twigs, leaves, and blossoms to form handles and finials, rank among the finest examples of porcelain modeling. They are colorful and decorative as well, even in a modern setting, and therefore particularly appealing and desirable.

The artist of that playful rococo era, the mid-eighteenth century, sought to recreate everything that caught his eye. The superb cool and plastic quality of Meissen porcelain lent itself especially well to representation of objects whose natural shapes and textures ideally suited and could be translated into the prevailing style. What could be more challenging than the many varied forms of nature, the fruits and vegetables, both common and exotic, in all their radiance and freshness? Like the human figure, these other forms of life provided exciting lines and rhythms in composition, combined with an endless diversity of shape and color.

Whether modeled as a delicate pink-petaled, full-blown rose, or as an electric bright yellow lemon lying on a flower-encrusted bed of leaves, or as a

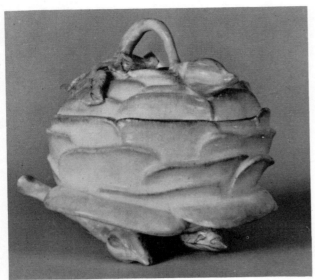

A covered dish in the shape of a rose, standing on modeled buds as feet, its cover finial as a twig terminating in modeled leaves and another bud; naturalistically colored in rose pink and green; porcelain of Meissen, ca. 1745.

massive bunch of grapes of luminous blue contrasted with a green stem handle and leaves appropriately touched with autumn hues, Meissen's variety of covered dishes remains unsurpassed in the artistry of porcelain modeling and coloring. Lettuces, cabbages, artichokes, and bunches of asparagus in their porcelaneous perfection joined in a dazzling array suggesting the most tempting vegetable garden.

The predilection for porcelain fruits and vegetables rapidly spread to other factories, most notably to Chelsea, where these novelties were profusely imitated in the Kaendler manner; however, they also reflected each modeler's own characteristic touch. Chelsea, like Meissen, excelled at exquisite miniature objects, or "toys." Individual asparagus stalks and peapods—closed, barely split open, or parted just far enough to reveal a row of finely modeled peas—served as delightful table decorations. Three stalks of asparagus were imaginatively modeled together to form knife and fork rests. Perfume bottles and needle cases were shaped as miniature gourds, plums, apples, broccoli, or cauliflowers.

The unqualified success of the porcelain potters quickly inspired faïence entrepreneurs everywhere. At Delft, Marseilles, Strasbourg, Sceaux, Brussels, Höchst, Holitsch, and at numerous smaller or lesser known, but hardly inferior, workshops the production of vegetables and fruits began to flourish. The

softer contours achieved in modeling faïence seemed even more favorable to naturalistic representation. Quality was consistently excellent, quantity plentiful, and variety overwhelming.

Though striving for realism the modelers and decorators were often carried away when faced with the unlimited possibilities of their plastic material and colorful palette, that differed somewhat from one factory to the next. Sometimes they idealized, superimposing their own image of a perfect specimen. Or in their flights of fancy, the artists would add a frog, a snail, a small bird, or a flower perched atop a vegetable tureen as a finial. Thus reasonably naturalistic decorative accents were cleverly turned into functional devices. In a step beyond realistic representation the modeler would, in a whimsical mood, attach a miniature dog, melon, or artichoke as a knob or handle to a larger vegetable or fruit dish. A covered dish might be modeled to simulate a basket containing strawberries or other assortments of small fruit or berries.

Manifold compositional variations determined the positions of these ceramic sculptures. Fruits were placed upright, with the stem of an apple or pear enhanced by a solitary leaf or blossoms. Cabbages, with their spreading outer leaves unfurled, looked as though they had been picked right out of the cabbage patch; yet the closed center might lift to

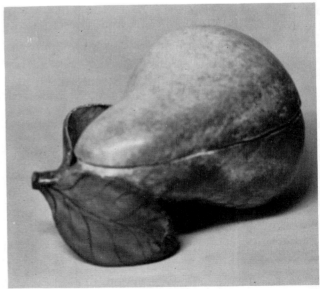

A covered dish in the shape of a pear, its stem and leaves forming the handle and base support; naturalistically colored green with touches of rose pink; faïence of Strasbourg, middle of the eighteenth century.

An arrangement of yellow and orange fruit attached to a fluted white-glazed bowl; faïence of Moustiers, middle of the eighteenth century.

Many small specimens were gracefully shaped in one piece such as apples, pears, and lemons astonishingly and deceptively real because of textural imitation achieved by skillful modeling and coloring. As the artists continued to allow their fantasies free reign, however, the objects tended toward stylization. Delft was particularly noted for its individual fruits, sometimes casually placed on an attractively shaped leaf.

The creativity of the modelers advanced beyond shaping single specimens and halving fruits and vegetables in the middle to produce large and small tureens. Another amusing invention was the *trompe-l'oeil,* a dish or platter usually gaily painted around the border with floral designs typical of the factory, its center naturalistically decorated with attached arrangements of fruits, vegetables, nuts, olives, or flowers. The most appetizing meal might be concocted consisting of an enticing vegetable platter of asparagus, celery, and cucumber followed by a dish of apples, cherries, or an assortment of nuts as dessert. Some factories excelling at *trompe-l'oeils* were Marseilles, Strasbourg, Rouen, and Sceaux.

reveal a cabbage tureen. Most of the numerous melons and lemons were conceived as lying on their sides, sliced in half horizontally to form bowl and cover, their stems serving as handles, and a flower, fruit, or animal as a knob.

Some of the specimens were simply glazed all white, elegantly showing off their surprisingly serene or unruly rococo forms. Sometimes the object's surface was smooth, with a softly glowing glaze, decorated in rather exaggerated but essentially true colors, or the delicacy of a fruit was accentuated by finely shaded pastels. The texture might similarly be indicated by a painted pattern, or at great pains to recreate a vegetable or fruit to naturalistic perfection, in particular the many cabbages and melons, a modeler would carefully detail with verisimilitude the texture of his subject. Some shapes only hinted subtly at indentations with faintly incised lines or gently curved molding. A rare inspiration might be the painting of a very realistic insect on a fruit.

Whether round, oval or irregularly shaped, smoothly glazed or encrusted with flowers or other ornamentation, naturalistic or illusory, vegetables and fruits formed flawless and pleasing compositions as seen from every view and angle. Large tureens, small decorative specimens, miniature "toys", and *trompe-l'oeils,* all the vegetable and fruit creations in ceramics became a collector's delight. These eighteenth century rococo variations on a theme, later copied ad infinitum with varying degrees of success, deservedly remain as highly prized today as when they were first conceived more than two hundred years ago.

4
Cups and Saucers

For budget-minded collectors of eighteenth century porcelain, there is no need to despair. While it is true that for the average collector many objects are too prohibitive to acquire, enough beautiful fragile porcelains remain available to the individual who is understandably intimidated by exorbitant prices. An enterprising person of limited means, but with an imaginative mind and a genuine love for antique porcelains, can search for and discover objects that will satisfy his discriminating taste. Thus, gradually he can build up an unusual collection.

If, for example, he concentrates on cups and saucers, he will find that their supply seems unlimited and their variety inexhaustible. And small wonder indeed. The strange custom of drinking tea and coffee had been introduced to one European country after another in the sixteenth and seventeenth centuries. Chocolate had been brought back to Spain by Columbus in 1502 from his fourth voyage to the New World. The Spaniards cleverly managed to keep the secret of this drink for a hundred years, after which it slowly became known like tea and coffee. All three beverages were expensive luxuries and accessible only to a few wealthy connoisseurs of exotic tastes.

By the time the eighteenth century arrived the coffee, tea, and chocolate drinking habit had become accepted among the European nobility and aristocracy. The discovery of porcelain almost became mandatory, so that proper and worthy vessels might be available from which to drink these liquids. Bona fide physicians, quack doctors, and numerous other more or less qualified commentators voiced their opinions on the reputed healing powers, medicinal uses, and rumored dangers of imbibing tea or coffee. Whether fact or fiction, these statements only served to publicize the beverages and made them much more tempting and desirable. Johann Sebastian Bach composed his famous *Coffee Cantata* in 1732 as a women's protest against propaganda advising abstinence then being disseminated in Germany, because many doctors had claimed that the consumption of coffee caused sterility.

In any event, even the considerable importation of highly prized porcelain from the Orient did not seem to fill the need. When the secret of making it was independently discovered in Europe—soft paste in France at the end of the seventeenth century, hard paste in Germany at the beginning of the eighteenth—cups and saucers immediately became the major item of manufacture.

Among the earliest cups were shallow tea bowls, without a handle, and tall chocolate cups, with two

44

A handleless cup and saucer with gold chinoiserie decoration, the cup gilded inside, the saucer with a wide lobed gold-ground border; porcelain of Meissen, ca. 1720.

A handleless cup and saucer, decorated in colors with East Indian flowers and ornaments; porcelain of Meissen, 1730-1735.

A handleless cup and saucer, decorated in colors with a coat of arms on the saucer, chinoiseries *on the cup, and a diaper pattern inside the cup; enhanced with a gilt lacework border; porcelain of Meissen, 1725-1730.*

A cup and saucer with a sea-green ground, painted in colors on the saucer and in reserved panels on the cup with East Indian flowers, birds, and insects; porcelain of Meissen, 1730-1735.

A cup and saucer decorated in polychrome with putti *picking apples and children riding a donkey, surrounded by elaborate* Laub und Bandelwerk; *porcelain of Meissen, ca. 1730;* Hausmalerei *by Bressler.*

A double-handled cup and saucer, painted in colors with Chinese figures, flowering sprigs, and butterflies; porcelain of Meissen, ca. 1735.

A two-handled double cup with open latticework in the lower part; decorated in colors with scattered sprigs of East Indian flowers; porcelain of Meissen, ca. 1735.

An octagonally lobed cup and saucer decorated in colors with bouquets of flowers; soft-paste porcelain of Vincennes, 1753.

A cup and saucer with a molded basket-weave border and an elaborately modeled handle terminating in a female head; decorated in polychrome with East Indian flowers, butterflies, and insects; porcelain of Meissen, ca. 1735.

A cup and saucer with molded prunus blossoms; soft-paste porcelain of Saint-Cloud, ca. 1735.

A cup and saucer (trembleuse): the saucer with a recessed center, the cup with an interlaced handle; decorated with garlands of bluebells enclosing fields of gilt-stippled ground, superimposed by wreaths of polychrome flowers; the rims and handle embellished with gilding; soft-paste porcelain of Sèvres, 1772; artist: Thévenet, aîné.

handles. Another interesting early shape was the *trembleuse,* popular at the French soft-paste porcelain factory of Saint-Cloud but also produced at Meissen, Vienna, Venice, and most other subsequently established manufactures. The *trembleuse* consisted of a slender, high cup—handleless, with one, or with a double handle—standing on a saucer with a finely modeled gallery to keep the cup from sliding. These *trembleuses,* it is said, were intended for ladies, who were served their morning chocolate in bed, or for elderly people with unsteady hands.

The earliest known dated piece of porcelain made at the Vienna factory during the Du Paquier period in 1719 was a white-glazed *trembleuse* with a fluted body and two handles, bearing the inscription "Honor to God alone and none other" (*Gott allein die Ehr' und sonst keinem mehr*). The saucers of *trembleuses* produced later, beginning about the middle of the eighteenth century, were modeled with higher, more ornate lattice-work galleries.

Cups and saucers of the eighteenth century were not necessarily produced in sets but even those manufactured for services of various sizes were all individually painted by the factory painters, with variations on a particular subject, so that no two cups and saucers were exactly alike. This is particularly noticeable when a painter took liberties in using engravings as models.

Hausmaler, who were independent porcelain decorators, often pilfered white pieces from the factory and painted them at home or in their own small workshops. Some of the *Hausmalerei* examples evidence superior artistry, others are naïve and amusing in conception or a little stilted in execution. All are interesting because of the diversity of their decoration and the very original and individualistic style employed by the artists, who were not bound by any factory rules and limitations governing subject matter, placement, and colors.

A cup and saucer made as a part of a *déjeuner* (a coffee, tea, or chocolate set for one person) will, of course, be unique as are all those other individual cups and saucers created just once, each as a separate work of art. The original purpose of producing cups and saucers had no doubt been to serve the new beverages that had become a vogue. When the stunning new porcelains were first successfully made, the factories and their most prominent modelers and painters competed in creating ever more breathtaking and aesthetically satisfying objects. It is questionable whether ultimately the

A cup and saucer decorated in polychrome with German flowers; soft-paste porcelain of Tournai, ca. 1760.

A cup and saucer (trembleuse), *painted in polychrome with birds and flowers; porcelain of Chelsea, gold-anchor period, ca. 1765.*

A double-handled cup and saucer (trembleuse) *with a gold diaper pattern on a blue ground; the reserved panels painted in colors with trophies; porcelain of Chelsea, gold-anchor period, ca. 1765.*

finest examples of unique cups and saucers were intended for actual use. Many, in fact, were couched in especially made-to-order leather cases and presented as gifts by one sovereign or nobleman to another.

These early one-of-a-kind cups and saucers belong to the most expensive examples. They include the first Meissen specimens painted in gold or polychrome with subject matter borrowed from the

A cylindrical cup and saucer with a light blue ground, painted with ornaments in grisaille; the broad, gilt-bordered, deep royal blue reserves decorated in rich gold relief, of varying shades, with diverse still lifes including trophies, a bird cage, birds, fish, and flowers; the reddish brown border with a Greek fret; porcelain of Vienna, Sorgenthal period, dated 1797.

Orient: Chinese figures at various pursuits in garden settings, East Indian flowers, and motifs copied from Japanese Imari and Kakiemon porcelains. European harbor and merchant scenes were also much favored. These miniature paintings on cups and saucers were surrounded by elaborate lacework borders in gold or colors. The Du Paquier factory in Vienna invented an intricate, lovely ribbon and foliage pattern. The Vezzi factory in Venice not only designed simple elegant ornamental motifs, but in bursts of rich fantasy also added birds, monkeys, and other animals to its Meissen and Vienna-inspired decoration. The sole embellishment of some of the first white-glazed Meissen examples consisted of prunus blossoms or stylized acanthus leaves molded in relief. Other factories and even Meissen later on repeated this refined decoration.

Gradually with the emergence of the rococo style, greater emphasis was put on the shapes of handles that the modelers enhanced with an upward sweep, a shell motif, or a little twirl near the bottom. Sometimes the handles simulated stems, terminating in molded blossoms on the cup, or the cups and saucers themselves were molded in relief, with floral and rococo motifs. The cup lost its early, gently outward flaring rim, and the saucer began to vary slightly in depth and size. Interlaced handles were introduced by the French in the 1750's. The Louis Seize and neoclassical styles made the cylindrical coffee-cup shape popular. But the plentiful production of high and low bowl-shaped cups was continued throughout the century by all the European factories.

By mid-century, Western European decoration had to a great extent replaced the early Orientally inspired designs and subjects. German flowers, ordinary garden flowers so-called to distinguish them from the Oriental kind, were painted with freshness in ever varying arrangements and colors. Bird, animal, and fruit decoration was finely applied. The artists depicted peasant, miner, or other workmen at their tasks. They rendered comedy and domestic scenes with humor and painstaking care and detail. Landscapes, river scenes, and figures in gardens or in landscapes with ruins, surrounded by rococo trellises and ornaments, were among other beautifully executed miniature paintings on porcelain cups and saucers. An increasing number of accomplished and specialized artists at the different factories worked from nature or after paintings and engravings.

Now and then a latecomer among porcelain manufactures would add its version of decoration inspired by Chinese and Japanese models. The results might be startling, amusing, or simply just as lovely as those achieved at Meissen, whose exquisite productions every factory sought to emulate.

As the consumption of tea and coffee became more prevalent, during the course of the eighteenth century, the demand for complete services also increased. After the initial difficulties of porcelain making had been overcome, the manufactures happily obliged their clients by supplying the costly treasures. As a result the second half of the eighteenth century was rich in the production of a large number of cups and saucers of great variety and differing quality. Many of these distinctive examples, subtly or simply decorated, remain for today's collector, who can appreciate and cherish a delicate hand-painted specimen that has survived for two hundred years or more.

However, the unique examples were not altogether neglected. At Sèvres, which produced numerous charming cups and saucers delightfully decorated with colorful sprigs and bouquets of flowers, precious resplendent ground-color cups and saucers were made during the third quarter of the eighteenth century. Meissen, too, repeated some of the ground colors of its earliest period; they are of fine quality, with their diversified subject matter painted in reserved panels.

Most European factories were known for one or another specialty. Saint-Cloud cups and saucers, decorated in blue only, featured a lacelike border lambrequin design. The Ginori factory at Doccia produced services with floral painting in colors based on an Oriental motif, that the Italians called the *tulipano* pattern. The Berlin factory had a predilection for scale patterns and Sèvres invented a number of different diapers to superimpose in gilt on its ground colors.

The Vienna factory embarked on its era of most elaborate and qualitative painting as late as 1784 under the directorship of Konrad von Sorgenthal, after whom the period (1784-1805) was named. A large number of individual cups and saucers were lavishly decorated by outstanding porcelain painters and glass enamelers with trophies and ornaments, mythological subjects, portraits, and views of cities, all well suited to the severe, straight, classical shapes of the cups and turned-up angular, rather than rounded, saucers. Some of the decorators specialized in exceptionally fine gilding, sometimes in relief or engraved, emulating the practice and opulent style originally introduced at Sèvres many years earlier.

The Sorgenthal period was the ultimate dramatic highlight of eighteenth century porcelain production in Europe. A sampling of the diversity of cups and saucers representing this century which passed through the baroque, rococo, and neoclassical eras cannot leave any porcelain enthusiast untouched.

5

New Pots for New Beverages

The age of the explorers and the subsequent burgeoning of international and intercontinental commerce gradually served to acquaint Western Europeans with numerous unheard-of customs and products.

The introduction of exotic imports such as tea and coffee stimulated the manufacture of proper vessels from which to serve them. Stoneware, pottery, and pewter jugs and tankards were being used for wines, ales, and other common liquids, but these heavy wares hardly seemed suitable for dispensing the strange new beverages. Exquisitely hand-wrought silver pots made by expert gold and silversmiths in France, Germany, England, and elsewhere were available, but they were expensive and did not readily satisfy the increasing demands of the nobility and aristocracy. For by the time the eighteenth century arrived, the coffee and tea drinking fashion had become accepted and popular among them.

Fine Oriental porcelain, which seemed to be the most appropriate and desirable material from which to serve the beverages, was being imported in considerable quantities through the several East India Companies. But Europeans, in spite of continuous and indefatigable experimentation, had not yet been able themselves to find the secret of porcelain manufacture, although the discovery of the proper formula appeared to have become an urgent necessity.

Finally, at the end of the seventeenth century, efforts at porcelain making were rewarded when at Saint-Cloud the first small pieces of soft-paste porcelain were successfully drawn from the kiln. And at Meissen, early in the eighteenth century, jubilation greeted the production of a fine hard translucent porcelain, equal in quality to the highly prized examples of the Chinese and Japanese. Naturally the first small objects to be manufactured included cups and saucers and a variety of pots. There were tall, well-proportioned, pear-shaped ones for coffee; smaller versions for milk and cream; squat and globular shapes for tea; and medium-sized pots, sometimes with wooden handles, for hot chocolate. The covers were domed or flat with plain knobs. Other accessories produced to complete sets for serving and drinking the new beverages included tea caddies, sugar bowls, spoon trays, and waste bowls. It should be of interest to collectors of pots to remember that each service might have several cups and saucers but only one tea, coffee, or chocolate pot. The pot is always the most desirable, rarest, and most valuable object of a set.

A teapot decorated in polychrome with birds and flowers in the Kakiemon manner; porcelain of Arita, Japan, ca. 1700.

A teapot with a molded mascaron spout, decorated with gilt chinoiseries *and ornaments; porcelain of Meissen, ca. 1725.*

A teapot of quadrangular Oriental shape, decorated with Chinese motifs in relief; white-glazed porcelain of Meissen, ca. 1720.

A coffeepot with polychrome decoration in the Höroldt manner of harbor scenes in reserves, framed by lacework borders enhanced with mother-of-pearl luster and gilding; painted with scattered East Indian flowers; porcelain of Meissen, ca. 1725.

A coffeepot painted in polychrome and gold with chinoiseries, *the cover and spout enhanced with ornaments; porcelain of Meissen, 1720-1725; Bayreuth* Hausmalerei.

A teapot with a molded mascaron spout, painted in polychrome and gold with Moors attending a lady, and scattered East Indian flowers and insects; on the reverse, Chinese bathing; porcelain of Meissen, ca. 1725.

A teapot, sugar bowl, and cup and saucer painted with farmer scenes in iron-red monochrome, and enhanced with gilt borders; porcelain of Meissen, ca. 1725; Hausmalerei.

The earliest teapots were modeled of simple globular shape with short, straight spouts and plain, round handles. Those of Böttger's brown stoneware, preceding the white porcelain, were frequently polished, glazed, cut, and faceted. The functional knobs on the covers were soon transformed into more elaborately modeled finials such as blossoms with leaves and stems. Applied prunus blossoms in relief in the Chinese taste or raised acanthus leaves in the European baroque style often enhanced white-glazed pots. The French soft-paste factories formed some teapots in the shape of melons.

Most of the early porcelain factories produced some pots imitating the Chinese K'ang Hsi shape: straight-sided pots either quadrangular or round with fluting, with a vertical basket-like, inverted U-shape handle. At Meissen, imaginative modeling resulted in applied mascarons in relief to decorate the gracefully curved, elongated spouts. Sometimes the spout itself terminated in an eagle's head and the handles might be decorated with a child's head. The pot itself was squat at the base, narrowing gently toward the top.

Painted decoration in enamel colors or underglaze blue imitated Oriental motifs such as East Indian flowers, *chinoiseries,* and Kakiemon designs. Some pots were daintily painted in gold only or decorated in gold and enamel relief with Chinese figures, birds, pagodas, and blossoming trees. Outstanding decoration was painted by the leading factory artists such as Johann Gregor Höroldt, Adam Friedrich von Löwenfinck, and their many talented followers and pupils. Other original and unusual ornamentation, sometimes amusing in its conception, was applied by painters or enamelers outside the porcelain factories who, like the Auffenwerths of Augsburg, owned kilns and worked independently and with their families, or supervised small decorating establishments.

Monochrome painting with exquisite shading of details was practiced at most factories or by the independent *Hausmaler*. The Du Paquier manufacture at Vienna invented designs consisting of intricate ribbon and foliage motifs as the sole decoration or to frame other subject matter, while the Meissen factory tended to prefer delicate lacework borders usually in iron red, gold, and purple, to surround its great variety of miniature painting on pots.

Kaendler at Meissen first introduced more elaborately modeled handles with shell and scroll motifs reflecting the baroque taste. Asymmetrical rococo molding of spirals and of fanciful curves and twists was added to handles and spouts toward the middle of the eighteenth century. Delicately interlaced

A coffeepot decorated with modeled vine leaves and bunches of grapes, the cover with interlaced twig handles; two handleless cups with molded prunus blossoms; white-glazed porcelain of Meissen, 1730-1735.

A coffeepot decorated in colors in the Kakiemon style with the banded hedge pattern; porcelain of Meissen, ca. 1735; silver-gilt mounting.

A teapot and sugar bowl with a sea-green ground, painted in reserves with polychrome East Indian flowers and insects; porcelain of Meissen, 1730-1735.

A sugar caster and a teapot with a modeled animal spout, decorated in colors with butterflies and East Indian flowers; porcelain of Meissen, ca. 1735.

handles were a novel contribution of the Sèvres factory. At Meissen, in a burst of creativeness, handles were modeled as stems with applied flowers terminating on the body of the pot. Kaendler in fact, with his unequaled ingenuity, conceived and successfully executed pots in the shape of animals, birds, and flowers. The bodies of pots were frequently enriched with molding such as flowers, ornaments, and basket-weave borders.

The imagination of modelers at the Italian porcelain factory in Venice was similarly fired by the sculptural possibilities offered by the new medium; they created pots with the most fantastically baroque-shaped spouts and handles.

An enormous diversity of exquisitely painted merchant and harbor scenes soon followed the first *chinoiserie* decoration. European flower painting of the common garden variety, usually referred to as German flowers, succeeded the stylized Oriental examples. At first rendered in a rather stiff and dry-looking manner, sometimes enhanced with carefully drawn shadows, these flowers (*Holzschnittblumen* or *Schattenblumen*), which were copied from botanical engravings, eventually loosened and brightened as though touched by sun and breeze. German flower painting was practiced at Meissen, Vienna, and other subsequently established German factories and, with slight variations, at times in more formal arrangements, appeared on pieces made at manufactures in France, England, and other European countries.

A coffeepot with a modeled mascaron spout, decorated in polychrome with harbor scenes alternating with panels of gilt ornamentation; porcelain of Meissen, 1735-1740.

A small teapot with polychrome and gilt decoration in the Watteau manner over underglaze blue; porcelain of Meissen, ca. 1735; Hausmalerei *by Ferner, ca. 1750.*

A cream pot on three feet, with engraved decoration filled in with Schwarzlot; *porcelain of Meissen; signed and dated by Canon Busch, 1749.*

Scenes after Watteau, surrounded by rococo ornaments, and many diverse subjects after well and lesser known engravings were painstakingly executed in colors and gold on large and small pots. River landscapes with castles or ruins; animal, bird, and insect painting; cupids and children; Italian comedy, sporting, and battle scenes; peasants, miners, and other workmen at their tasks or at rest became desirable subject matter. Ladies and their cavaliers seated in gardens sheltered by rococo arbors and trellises or strolling in exotic settings were popular painted themes, sometimes on pots of an ornately modeled rococo design.

As the new beverages became better known and when, after decades of debate over their putative merits or ill effects, interest in them by the privileged few began to infect the masses, the manufacture of porcelain in Europe, with its ex-

traordinary decoration, added to the pleasure of consuming them. Throughout the eighteenth century, however, Oriental pots were imported to supplement public demand and European production. Of particular interest and charm were pots with molded flower patterns, painted with matching colorful floral ornamentation. Some of the teapots or milk jugs, that continued to be precious to the Western market, were mounted in silver.

An immense variety of eighteenth century porcelain tea and coffeepots still exists to tempt today's collector. They were made by every factory, ranging from the most important and famous ones such as Meissen, Sèvres, and Chelsea to the smallest and least familiar in Thuringia, which often produced artistically astonishing specimens. One can choose from simple baroque and ornate rococo shapes or those of the more severe, angular, neoclassical forms made toward the end of the century. Similarly in the decoration, the choice of colors and subject matter is endless. Production, of course, increased greatly during the second half of the century when the problems of firing virtually had been overcome. Yet, each pot was individually made and no two will be exactly alike.

From the most elaborately painted early piece, perhaps with *chinoiseries* in reserves against a rich,

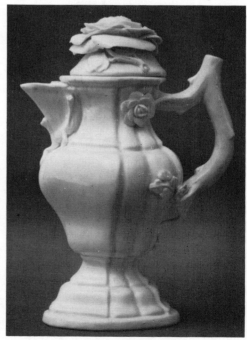

A paneled cream pot with a twig handle terminating in modeled foliage and blossoms on the pot, the cover with a large modeled full-blown rose; white-glazed soft-paste porcelain of Naples, ca. 1771.

glowing ground color, to a simple mid-eighteenth century example, modestly decorated with sprigs of flowers in monochrome or polychrome, there are porcelain pots available to every avid collector to satisfy his particular taste and requirements. Some pots are in such excellent condition that one wonders if they were ever used. Probably a good number were not. Because of their fragile and exquisite beauty, they never reached the tea table but were carefully kept in display cabinets as they are today. Yet once in a while it is pleasant to remember that originally these attractive pots were lovingly created to serve the exotic new beverages that we take very much for granted today.

6
Tile Pictures

Colorful tiles had been made for several centuries in the Near East, Spain, and Portugal to cover floors, ceilings, and walls before individual wall plaques became popular in Western Europe for purely decorative purposes.

In the ancient world, in such countries as Assyria, Babylonia, and Egypt, where it was customary to adorn walls with glazed faïence tiles, they constituted a major part of ceramic production. In Persia the art of making tiles underwent further refinement. Here some of the finest tin-glazed wall pictures were produced, colorfully painted in yellow, green, blue, white, and black.

Popular subject matter included figures of archers and intricate, symmetrical ornamental designs. Alternating eight-pointed stars and cross-shapes interlocked to form large panels. Individual tile segments frequently featured a complete composition. From about the thirteenth to the fifteenth century animal and plant motifs and sentences from the Koran formed the chief designs. Mosques as well as palaces were profusely decorated with tiles.

The Turks contributed stylized foliage and floral patterns on their Iznik wares of the sixteenth and seventeenth centuries. Copper-luster decoration was invented in the East and introduced by the Moors into Spain, but its quality was quickly rivaled and even surpassed by the superb craftsmanship evident from luster glazes on monochrome and two-color Hispano-Moresque wares and polychromed Italian majolicas.

In Spain, as in the East, the *azulejo* (from *azul* = blue) was originally associated with architecture; tiles served most commonly to cover the lower part of walls. At first, as the name suggests, the tiles were painted only in blue; polychromes made a later appearance. The earliest *azulejos,* dating from the fourteenth century, decorate the inside of the Alhambra. Of geometric design, small rectilinear monochrome tin-glazed pieces in white, grayish blue, green, brown, and black were joined to form larger tiles for walls, door panels, or friezes. A century later the process was simplified by using larger sections. Renaissance ornaments such as foliage, heraldic shields, and rosettes were eventually added to the Moorish designs.

From the fourteenth to the sixteenth century the chief tile workshops were situated in Seville, Toledo, and Triana. Valencia was noted for tiles decorated in blue with heraldic emblems and Gothic ornaments. Seville, the major tile-producing center that also supplied Portugal, was liquidated in 1610 after

A tile painted in polychrome with a design of foliage, flowers, and ornaments; Iznik pottery, Turkey, sixteenth century.

the ultimate expulsion of the Moors from Spain.

In Italy, as in Spain, ceramic tiles and plaques at first embellished houses architecturally. Simple wall and floor tiles gradually were supplemented by exquisite pictorial tablets, often framed like paintings. Well known examples are the fine polychromed relief compositions from the Della Robbia workshops. Many featured attractive religious subjects, such as Madonnas, saints, and cherubs, and were affixed to the outside of buildings over a door or window. Soon large and small dishes were virtually flattened and turned into plaques to afford a larger, smoother painting surface. They served as showpieces for finely painted compositions, some comparable to the best oil paintings of the Renaissance.

To the north, in Germany, where the climate dictated other customs and made other demands, tile production expanded into a totally different direction. True, at the end of the fourteenth century, architectural considerations here also played a part. When late Gothic-style houses were being constructed, handsome artistic appearance was stressed. Decoration consisted of relief ornaments of lions, scorpions, and grotesques. These plastic highlights, coated with a blackish lead glaze, were probably first introduced in Lübeck. Decorated bricks, glazed and pieced together, formed attractive designs to enliven the monotony of sheer walls.

Other tiles, tin-glazed and white, and partially painted in blue, were separated from one another by translucent lead-glazed foliage and rosettes.

The early German potters were known as Hafner (from *Hafen* = receptacle), whose main products were lead-glazed stoves or simple bowls and pots for everyday use. But soon their unpretentious blue and white stove-tile decoration developed into more colorful elaborate painting, frequently depicting biblical scenes. In the sixteenth century, in faïence centers as far apart as Hamburg and Nuremberg, potters created highly artistic tile stoves painted with ornaments, scrollwork, and stylized flowers in blue and white or polychrome.

Tile production in France was not as significant as in some of her neighboring countries. The French nobility scoffed at pottery, preferring precious metals, so that the artistry of French potters for a long time found greater appreciation among Italians than at home. Faïence did not really become popular in France until Louis XIV decided to have a pleasure pavilion built for his mistress, Madame de Montespan. Called the *Trianon de porcelaine*, it was actually a *Trianon de faïence*. Its roof, outside walls, and floors were covered with tiles from the early faïence factories at Rouen and Nevers. Additional large quantities were imported from Holland.

The Dutch had quietly and quickly become the major tile producers of the north. The custom of covering walls with faïence tiles had been introduced from Spain. From the beginnings of pottery making in Holland in the sixteenth century, tile production reigned foremost in Delft and other Dutch centers. In the seventeenth century a wealth of astonishing and delightful decoration of tiles flourished, mostly in blue or purple monochrome.

Shapes were rectangular or round. Frequently sets of four, six, twelve, or more small square tiles were joined to form large compositions. Subjects included grotesques, portraits, animals, *chinoiseries*, biblical scenes, land and seascapes, and floral designs and ornaments.

Often the Delft painting, be it of a city view or a floral composition, was of excellent quality. Sometimes the more primitive, amusing attempts had a special charm, unrivaled by any other of the European faïence factories. Beginning with simple rows of tiles running along the foot of a wall, or applied to dados in the kitchen, tiles soon surrounded the fireplace for practical reasons such as cleanliness

A plaque painted in colors with Saint Christopher carrying
the Christ Child, the modeled frame simulating wood;
faïence of Savona, seventeenth century.

and the material's excellent capacity to absorb and radiate heat.

The trend toward decorativeness in the production of tiles—their use as pictures on the wall, like paintings on canvas or board—became most prominent early in the eighteenth century, when the discovery of porcelain stimulated a new competitive inventiveness in faïence as well. The Dutch con-

tinued to be prolific and original with wall plaques of many diverse sizes and forms: rectangular, round, oval, or of symmetrical baroque shape. Vivid polychrome compositions vied with blue and white city views, domestic outdoor scenes, and bird, floral, and *chinoiserie* painting. Flower baskets, birds in a cage, children at play, and imaginative interpretations of biblical subjects were immensely popular. As the

58

*tile picture painted in colors with a mascaron sur-
rounded by elaborate baroque scrollwork; faïence of
Winterthur, seventeenth century.*

*A baroque-shaped plaque with a molded border suggesting
a frame, ornamented in underglaze blue and outlined in
dark green; the center painted in blue with chinoiseries;
faïence of Delft, early eighteenth century.*

*tile picture decorated in polychrome with a bouquet of
flowers; faïence of Strasbourg, middle of the eighteenth
century; carved wooden frame.*

decoration began to assume a more native character, *chinoiseries* and baroque themes gradually
lagged behind.

On the finer, more elaborate panels the borders
were often molded to simulate frames. Sometimes
they were embellished with intricate painted diaper
patterns imitating Oriental motifs that meandered
around and filled in the depressed areas created by
the molded designs.

Further north, influenced by the Dutch, the
English at Lambeth and Liverpool followed the new
fashion and produced numerous tiles, some notable
for their *chinoiserie* subjects.

In Italy, at the majolica center of Castelli in
particular, the painting of picture plaques developed into an outstanding art. Subject matter
favored on oil paintings became equally desirable on
pottery tiles in soft, predominently autumn-like
hues including yellow, blue, green, orange, and
brown. Dramatic biblical interpretations as well as
allegorical and mythological themes were produced
side by side with painstakingly executed pastoral
scenes.

At Meissen, where everything that could be
fashioned out of porcelain was made as soon as it
became feasible, finely painted porcelain pictures
were of course included, especially during the
rococo era. Other factories followed suit. Vienna, in
its first period under Du Paquier, was noted for
small, exquisitely painted panels featuring

chinoiseries and East Indian flower painting in lovely bright, yet soft, polychromes, combining iron red, purple, light blue, and green. Many of these delicate specimens were originally intended for the ambitiously planned porcelain rooms in the palaces of noblemen where they decorated the wood-paneled walls.

Another German factory known for superior porcelain decoration was active at Fürstenberg. In the 1760s the manufacture began to produce one of its specialties, small rococo-framed porcelain paintings, that portrayed Brunswick nobility as well as a variety of other subjects such as harbor scenes, landscapes, animals, and mythological themes in monochrome or colors. The extended modeled porcelain frames surrounding each of these delightful miniature paintings usually were gilded, or touched with gold to simulate wood.

At Vincennes and continuing at Sèvres, small finely painted oval or rectangular plaques also became a specialty. Usually they featured floral sprigs and fruit or birds painted in luminous polychromes, sometimes in reserves offsetting the famed ground colors of the factory. Individually framed or applied as furniture panels, they certainly deserved lavish praise for their quality, simplicity, and elegance. Others following the Sèvres vogue with worthy examples were Tournai and some of the English factories.

Toward the nineteenth century, porcelain picture painting became essentially derivative. Quantity and decorativeness prevailed over artistic quality. The overall ornate multicolor floral decoration and crowded neoclassical compositions on large panels seemed somehow too massive and totally unsuited to the fragility of porcelain. However, a craft that had originated as utilitarian and to enhance architecture had developed, flourished, and finally peaked during the era of fine faïence and porcelain production into an exceptional and popular decorative art.

7

Cats in Ceramics

Cats have been a favorite subject in literature and art throughout the ages. In our time we need only turn to *Old Possum's Book of Practical Cats* or the *Just-So Stories*. What child or adult, for that matter, is not captivated by the ingratiating charm of T. S. Eliot's Jennyanydots, who "sits and sits and sits and sits" or is fascinated by Kipling's proud independent feline, who stubbornly insists, "I am the cat who walks by himself and all places are alike to me."

The artistic depiction of cats reaches far back into antiquity. The cat's recorded history of more than 4,500 years is one of extremes. The seemingly harmless household pet has aroused the full range of emotions from affection to fear; it has inspired religious cults as well as persecution and violent acts.

Savage tribes valued the cat and tamed it to hunt, fish, and guard the grain. The cat was regarded as a totem, like the bull and the ram.

The ordinary cat was first venerated in all of Egypt. The goddess Bast, variously identified with Artemis, Aphrodite, Venus, and Freya, was commonly pictured with the head of a cat. Similarly, the sun god Ra was sometimes represented with a cat's head, while Isis was depicted with the ears of a cat. At shrines erected especially for cats, offerings were made to their images of wood and bronze.

Egyptian cats fared equally well as domestic pets.

When one died, all members of the household were required by law to shave off their eyebrows as a sign of mourning. Killing a cat was punishable by death. To export a cat was prohibited and agents were sent out to retrieve those animals or their descendants, illegally taken out of the country. Bubastis, the city sacred to cats, served as their major burial place, although at Beni Hassan as many as 180,000 cats were found. They were embalmed and wrapped in linens like humans. Innumerable carvings and paintings of cats decorated tombs; feline themes were used in rich exotic jewelry designs.

While the Assyrians, Babylonians, and Israelites apparently did not know the cat as a domestic animal, it became an economic necessity to the Greeks. Probably introduced to Mediterranean countries by the seafaring Phoenicians, cats were adopted by the Greeks, who were actually more familiar with dogs, as rodent eliminators and gradually assumed an indispensable household position. Representations of cats have been found on Greek coins, lamps, vases, and grave steles. A stone relief of the sixth century, before Christ, at the Athens National Museum shows both a cat and dog on a leash.

In ancient Rome, where the cat's independent character apparently was recognized for the first

A sugar bowl with the figure of a cat as a finial; painted in sepia with a continuous harbor scene and enhanced with gilt borders; porcelain of Meissen, ca. 1730.

A snuffbox in the shape of a cat with brown markings on a yellow body; the lid painted inside and outside with polychrome sprigs of flowers; soft-paste porcelain of Mennecy, ca. 1750; silver mounting.

A scent bottle in the shape of a cat with brown markings on a white body; porcelain of Gotha, Thuringia, ca. 1775.

time, the animal was chosen as a symbol of liberty and freedom. The goddess of liberty was pictured with a cat at her feet in a temple dating to the third century before Christ.

This symbol of independence recurred throughout history, from the time of warring Teutonic tribes to the French Revolution. The Dukes of Burgundy in the Middle Ages depicted the cat on their banners and heraldic emblems and the sixteenth century Dutch associated the feline characteristic with their struggle for liberation from Spanish oppression.

In England cats became great favorites from the time they were introduced, when the country was a Roman colony. Saint Patrick is reputed to have been aided by cats when he cleared Ireland of snakes, and Pope Gregory the Great owned a cat of which he was very fond. During the reign of Henry the Fowler in Germany in the tenth century, when cats were scarce and valuable, a heavy fine was imposed if they were injured. Architectural decoration in Spain and France featuring cats attests to their popularity in these countries.

Germany suffered a veritable cat craze in connection with the love and fertility rites practiced in honor of the Norse feline goddess Freya. In 1484 Pope Innocent VIII ordered thousands of participants in the worship of Freya burned as witches. Cats were executed as well.

In France this hysteria eventually developed into the use of the "cat organ," a small torture chamber equipped with pedals, that housed cats. Pressure exerted on the pedals caused the cats to scream, producing the so-called music. In other instances, cats were dipped in oil and set afire.

In a contrasting spirit, cats were lovingly depicted in serene Italian paintings of the Holy Family. Among famous painters, Dürer pictured a most ferocious cat, while Breughel created one of many charming versions of cat concerts. The cat as an animal subject became increasingly popular with artists such as the Teniers, Coypel, Cochin, Watteau, Boucher, Greuze, Goya, and others.

In China the cat as a household pet has a long and varied history inextricably associated throughout the ages with naturalistic and stylistic artistic depiction in bronze, stone, scroll painting, ceramics, and ivory. It is told that when Buddha died, the cat refused to pay its respects so that on scrolls depicting

A night-light holder in the shape of a crouching cat, its speckled blue glaze with brown and yellowish highlights; Kuang-tung stoneware, China, eighteenth century.

the scene the cat is missing. In the thirteenth century, for the first time, the cat was pictured with the mourners but set apart, shunned by the other animals.

The cat enjoyed favor and popularity in Japan where it was introduced by the Chinese. In Siam the cat was believed to be endowed with royal qualities.

In the eighteenth century, when the cat had returned to good graces everywhere, its artistic portrayals flourished, becoming perhaps most naturalistic, attractive, and universally admired. The beauty of the feline shape, eyes, and soft fur was stressed. Its characteristic wary stance or beguiling relaxed repose was caught by sensitive able artists. These were not only painters and sculptors but also masters in the decorative arts.

With the discovery of porcelain manufacture at Meissen and subsequently at other European centers, a new medium became available—though long known in the Orient—well suited to accentuate the insinuating and endearing feline charm. Sculpted individually or in the company of other animals such as birds, dogs, or mice, the cat reached a new unchallenged superior status.

Without attaining a religious aura inspiring reverence, cats were simply loved and adored stimulating a great demand for fine artistic representation. The major, as well as lesser known, eighteenth century ceramic factories, especially in Germany and France, obliged with delightful specimens. The exquisitely modeled and finely painted cat-form porcelains of this period, sometimes ingeniously shaped as scent bottles or snuffboxes in true rococo style, remain and still are highly prized collector's items.

8
New Vessels for an Ancient Cult

The fragile porcelain censers of the eighteenth century represented the culmination of making new vessels in a new medium for an ancient cult.

The use of incense is as old as human history. In ancient times the primitive rite of sacrificing animals was often accompanied by the burning of incense. The twelfth century Spanish philosopher Maimonides maintained that, in addition to counteracting the odors arising from animal sacrifices, incense animated the spirit of the priests. As some of these religious practices became more refined, incense eventually replaced live offerings.

The Bible frequently refers to the use of incense in a variety of customs and situations. Garments and beds were perfumed with myrrh, aloe, and cinnamon. Brides and noble guests at festivities were sprinkled with incense. A brazier with incense was passed around after meals.

In pagan rites, an emperor might be honored as a deity at a ceremony where incense was smoked. When Christianity supplanted heathen cults, incense as a part of worship was introduced into the church. A thurible was carried before the pope in procession.

In ancient times because of the extreme heat in the Orient, the utilization of aromatic substances was far more widespread in the East than in the West. Odors that arose from the burning of resins and spices were desirable for sanitary and domestic habits, as well as for acts of worship in religious ceremonies. Under primitive hygienic conditions, in hot, often humid, climates, the diffusion of perfumes to obliterate disagreeable odors provided welcome relief. In time the practical application of incense extended everywhere to deodorization and disinfection, particularly during periods of epidemics.

For these diverse purposes of fumigation throughout the ages, suitable receptacles and dispensers were required. In those objects which have survived we possess a heritage of a great variety of antique censers, usually made of bronze or other precious and base metals, but also of earthenware from the times when the art of making ceramics was known.

The Egyptian vessels were obligatory for offering libations of wine and incense to the sun god. In the Far East censers were important to the Hindus, who used incense from remote antiquity in worshiping the gods and during the rites of burning their dead. Incense burners continued to be essential to Buddhists, who adopted many Hindu customs. Moslems

Three tile pictures decorated in blue (top) and manganese purple (bottom) with biblical themes: Jacob's dream, Jacob wrestling with the angel, and Jonah and the whale; faïence of Delft, seventeenth century; wooden frames

A tile picture painted in varying shades of blue with an arrangement of flowers and fruit, surrounded by foliage and scrollwork ornaments; faïence of Zurich, third quarter of the eighteenth century; carved wood frame.

A tile picture painted in manganese purple camaïeu with a village view, partially surrounded by rococo ornamentation; faïence of Zurich, third quarter of the eighteenth century; carved wooden frame.

A pair of plaques with molded borders suggesting frames, enhanced with gold, the upper parts with modeled wreaths of flowers tied with ribbons, decorated in colors; the pictures painted in polychrome in the Watteau manner with figures in landscapes; porcelain of Copenhagen, ca. 1780.

A pair of cachepots, gracefully waisted, with a scalloped rim and modeled berries as handles; painted in polychrome with blossoming branches and scattered insects; faïence of Marseilles, third quarter of the eighteenth century; Veuve Perrin.

A collection of modeled flowers, naturalistically colored; soft-paste porcelain of Vincennes, middle of the eighteenth century.

*An octagonally shaped coffeepot, creamer, sugar bowl, and
cup and saucer with a yellow ground painted in polychrome
within reserved panels with blossoming sprigs and flowers
in the Kakiemon style; porcelain of Meissen, ca. 1735.*

A pair of figures of La Petite fille au tablier *and* Le
Porteur d'oiseaux; *soft-paste biscuit of Vincennes, 1752;
models by Blondeau after Boucher.*

A finely fluted jar with a petal-shaped cover and a brownish celadon glaze; porcelaneous stoneware of China, Yüan dynasty, 1280-1367. A jar on three small feet with an olive green celadon glaze; stoneware of China, Ming dynasty, 1368-1644.

A jar with ornamental relief molding and a cucumber-green glaze; stoneware of China, Ming dynasty, 1368-1644.

A two-handled creamer and underdish, painted in colors with chinoiseries *surrounded by lacework borders in purple, iron red, and gold; porcelain of Meissen, ca. 1725.*

A vase decorated in underglaze blue with a bird amidst flowers and foliage, and with ornamental borders; porcelain of China, Wan-li period, 1573-1619.

A large dish painted in underglaze blue and polychrome enamels with a bird in flight and another amidst blossoming shrubs and rockwork; porcelain of China, "Transitional" period, second quarter of the seventeenth century.

A winepot with a thick glaze of green and reddish brown, speckled with black, dissolving and blending into grayish white; porcelaneous stoneware of China, seventeenth century.

A large vase, richly decorated in underglaze blue with figures at various pursuits in interior and outdoor scenes; porcelain of China, K'ang Hsi period, 1662-1722.

A trompe-l'oeil *dish, decorated with blue flower sprigs, in the center an arrangement of walnuts and almonds, naturalistically modeled and colored; faïence of Rouen, middle of the eighteenth century. A covered dish in the shape of a melon, its stem and leaves serving as a handle and base support; with a miniature melon as a knob; decorated in yellow and green; faïence of Frankfurt/Main, middle of the eighteenth century.*

A pagoda figure of polished brown Böttger stoneware; Meissen, 1712-1715.

An incense burner in the shape of a basket, set on a rockwork and foliage base, the cover with an assortment of modeled flowers; white-glazed soft-paste porcelain of Mennecy, ca. 1750.

A potpourri vase on a rockwork base embellished with modeled flowers and foliage; white-glazed soft-paste porcelain of Vincennes, ca. 1750.

An incense burner with a rose finial on a green stem; encrusted with tiny blossoms touched with rose coloring; soft-paste porcelain of Mennecy, second quarter of the eighteenth century.

also required censers for their religious ceremonials. The existence of innumerable Chinese, Japanese, and Indian receptacles of many eras, differing in form and material, attests to the prevalence of incense burning practices.

From the Orient the fumigation customs were introduced to Greece and later to Rome, from where they were finally absorbed by the Christian world. Each civilization, in turn, contributed its representative censers, their distinction depending on their specific function, the particular gums and plants used, and the style and fashion of the day.

By the time porcelain censers were first produced in Western Europe in the eighteenth century, the custom of burning incense had undergone many changes. The sacrifices of the ancients were all but forgotten, and in an age of enlightenment one no longer tried to please the deity with the aroma of myrrh and frankincense.

The use of incense was almost entirely domestic,

An incense burner elaborately modeled in the rococo style, standing on three feet, the openwork cover with a rosebud finial; outlined and decorated in reddish purple and green; porcelain of Nymphenburg, ca. 1765; hinged gilded metal mounting.

these vessels were, of course, produced for smoking incense; others by their shape and size indicate that they were made primarily to hold flower petals.

Following the baroque and rococo styles generally observed in the production of porcelain as well as faïence, which flourished concurrently with porcelain, the artist's inventiveness soared as he modeled and decorated incense burners and potpourri jars. Modelers and painters at the major European porcelain factories, particularly in France and Germany, impressed their artistic individuality on this specialized form of ceramic production.

Sometimes they were influenced by Oriental models. Among the first figures produced at Meissen in Böttger's brown stoneware and subsequently in the earliest white porcelain were small seated

A potpourri vase with a flower finial; the body overlaid with a finely modeled open network with molded flowers at the intersections; the reserved panels, within rococo cartouches, decorated in colors with flower bouquets; faïence of Münden, Hanover, 1750-1760.

essentially to eliminate unpleasant odors, but also to enhance a luxurious environment, to please and intoxicate the senses. The development of a sensuous appreciation of perfumes had reached its peak. Gradually a subtle line of distinction could be drawn between the words incense and perfume, which originally had been identical in their meanings. The term perfume was extended to encompass everything aromatic, from smoking incense to the fresh smells of fruit, exquisite diverse fragrances of flowers and, finally, even including artificial essences. The word incense through a process of limitation became associated almost exclusively with frankincense.

Consequently, eighteenth century porcelain censers of the most imaginable variety, of large and small shapes, from human to vase form, have loosely and interchangeably been called incense burners, *brûle parfums*, or potpourri jars and vases. Some of

Buddhas ("pagoda" figures). With grinning faces, Chinese looking, yet oddly westernized, they were intended as censers, modeled with hollow bases and open mouths as apertures for the emanating smoke. The artists and patrons of the soft-paste porcelain factories in France—Saint-Cloud, Chantilly and Mennecy—also had a penchant for Oriental models.

But most commonly, the modelers fashioned censers in the shape of baskets filled with fruit or flowers, potpourri jars encrusted with modeled applied blossoms and covers pierced in dainty designs, vases enhanced with elaborate open latticework, and bulbous openwork pots standing on delicately turned rococo feet. They may be startlingly beautiful in all white, the French examples showing off a fine soft paste and glaze, or their lovely molded and pierced designs may be or-namented with touches of color.

Some German porcelain specimens were exquisitely decorated with flower painting or a variety of indoor and country scenes, executed after paintings and engravings by leading artists such as Boucher, Watteau, and Nilson. Faïence jars frequently featured beautifully modeled applied blossoms, richly and naturalistically colored.

Censers were fashioned in appropriately attractive and dainty designs to match the redolent pastilles and petals they were to contain and whose fragrance they were to diffuse. Sometimes these precious vessels were mounted in gilded bronze or other metals. The Psalmist sang, "Ointment and perfume rejoice the heart." The censers alone had become a joy to behold; the purpose for which they were created became secondary.

Part II

Women in Ceramics

9
Artists: Sabina, Seraphina, and Others

The tantalizing fact about eighteenth century ceramics is that most of the small, finely sculptured and delicately painted objects are not signed. Knowing the names of modelers and decorators active at various porcelain and faïence manufactures enables us to make attributions, but rare indeed is a signed specimen by artists such as Löwenfinck or Auffenwerth! Such a discovery is comparable to finding a Leonardo, Raphael, or Rembrandt. And then the question of authenticity may arise.

We can identify Kaendler's work from the detailed descriptions contained in the Meissen factory records, for his models themselves were never signed. We know that artists were actually prohibited from marking their work, but sometimes we discover initials that were added surreptitiously, usually causing conjecture and debate rather than providing definitive answers. Even *Hausmaler,* the independent artists flourishing outside the factories, who frequently conducted sizeable workshops, generally preserved a certain anonymity, perhaps because some of their porcelains had been illicitly obtained. We identify their hand by their style, colors, and subject matter.

It is even more intriguing to investigate the extent of female participation in the development of eighteenth century porcelain and faïence. The near-vagabond existence of many itinerant arcanists and potters was hardly appropriate for a respectable young girl or woman. It may have been the age of enlightenment, but not of women's equality.

Yet we know that women were involved in this new art form. At the very beginning of porcelain manufacturing, Böttger sent quantities of precious white-glazed examples to Augsburg, the famed center for fine metalwork, to be mounted by the goldsmith Elias Adam. Adam, who bought many of the specimens, passed them on to Johann Auffenwerth's workshop for decoration.

Few collectors realize that not Auffenwerth alone painted on the porcelains; at least one of his daughters, Sabina, was also a gifted and active decorator. An eighteenth century Augsburg source, dated 1765, reveals that "white Saxon porcelain was painted here with skill and artistry. Bartholomeus Seuter, the silk dyer, a man of great skill and pleasing ingenuity in the art of enameling; Johann Auffenwerth, a goldsmith; and his daughter, Frau Hosennestlin (whom I mention regardless of the fact that she is no longer active as an artist), did the same kind of work and decorated the pieces with gilding and silvering, which was very highly prized.

A teapot (detail) decorated in colors and gold with a satyr and nymph surrounded by elaborate ornamentation, crowned with a basket of flowers flanked by two birds; porcelain of Meissen, 1720-1725; Hausmalerei by Sabina Auffenwerth, ca. 1730.

A hexagonal tea caddy, its panels alternately painted in iron red and purple with putti *and with silver ornaments; porcelain of Meissen, ca. 1725; Hausmalerei by Johann Auffenwerth.*

Thus great art may be found where it is least expected."* Sabina Auffenwerth, born in 1706, married the Augsburg engraver and publisher, Isaak Heinrich Hosennestel, in 1731. As the talented daughter of an innovative artist, she was no doubt encouraged to develop her artistic inclination and ambition.

Auffenwerth *Hausmalerei* on Böttger and early Meissen porcelain is dated from the 1720s, until Johann's death in 1728, but no doubt the workshop, including family members, continued for sometime afterwards. Decoration consisting of finely executed *chinoiserie* silhouette painting in gold and silver expanded to include iron red and purple. The variety of subject matter taken from French and Dutch engravings increased. Imaginatively conceived family scenes in indoor settings appeared, as

* Stetten, Paul von, *Erläuterungen der in Kupfer gestochenen Vorstellungen aus der Geschichte der Reichsstadt Augsburg;* see Selected Bibliography.

*A coffeepot (detail) decorated in colors and gold with
Venus and cupids, surrounded by fanciful ornamentation
of scrolls and diaper patterns, and surmounted by a basket
of flowers and a pair of birds; porcelain of Meissen,
1720-1725; Hausmalerei by Sabina Auffenwerth, ca.
1730.*

well as comedians and musicians after Watteau,
cavaliers and their ladies, hunting and battle scenes,
portrait busts, and mythological and allegorical
themes.

They were delicately painted on coffee and
teapots, cups and saucers, beakers and sugar bowls,
usually framed by elaborate and intricate baroque
lacework designs featuring scrolls, dots, and diapers. Flesh tones were picked out in iron red, dresses
were painted in shades of purple monochrome.

Gold and silver were reserved for the surrounding
embellishments. Since enameling of superior quality on copper and other metals had originated in the
goldsmiths' workshops, the Auffenwerths soon extended their proficiency with colors to polychrome
decoration on Meissen porcelains.

Where Johann Auffenwerth's artistry ended and
Sabina's, or that of some of the workshop assistants',
began is almost impossible to determine. There
have been recent, entirely plausible attempts at

A coffeepot (detail) decorated in colors and gold with Zeus courting Callisto, surrounded by ornamental lacework, scrolls, and diaper patterns, and crowned by a basket of flowers with a bird perched on each side; porcelain of Meissen, 1720-1725; Hausmalerei *by Sabina Auffenwerth, ca. 1730.*

attributions, and some painting by Sabina has now been positively identified. A coffee service, decorated in colors with *chinoiseries,* whose coffeepot bears the initials I.H., for Isaak Hosennestel, is reputed to have been painted by Sabina as a wedding present for her husband. Among other objects studied are specimens finely painted with mythological figures, surrounded by the typical, exquisitely rendered Augsburg ornamentation. Tiny birds and baskets of flowers form delightful, subtle highlights in the lacework designs.

A somewhat later cup and saucer has also been tentatively assigned to Sabina. This specimen, bearing an Augsburg luster mark and dating to about 1740, is decorated in relief with flowering prunus sprigs, which are enhanced with touches of yellow and green, and with purple outlines. In addition, the cup and saucer is painted in iron red, blue, green, and dark purple with German flowers, coming into vogue just then in Vienna and Meissen. It is quite possible that Sabina had been quietly and busily painting on porcelain in Augsburg throughout the years, keeping her eye on the fashions of the moment. We see that as late as 1765 she was well

remembered together with the two famous Augsburg names, those of her father and Seuter. Thus
collectors contemplating an example of Augsburg
Hausmalerei might keep in mind Sabina Auffenwerth and reserve some credit for her.

Another name sacrosanct to connoisseurs of early
Meissen porcelain and German faïence is that of
Adam Friedrich von Löwenfinck. His younger
brothers, Carl Heinrich and Christian Wilhelm, also
ceramic workers, are lesser known. Virtually unknown is Adam Friedrich's wife, an artist in her own
right. Born in Fulda in 1728, Maria Seraphina
Susanna Magdalena Schick was the daughter of the
painter Johann Schick, who as an influential court
official was connected with the Fulda faïence and
porcelain manufacture. Seraphina probably met
Adam Friedrich soon after his arrival in 1741, when

A cylindrical tankard decorated in purple monochrome
with a shepherdess seated in a landscape; surrounded by
an elaborate rococo scrollwork and shell border; faïence of
Künersberg; Hausmalerei, signed and dated: Augsburg, anno 1748, Anna Elisabeth Waldin, Eine
geborne Auffenwerthin.

A double gourd-shaped vase decorated in polychrome with
sweeping floral designs in the Oriental style; faïence of
Fulda, 1741-1744; painted by Adam Friedrich von
Löwenfinck.

he and his brother Carl Heinrich were decorating
faïences at the establishment.

Though we have no proof and Seraphina was still
a child, she may already have been trying her hand
at painting on faïence. We do know that most
ceramic workers, including the Löwenfinck
brothers, were apprenticed at a young age. Thus
Seraphina's early mastery over her medium comes
as no surprise. A rectangular plaque signed
M.S.S.M. Schickin pinx. 1745 depicts Saint John
Nepomuk, sensitively painted in manganese purple
and black.

That same year Adam Friedrich left Fulda to find
a more lucrative position elsewhere, enabling him to
support his future wife. He moved to Mainz where
he lived with Seraphina's uncle, the gilder Ignaz
Schwang. In 1747 Seraphina was married to Adam

A handleless cup and saucer decorated in colors and gold with chinoiseries, *surrounded by ornamental borders of scrollwork, a basket of flowers and birds at the top, and mascarons at the bottom; porcelain of Meissen, 1720-1725; Augsburg* Hausmalerei, *attributed to Anna Elisabeth Wald, ca. 1740.*

Bottom of Künersberg faïence tankard, showing signature.

Friedrich and followed him to Höchst, where he now seemed securely settled as director of the prestigious factory founded by him and two wealthy Frankfurt merchants.

Only one other specimen authenticated by Seraphina's signature is known. It is a faïence plaque that must be dated after 1747 because it bears her married name, *Seraphina de Löwenfincken.* Delicately painted in purple monochrome, the plaque pictures a southern landscape with buildings and the figure of a man fishing in a stream crossed by a bridge.

In all probability Seraphina enjoyed a long decorating career unheralded as befitted an eighteenth century lady, the daughter of an acknowledged painter—who also happened to be a Fulda mayor and senator—and the wife of a superior young artist in a new medium. Perhaps it is because of her privileged position that her name as a painter is recorded at all, since signatures were rare exceptions rather than the rule.

In 1749, when Löwenfinck objected to the unjust distribution of profits from the Höchst factory and insisted that like the financiers he was entitled to an equal share, he was relieved of his post. With Seraphina, Adam Friedrich journeyed to Strasbourg where he probably instructed Paul Hannong in the application of enamel colors on faïence, a process then still unknown at the factory. Hannong appointed Adam Friedrich director of his nearby Haguenau manufacture. Here his wanderings ended; after his death in 1754, Seraphina took over

Two plaques painted in colors with chinoiseries, and embellished with ornamentation; porcelain of Meissen, ca. 1725; Augsburg Hausmalerei, attributed to Anna Elisabeth Wald, 1730-1735; from a silver-gilt Augsburg guéridon by Johann Engelbrecht, 1723-1735.

Three plaques painted in colors with chinoiseries and with various diaper patterns and scrollwork; porcelain of Meissen, ca. 1725; Augsburg Hausmalerei, attributed to Anna Elisabeth Wald, 1730-1735; detail from a silver-gilt Augsburg guéridon by Johann Engelbrecht, 1723-1735.

A collection of modeled garden flowers, naturalistically colored; soft-paste porcelain of Vincennes (excepting the tulips which are Meissen), middle of the eighteenth century.

the direction, a position she retained for several years.

In 1763, now known as the wife of Captain De Becke, she was called to the faïence factory of Ludwigsburg, then employing twenty-four workmen, where she was appointed codirector. In 1775 she assumed full charge, and for twenty years proved to be as capable an administrator as she was a gifted artist. It is said that at Ludwigsburg Seraphina compensated her workers with faïences instead of money. In order to realize actual payment, they had to sell the specimens. She shrewdly trained her potters and decorators to be salesmen as well. Widowed a second time, after a long and diversified career in ceramics, Seraphina died in 1805.

Sabina Auffenwerth and Seraphina Löwenfinck are just two prominent names in eighteenth century ceramics. At Bow, Sarah Wilcox, a daughter of the painter and potter Thomas Frye, was active as a decorator of figures and groups.

Many women are known to have been employed as painters by the Meissen factory. Though they excelled at such fine details as the decoration of laces on the dresses of figures, they received only a third of the salary paid to male painters.

At Vincennes, forty-six girls were engaged exclusively to model exquisite white or naturalistically colored porcelain flowers such as roses, lilies, pinks, carnations, and camelias. The girls are remembered anonymously, as a group, and ultimately, it is probably unimportant whether their names are listed or not. Significant is the fact that they created some of the loveliest and most fragile of all porcelain sculptures. Among the identified decorators at the Sèvres factory, many were women, the majority excelling at flower painting.

Perhaps names of other artists will surface in the future. Current investigations are yielding information on another daughter of Johann Auffenwerth, Anna Elisabeth, born in 1696, who in 1722 married Jakob Wald. Two Künersberg faïence tankards, signed by her, are known. There is speculation that, like her sister Sabina, Anna Elisabeth Wald painted on Meissen porcelains at Augsburg; some exquisite *chinoiserie* examples have been attributed to her.

Considering the status of women in the eighteenth century and the dearth of documentation, it is gratifying to know that these ladies played a modest but significant role in the era's ceramic art.

10
Entrepreneur: Veuve Perrin

With the exception of one prominent faïence entrepreneur in the south of France, all the familiar names are those of men. The productions of Marseilles are among the most beautiful and treasured of eighteenth century faïences, and because of their desirability and rarity, they have been copiously imitated into our day, complete with the mark of Veuve Perrin, the woman responsible for them.

Pierrette Caudelot Perrin was the wife of Claude Perrin, a native of Nevers, who, in 1740, established a faïence factory at Marseilles. After his death, from 1748 to 1793, his widow carried on. It was under her energetic direction that the factory achieved its extraordinary distinction and recognition. Highly enterprising, Veuve Perrin knew what she wanted and demanded it from her associates and workmen. She thoroughly understood her material and explored all its possibilities, skillfully applying to best advantage the lessons learned from Meissen and other porcelain manufactures. Not only did Pierrette Perrin experiment and let her artistic fantasy reign, but she carried her ideas through to perfection.

Having developed superior techniques, she was able to produce an enormous variety of original shapes, often modeled after contemporary silver

A plate decorated in colors with an East Indian flower design; faïence of Marseilles, third quarter of the eighteenth century; Veuve Perrin.

objects including tureens, cachepots, bouquetiers, glass coolers, centerpieces, and pitchers, besides the smaller articles such as mustard jars, sugar casters, sauceboats, and innumerable dishes and platters so fine in the quality of their faïence and decoration

79

A plate decorated in colors with flowering branches and a bird in flight; faïence of Marseilles, third quarter of the eighteenth century; Veuve Perrin.

A plate with a sea-green ground, the border decorated in colors and gold with bows alternating with floral arrangements, the center with a sprig of flowers; faïence of Marseilles, third quarter of the eighteenth century; Veuve Perrin.

A plate painted in colors with animals in a landscape; faïence of Marseilles; third quarter of the eighteenth century; Veuve Perrin.

A plate with an openwork border, decorated in polychrome with flowering sprigs and a butterfly; faïence of Marseilles, third quarter of the eighteenth century; Veuve Perrin.

A cachepot with a scalloped rim, painted in colors with a fish still life; faïence of Marseilles, third quarter of the eighteenth century; Veuve Perrin.

that each was a masterpiece, comparable to the best in porcelain.

Faïence production, past its peak at other centers, experienced a dazzling revival at Marseilles. The exuberance of an extravagent rococo came into full play. Plastic decoration in the form of cherub finials, and modeled applied flowers, foliage, and fruit enriched many specimens. Brilliant and colorful painting in the high-temperature kiln was soon superseded by soft polychrome enamels, subtly enhanced with gilding. Marseilles's ground colors, green ranging from pale aquamarine to turquoise and a luminous yellow, remained unsurpassed anywhere.

The extraordinary beauty of the geographic locale, the lovely land of Provence, was translated into faïence. Marine subjects, fish, seaweeds, the Marseilles coast and the port itself, seascapes or landscapes with distant, gently rolling hills, all suffused by the region's special atmosphere of warmth, light, and color, received their proper exposure.

Veuve Perrin's productions reflected her period in numerous diverse ways. The full-blown, somewhat unruly rococo shapes soon tapered to more sedate, gently curved Louis XVI forms. Decorative themes included the era's predilection for ruins and a romantic vogue for gracefully rendered Oriental motifs. Flower painting, as at Meissen, continued to be fashionable throughout Pierrette Perrin's directorship, sometimes leaning toward Oriental stylization or reflecting an elegant, delicate French rococo. Veuve Perrin herself favored certain flowers: the rosebuds, jasmine, daisies, convulvus, and ranunculi that repeatedly appeared on her faïences. Themes from Pillement's engravings were deftly borrowed with characteristic charm and good taste.

About 1755 Veuve Perrin had engaged Honoré de Savy, primarily to instruct the apprentices in enamel painting. He remained associated with her until 1770, although he established his own workshop in 1764. From 1775 to about 1780, Veuve Perrin worked in partnership with François Abellard. Later she was assisted by her son, Joseph, until her long direction of the manufacture ended with her death. Her faïences, which we treasure today, are the legacy of one eighteenth century woman's imagination, resourcefulness, and business acumen.

11
Patron: Madame de Pompadour

When in 1745 King Louis XV established Jeanne Antoinette Poisson le Normant d'Etioles at Versailles as his *maîtresse en titre,* she accepted the King's favor and her new status graciously but hardly with surprise. The daughter of an officer, she had been raised by a wealthy financier who, undoubtedly recognizing in her the desirable prerequisites, deliberately educated her for the role of mistress to a king. This fanciful idea was later reaffirmed in the young girl's mind by the prophecy of an old woman. Years after the prediction had become fact, the King's mistress, now the Marquise de Pompadour, gratefully remembered the woman with a pension. In the meantime, however, she had married the nephew of her benefactor, whom she left immediately after the King became enamored of her.

Trained for her unique position from childhood, Madame de Pompadour with ease and inner security assumed a powerful role at court, particularly as a patroness of the arts. She was soon acclaimed for encouraging all forms and aspects of the arts and the resulting wealth of astonishingly beautiful objects created. At the same time, she was condemned for her outrageous extravagance.

But all her châteaux, furniture, rugs, tapestries, sculptures, porcelains, and paintings had to be paid for. She inspired and gainfully employed architects,

painters, *ébénistes.* Among her best and favorite artists ranked Boucher, Van Loo, Bernard van Riesen Burgh, Guérin, Falconet, Caffiéri, and Pigalle. The Gobelin and Savonnerie factories worked under her patronage. Her protection of an artist assured his fame. But she also possessed the instinct and knowledge to select those truly gifted and qualified to enhance the style of living, surrounded by art, that she had chosen for herself, the King, and their entourage. She was not content only to rule as a queen of fashion; her imagination and good taste favorably influenced her artists. Artistically inclined herself, she created, under the guidance of Boucher, a number of charming engravings, mostly after his drawings of *putti.*

Madame de Pompadour pursued her interest in the decorative arts with comparable zeal. As a great admirer of imported Chinese and Meissen porcelains, she was ambitious for France to produce porcelains of at least equal quality. The King was persuaded to support the factory existing at Vincennes, founded in 1738 by two rather unreliable artists, Robert and Gilles Dubois, but operated by capable porcelain enthusiasts under a royal privilege since 1745. In 1751 the King became a major shareholder, and stringent prohibitions concerning the competitive manufacture of porcelain

A pair of figures of Le Moissonneur *and* La Moissonneuse; *soft-paste biscuit of Vincennes, 1752; models by Blondeau after Boucher.*

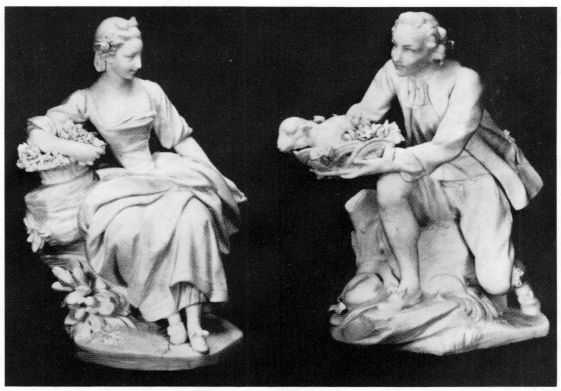

A pair of figures of La Bergère assise *and* Porteur de mouton; *soft-paste biscuit of Vincennes, 1754; models by Fernex after Boucher.*

A figure of Madame de Pompadour as L'Amitié au coeur; *soft-paste biscuit of Vincennes, 1755; model by Falconet.*

A group of figures picturing La Vache; *soft-paste biscuit of Sèvres, 1759; model by Falconet after Huet.*

elsewhere in France were enforced. The royal cipher of interlaced L's, used only occasionally before, was officially adopted as the factory mark in 1753.

Enjoying the active support of the King and the spirited Madame de Pompadour, the Vincennes establishment employed knowledgable chemists and fine artists and expanded rapidly. By 1756 larger quarters were required and the factory was transferred to Sèvres, near the château of Bellevue, the Marquise's favorite residence. Under her supervision, the manufacture was surrounded by beautiful landscaped gardens and fountains, giving it the appearance of a palace. Sèvres artists were permitted hunting privileges generally extended only to the nobility.

However, because of financial losses suffered by the move to Sèvres, the King took over the manufacture completely in 1759. An annual exhibition and sale of Sèvres porcelain was organized to be held at Versailles. The King determined the prices, which were high. Attending noblemen, when they believed themselves unobserved, might now and then pocket a small cup. But nothing escaped the wary royal eye. The following morning the cashier from Sèvres would appear at the nobleman's door with the saucer the offender had been unable to take and a bill for the purchase.

The Marquise de Pompadour also participated in the various exhibitions and bazaars to promote the distribution of the porcelains. She was a clever and successful saleslady, shrewdly questioning the civism of those who did not buy the porcelain. But her true moment of triumph came when she was able to send as a present to the Saxon king some choice examples of the Sèvres factory's productions. Though quite different from Meissen's hard-paste porcelain, the Vincennes and Sèvres objects demonstrated superb technical skill and artistic perfection. At their best, their tastefulness and delicacy were unsurpassed. The enamel color decoration fused beautifully with the soft porcelain.

At the factory, the Marquise herself was a constant source of inspiration. Beginning in 1749 and well into the next decade, the much-desired ground colors were invented. When the famous, highly valued, lush, rose-pink ground color was first successfully developed in 1757, it was named *rose Pompadour* in her honor. About the time of her death of consumption at the age of forty-three, in 1764, the color was discontinued. In 1752 the

A two-handled tray with a yellow-ground reserve in the center, painted in colors with trophies of love and friendship and surrounded by garlands of roses and blue ribbons tied in bows; the border decorated with four blue-ground medallions, each painted with the altar of love bearing a heart, set in a design of scalloped yellow-ground reserves, separated by cupid's arrows and connected by festoons of roses; enhanced with gilt lacework ornaments; soft-paste porcelain of Vincennes, 1753.

A sugar bowl with a modeled and naturalistically colored floral knob and molded prunus blossom decoration; enhanced with a gilt dentil border; white-glazed soft-paste porcelain of Vincennes, 1754.

A small tray with a rose Pompadour border enhanced with gilding, and a design of blue and gilt discs alternating with gilt foliage ornaments, interspersed with green sprigs bearing red berries; the center with a gilt circle wreathed by green sprigs with red and blue berries; soft-paste porcelain of Sèvres, 1760; artist: Thévenet, père.

An oval bowl decorated in blue and gold with a diaper pattern, the reserves painted in polychrome with cupids; soft-paste porcelain of Sèvres, 1767; artist: Dodin; on metal branches a variety of naturalistically modeled and colored flowers; soft-paste porcelain of Vincennes, middle of the eighteenth century.

Marquise ordered a series of eight figures of children, modeled by Blondeau after drawings by Boucher, that were glazed and painted in colors. When she learned of the factory's new biscuit productions, she ordered the same set of figures in unglazed porcelain, perhaps even more appealing in their soft whiteness. The enchanting models were inspired by a popular ballet pantomime of the day.

The Marquise naturally had to cope with numerous enemies at court, envious of her favored and influential position with the King. Many of her projects were severely criticized including her inter-est in white unglazed porcelain. However, her enthusiastic reception of the captivating models soon silenced those opposing the production of biscuit. The enterprising director of the factory, Jean-Jacques Bachelier, encouraged by Madame de Pompadour's unequivocal endorsement, continuously ordered from Boucher new sketches for figures and groups. The delightful children of his drawings now became available in a completely new version, as exquisitely refined all-white sculptures with a soft dull finish. That rare blend of sweetness and nonchalance, of elegance and rusticity, was depicted three-dimensionally. There were little girls, intent on some task or gazing fondly at a bird's nest, at some flowers in a basket, or perhaps at a little boy. The boys, with tousled hair and serious or pouting mien, expressed longing for sympathy and love.

A cup and saucer with a marbled rose Pompadour and blue ground, enhanced with gilding; the reserves painted in polychrome with bouquets of flowers; porcelain of Sèvres, 1760.

Several models were made for the dairy of Madame de Pompadour's château at Crécy. They included the youthful pastoral figures of *Le Porteur de mouton* and *La Bergère assise* by Jean-Baptiste de Fernex after Boucher drawings. Most of the earliest figure modeling was realized after subjects of Boucher's fecund imagination. An array of shepherdesses and milkmaids was joined by mythological figures or characters from currently popular comedies. The modelers rarely depicted actual personages, but when they did, such individuals were cleverly and poetically pictured in allegorical guises. Madame de Pompadour herself was associated with a heart upon an altar, the symbol of friendship and love. Falconet modeled a biscuit statuette of the Marquise standing next to a high round pedestal adorned with modeled festoons of roses. Gracefully arching her back, she extends her arms across the altar, in one hand holding a heart.

The decoration of a fine Vincennes porcelain tray, probably made for the Marquise, in part features tiny vignettes painted with hearts upon altars. The predominating yellow and blue color scheme of the tray's decoration reflects the Marquise's predilection for the combination of these two favorite colors.

Another specialty of the Vincennes and Sèvres factory supported by Madame de Pompadour was its soft-paste porcelain flowers. A large variety of garden flowers—lilies, roses, carnations, and pinks—were naturalistically modeled and daintily touched with pastel colors. Many were later mounted on metal stems to be placed in Vincennes, Sèvres, or Meissen porcelain flowerpots and vases, settings in which their naturalistic representation was completely convincing. The blossoms were of such exquisitely detailed perfection that their true-to-nature execution inspired the Marquise with an idea to surprise the King.

One day in the midst of winter, it is said, she invited him to one of her magnificent châteaux, where she received him in her luxurious apartment next to a hothouse. As they strolled into this summery retreat, the King found himself surrounded by an abundant, varied, blooming floral display. He praised the tasteful arrangement and the individual flowers themselves, commenting on their perfection of form and color, as well as their aroma. The Marquise was delighted with the success of her plan, for the King momentarily had actually believed he was walking in a garden of real flowers. The beautiful porcelain blossoms, enhanced with artificial fragrances, had faithfully imitated nature with utmost delicacy.

Madame de Pompadour had initiated a new vogue. Large orders for Vincennes flowers were placed with the manufacture by many courtiers and others of wealth and position. But as usual the Marquise's detractors voiced their displeasure. One of these intrigants, the Marquis d'Argenson, who resented her presence and power, testily recorded in his memoirs that the King had ordered more than 800,000 livres worth of Vincennes porcelain flowers with vases for all his country houses and the Marquise de Pompadour's château of Bellevue. The Marquis was incensed over this scandalous luxury that depleted the royal coffers and was the talk of Paris.

No doubt the Marquise's artistically inspired extravagances contributed to the eventual downfall of the monarchy. For the present, however, her perceptive aesthetic sense and appreciation of art in all its manifestations created and fostered immensely pleasurable hobbies and diversions.

When she came to power, the rococo style with its playfulness, its trellises and arabesques, and its sophistication despite arch simplicity seemed to be bursting into full bloom. Slowly the intensity of its intricate spiraling movement, its unpredictable twists and turns, and its wealth and joy of flowers and ornamental enhancements diminished. Lines became simpler and straighter, turning into an elegant, modified style heralding the neoclassical era in which shapes were less contorted and more serene, ornamented with decorously arranged festoons, ribbons, and bows.

For nearly two decades the Marquise de Pompadour reigned supreme as patroness of the arts, shepherding her artists through the turbulant rococo period and well into the classical revival. They, in turn, through their artistry paid hommage to her, leaving a lasting memorial in their creations.

PART III

The Specialist's Corner

12
A Glance at Chinese Porcelain

Even today the Chinese and their culture are strange to the West. Despite an old and continuous interest in this remote part of the world, we still find the Far East intriguing rather than comprehensible. Constant improvement in modes of travel and communication, and the present mobility of peoples everywhere would foster the belief in greater understanding and appreciation of these foreigners. But while the Chinese are friendly and hospitable to outsiders, they live in a closed society and a dearth of information exists. Yet from their art we are able to glimpse and learn something about them and their past, their character, traditions, and pastimes.

The current fashionable interest in everything Chinese is sporadic and superficial; perhaps it will deepen sufficiently to reveal to us, through the various media as well as actual contact, the refinements and painstaking care that produced the unique ancient art of ceramics and how it developed through the centuries. At the same time we can profit from the texts of European travelers with their finely rendered illustrative engravings that served to inspire eighteenth century Western artists in their own adaptations of *chinoiseries,* then equally in vogue in Europe.

Chinese ceramics are also easily accessible for educational purposes and visual gratification in most art museums. For the collector of antique porcelains looking for a specific area of collectibles, a wide and varied field opens up offering a panorama of wonders and delights, posing puzzles and challenging questions, some yielding answers, others defying resolution and remaining inscrutable until a future date, perhaps forever. Of course the serious scholar and curious collector will persist in their quest for documentation.

The collector's real problem is whether to specialize or diversify his interests. It seems logical to follow one's aesthetic dictates, that would probably, at least inititally, mean acquiring objects regardless of their dynastic origins. Diversification in acquisition would certainly aid in learning about the Chinese and their art, and in comparing styles and materials of different epochs. Ownership and repeated examination of one's possessions in the light of experience will prove continuously informative. Close scrutiny at first expands one's interest, trains and sharpens the eye, and eventually pinpoints one's personal preferences. Thus the neophyte collector turns into a specialist. Then, as an experienced collector, he may branch out once more, this time with more knowledge, but again guided by his

A bowl with a carved peony design under a green celadon glaze; porcelaneous stoneware of China, Sung dynasty, 960-1279.

taste, that by now may have changed.

Whatever the period or the method of collecting, the choice of objects appears inexhaustible. Personal preferences may depend on several factors such as form, size, and color. The great variety of objects, modeled and painted throughout a millenium of ceramics production, will surely provide a favorite area of interest to every prospective collector, at the same time opening the doors to a formidably strange but also perpetually appealing and enchanting civilization.

Centuries of upheaval and transition, both political and religious, caused by internal and outside forces, and of cyclic progress and decadence lie between the simple early earthenware shapes of the T'ang dynasty (681-906) and the elaborately decorated fine porcelains of the Ch'ien Lung reign (1736-1795). They reveal numerous changes of discipline as well as of style, of different means and variously achieved goals. Predominating ceramic shapes always were dishes, bowls, and vases, along with many other forms including figures.

Beginning with the T'ang period and through the Sung dynasty (960-1279), we are struck by the effectiveness of simple shapes. The bowls and jars are extraordinarily beautiful and serene; the directness of line and form carries just the right balance of tension and release. The figures of the T'ang dynasty in their fixed poses tell much about themselves, revealing admirable character traits transformed into art. The dancing ladies and musicians are poised, dignified, and demure, while the temple guardians and warriors display fierce pride, courage, and patience. Even the animals, the camels and horses, appear as noble and heroic figures.

The overall clay or buff color of the figures, sometimes partially glazed and highlighted with touches of pigment, stresses the tautly severe yet graceful forms. Their attributes are universal, their execution is uniquely Chinese.

Sung bowls vary from small, fragile, thin-walled vessels, shallow or conical in form, sometimes gently lobed or notched, to the massive celadon wares. The diversity of these objects, within a basically circumscribed range of shapes, is truly amazing. Their understated classic simplicity is enhanced by a narrow choice of glazes; some specimens are finely incised under the glaze with stylized floral motifs. To the uninitiated, the smaller objects may appear insignificant; to the connoisseur, their very modesty and restraint are particularly appealing and indicative of the Chinese character.

The Yüan dynasty (1280-1368) continued the Sung tradition though gradually some distinctive changes became apparent, among them some heavier potting and a concentration of black foliage and figure drawing against a buff or turquoise ground, heralding the long and highly productive Ming dynasty (1368-1644).

A broadening in diversity of shapes and a veritable burst of color characterized the era of the Ming emperors. This period spanning three centuries

A stem cup painted in underglaze blue with a dragon design; porcelain of China, Yüan dynasty, 1280-1367.

A bowl decorated in underglaze blue with a lady in a pavilion in a mountainous landscape; porcelain of China, Hsüan-tê period, 1426-1435.

resembles the Renaissance in Western Europe with its lavish, multifaceted, artistic production. In ceramics this thrust forward was translated into the development of elaborate forms both large and small, including jars, vases, bowls, and dishes, with fine fluting, valanced borders, or of floral shapes. Figural roof tiles and pillows became popular. A variety of imaginative smaller objects was produced such as winepots and incense burners, or utensils for the calligrapher or poet's use including brush holders, water droppers, and boxes for sealing wax, sometimes attractively modeled in animal or flower shape.

Among the great inventions of the early Ming dynasty were ground colors of astonishing beauty—copper red, yellow, and dark blue. Where during the Sung era attention had been focused primarily on shape, with the distraction of color, during the Ming dynasty efforts were divided be-

tween shape and color, perhaps even tilting in favor of brilliant color rather than dwelling on an object's sculptural excellence and delicacy.

The dishes covered with rich, thick, single-color glazes and jars decorated with painterly designs in two, or more, colors such as deep red and green are outstanding, unequaled achievements of the Ming artists. Another important invention was the bold and handsome underglaze blue painting of stylized floral and foliage ornamentation against the porcelain's fine white ground. An immense quantity of such blue and white wares was produced whose variety of subject matter ranged from extremely fine to quite provincial in the quality of its execution.

But the Ming painters, particularly during the later reigns, did not stop at underglaze blue decoration. They combined it in their designs with enamel colors including iron red, green, yellow, turquoise, and aubergine, thus creating the Ming five-color

A figure of Kuan Yin; white-glazed porcelain of China, Ming dynasty, 1368-1644.

schemes. Large fish bowls, numerous temple jars of all sizes, and small cabinet items were decorated in these colors with sweeping foliage and floral motifs, sometimes featuring fantastic animals and birds.

A special group of vases and bowls, usually of massive, bulbous shapes with incised designs or raised floral and other ornamental molding were painted in combinations of blue, purple, and turquoise.

Styles, qualities, and above all, taste varied throughout this era. There was an extraordinary amount of experimentation and innovation with shapes, colors, and designs. The porcelaneous stonewares of earlier periods were being replaced by the translucent, finer porcelains that inspired great creativity in modeling, as well as application of colors. It should be difficult not to discover examples to one's taste in this wealth of ceramic production from modest small provincial jars or delicate, elegant *blanc de Chine* objects to priceless blue and white or single-color dishes.

In a land as large as China where the ceramic industry was so highly developed and widespread, kilns produced an unimaginable number of objects; the choice is endless. Specimens are frequently similar, hardly ever identical. In addition to new precious objects, popular styles of the past were continued or repeated, with or without changes, such as the splash-colored or partly glazed wares of

the T'ang dynasty and the Sung celadons. On the whole, Ming productions, particularly of the later reigns, convey a somewhat heavier impression but, one must hasten to add, some of the finest, rarest, and most prized pieces, dazzling to the eye and poetic in feeling, date from this era.

Toward the dynasty's end and early in the seventeenth century a decline set it, with the exception of some unusual transitional objects including slender vases, tankards, and double gourd-shaped vases, noted for their fine deep blue underglaze painting of figures and foliate ornamental designs. Some of the specimens were decorated in brilliant polychromes in the best Ming tradition, but in a somewhat more expansive manner, heralding a new epoch in Chinese ceramic art.

With the ascent to the throne of K'ang Hsi (1662-1722), the second emperor of the Ch'ing dynasty (1644-1912), began another era of great advances and refinements in ceramic decoration combined with considerable changes in taste. It was a period of great pictorial art, of visual challenge, of detailed decoration depicting Chinese life and philosophy. In time as well as style this epoch was comparable to the splendor and extravagance of the baroque in Western Europe, and K'ang Hsi has been compared to his French contemporary, King

A plate decorated in underglaze blue with a stylized flower and foliage design; porcelain of China, K'ang Hsi period, 1662-1722; with the Johanneum inventory mark of the Royal Saxon Collection, Dresden.

A tall vase painted with four concubines in various poses and a border design in iron-red monochrome, enhanced with gilding; porcelain of China, K'ang Hsi period, 1662-1722.

Louis XIV. No doubt there is an artistic affinity. How beautifully do the finest K'ang Hsi porcelains, often elaborately mounted in French *bronze doré*, add the ultimate touch of perfection to a room of prized eighteenth century French furniture!

During K'ang Hsi's reign the kilns of Ching-tê Chên commenced production with bursts of resplendent color: pulsating underglaze blues of intense dark and soft lighter shades painted on the finest, whitest porcelain; clear, fresh enamel colors applied sparingly or profusely, as the decoration might warrant; overall single-color glazes, technically and aesthetically the most astounding achievements, recalling early Ming examples, but now ever more diversified. Finally there were the creamy white-glazed specimens, many from Tê-hua in the province of Fukien, so perfect in their purity and translucency.

Novel shapes provided additional excitement. Large bulbous forms, though not totally abandoned, gradually gave way to a preponderance of tall, slender jars and vases, with narrow or widely flaring necks. They were boldly conceived, soaring in movement, yet serene to behold. In the decoration, this was perhaps the period that most explicitly and generously provides us with an insight into the Chinese way of life. During earlier dynasties potters had concentrated on stylized incised, molded, or painted floral and animal ornamentation, stressing the Chinese affinity to nature. In the Ch'ing dynasty, symbolism deriving from nature, which pervades the Chinese life, gained in significance. Thus we are constantly shown natural phenomena—animals, birds, flowers, trees, and fish—as emblematic of the seasons, happiness, connubial bliss, or longevity, and other states of mind, conditions, and emotions.

But in addition to symbolic painting of prunus (spring), peacock (beauty and dignity), tortoise (strength and longevity), fish (abundance and fertility), or dragon (power), among others, large and smaller vases and bowls treat us to an endless variety of interior and outdoor scenes, illustrating all aspects of Chinese life. Indoors we observe the ladies at work, or play, or minding their frolicking children. We see their furniture, their vases filled with flowers, the arrangements of their houses and rooms. We note their colorful dress and elegant coiffures. We become aware of a demure pose, an acquiescent inclination of the head, of silence, patience, meditation, or a smile. These are busy, tranquil, and cheerful settings.

Outdoors we watch the men, astride their galloping horses, swords drawn for battle, or simply in pursuit of an animal during a hunt. Here the subject is as exciting as the brilliant colors with which it is depicted. Sometimes the scenes are rendered in shapes of deep underglaze blue, with an equally vivid effect. The men sport even more elaborate costumes of which we can study the fine details. Often there is a hint of humor in the way these subjects are deftly yet carefully drawn. At times a lively rabbit or dog underfoot will provoke a viewer's smile. Borders are mostly enhanced with diaper or foliage designs.

Quite different from decoration depicting an active, harmonious family life or vigorous outdoor pursuits are the quiet scenes from nature, frequently and perhaps most successfully executed in underglaze blue on tall vases. Great boulders rise into mountains, the streams far below are dotted with tiny boats or crossed by an arched bridge. Sometimes a philosopher alone, or in the company

A figure of a mythical horse, decorated in yellow, green, and aubergine enamels on biscuit; porcelain of China, K'ang Hsi period, 1662-1722.

of friends and disciples, contemplates the beautiful and grandiose scene. The insignificance and transitoriness of man is contrasted with the eternal majesty and pervasiveness of nature. The constancy of the seasons and their renewals are lovingly represented by the porcelain painter's bold and caring brush strokes. Occasionally the landscape painting is enlivened by the depiction of wild life such as gracefully leaping or silently attending deer.

Many vases celebrate a single season with their overall decoration of prunus or peach blossoms. The painting may be scant, leaving large areas of the porcelain gleaming white, or profuse, covering the entire surface.

The same subjects, of course, occur in polychrome painting on bowls and vases where usually one color predominates, most popularly the *famille verte*, or the rarer and highly prized *famille noire* and *famille jaune*.

The impact and nobility of the K'ang Hsi shapes

A large dish decorated in famille verte *enamels with birds amidst blossoming trees and shrubbery, surrounded by an ornamental diaper and floral border; porcelain of China, K-ang Hsi period, 1662-1722.*

A tall vase with a powder-blue ground, decorated in gold with birds surrounded by elaborate floral and foliage motifs; porcelain of China, K'ang Hsi period, 1662-1722.

A vase, modeled after a bronze shape, with a rose-pink glaze; porcelain of China, Ch'ien Lung period, 1736-1795. A lotus-shaped water pot standing on three small feet, with a finely molded fish inside; the biscuit with a deep purple glaze; porcelain of China, K'ang Hsi period, 1662-1722.

A collection of small vases: (from left to right) decorated with figures in underglaze blue; glazed blue; blanc de Chine, with a modeled lizard around the neck; glazed dark blue with traces of gilt decoration; with lotus-petal molding and painted with figures in underglaze blue; porcelain of China, seventeenth to eighteenth century.

A collection of miniature single-color vases: (from left to right) dark red flambé; crackled gray; turquoise; iron rust, with thickly run grayish green at the neck; peach bloom; porcelain of China, eighteenth century.

A pair of brush rests, in the shape of carps cavorting amidst waves, decorated in iron red and green; a whistle in the shape of a boy, decorated in iron red, yellow, blue, and black; porcelain of China, Ch'ien Lung period, 1736-1795.

*A group of figures of Callot dwarfs, the man sitting on a
pigsty from which a pig peeks forth, the woman standing
behind him, holding his forehead; white-glazed porcelain
of Meissen, ca. 1720.*

(Left) A group of figures of Callot dwarfs, the man standing on a hexagonal base, carrying an infant on his back and holding a pouch in one hand, a dish in the other; decorated with gilding and showing traces of black; faces and hands flesh-colored; porcelain of Meissen, ca. 1720. (Right) A figure of a Callot dwarf as an Indian woman. allegorical of America, standing on a hexagonal base with a gilt border; the woman with black hair and wearing a band of white feathers and a gilt cloth; the face and body tinted a light copper brown; porcelain of Meissen, ca. 1720.

An elaborately shaped rococo tile picture with molding simulating a frame; painted in blue with the baptism of Jesus; faïence of Delft, dated 1767.

A large dish decorated in golden yellow with a stylized foliage design around a coat of arms; Hispano-Moresque earthenware, sixteenth century.

A pair of albarelli *decorated in colors with foliage and ornamental borders, and an inscription in an oval medallion enhanced with floral and foliage motifs; faïence of Alcora, eighteenth century.*

were perhaps most effectively displayed through the application of the wide variety of single-color grounds or glazes, perfected during this reign. The brilliant glazes on the smooth hard surfaces both stressed and harmoniously balanced form and color. The complementary intensity of these primary attributes aroused tension that was released by strong, gracefully flowing movement.

Mirror black, powder blue, apple green, *sang de boeuf*, peach bloom, *clair de lune*, coral red—each color has its particular virtues and beauties and claims its own admirers. Glazes may appear highly polished, fatty-looking, or crackled. A rare *café au lait* ground was sometimes used in combination with underglaze blue painting in white reserves or with *famille verte* decoration.

Another specialty, actually begun during the Ming dynasty, but developed and refined in the K'ang Hsi reign, were objects decorated with enamel colors, frequently in combinations of yellow, green, and aubergine on the biscuit, or unglazed porcelain. These included many small cabinet specimens such as figural water droppers, brush rests, and libation cups.

One marvels at the enormous variety of shapes produced during the sixty years of the K'ang Hsi reign. They were mostly simple and strong, even severe, and included figural subjects such as birds, horses, sages, philosophers, poets, children, and deities. Similarly, it is truly astonishing to witness the range and superb quality of striking colors and the skillfulness of their application, achieved within a relatively short period of time. The immediate impression of the era is one of high aesthetic goals, sophistication, vigor, and irrepressible joy in artistic expression. This ceramic artistry is vivid, serious and whimsical, entertaining and beguiling, in its diversity offering something to every taste.

The tentative introduction of a new, sought-after color, that had so far eluded even the knowledgable Chinese potters, came toward the end of K'ang Hsi's reign. It did not make a firm appearance in its own right until his successor Yung Ch'êng (1723-1735) ascended to the throne. This was the delicate rose-pink enamel, discovered by one Cassius of Leyden in Holland, whose secret soon leaked to ceramic centers in Europe and eventually to China. Predominently applied in combination with other enamel colors, particularly during the ensuing long reign of Ch'ien Lung (1736-1795), it gave its name to a great variety of *famille rose* wares—figural,

decorative and useful, of which large numbers were intended for export to Europe.

The brief Yung Ch'êng reign was noted for extraordinarily fine quality porcelains, some of egg-shell thinness, most delicately, tastefully, and painstakingly painted. It seemed to be a time for momentary respite, for restraint and subtlety, when the lively subject matter and the bright colors, especially the *famille verte* palette of K'ang Hsi, were abandoned. Dainty *famille rose* floral and bird painting against the luminous white porcelain was favored, frequently applied scantily, leaving large white-glazed areas.

Then the new riot of color, the *famille rose*, on curved, flared, lyrical shapes—the playful Chinese rococo—burst forth during Ch'ien Lung's reign. Ming dynasty and earlier forms and colors in lighter, often blander, yet very lovely adaptations were revived. Several novel glazes such as the turquoise "robin's egg" and various *flambés* were added to those invented during the K'ang Hsi period. They were mixed and mottled in contrast to the pure, clear, earlier colors and came in highly glazed, matte, and different crackle variations.

The strict, classical discipline of the K'ang Hsi shapes and colors loosened. The strong influence of the sweeter rose shade abundantly applied and gradually replacing the cool enamel green as a predominating color ushered in a wide range of Ch'ien Lung wares, softer and sensuous in appearance, graceful in shape, and pleasing in the decoration. Many different combinations of colors were introduced, including grounds of turquoise and iron red, or softly shaded rose and greens, to approximate naturalistic colors of fruit such as peaches. Once more painted decoration became ornate and ostentatious, revealing a wondrous, colorful life.

A great number of earlier shapes, particularly those of figures, were retained or expanded upon with variations and beautifully decorated in the resplendent *famille rose* enamels. The proud parrots in the greens, aubergines, and turquoises of the K'ang Hsi period were replaced by delicate ducks and prancing phoenixes colored in the *famille rose* palette.

As the reign progressed a certain decadence set in. The aesthetic appeal suffered through overdecoration, when in the depiction of Chinese life on vases, jars, and bowls, combinations of iron red and rose were stressed, accented by several other enamel colors such as yellow, green, turquoise, and blue. Toward the end of the eighteenth century the impact and stateliness of K'ang Hsi, the airy delicacy of Yung Ch'êng, and the lovely flowery effect of early Ch'ien Lung had become a memory.

As in European ceramic production the nineteenth century in China produced few noteworthy novelties in style, shape, or color. It was an era of repetition and adaptation rather than originality, of quantity and decorativeness superseding quality and artistry.

The patterns of Chinese life and environment had unfolded in the ceramic art throughout many centuries and different dynasties. Chinese artists had meticulously depicted the people, the impressiveness of their natural surroundings, their animals, birds, and flowers, never simply in imitation of nature but to praise, to emphasize symbolic meaning, dwelling on beauty, grace, and tranquillity. It might be to capture a contemplative philosopher, the fleeting moments of a blossom burst into bloom, a burdened mother carrying a blissfully smiling child, a deer hearkening in a silent landscape.

Modeled figures as well as painted decoration mirrored and inspired eloquence, grandeur, and humility, a respect for the endless details of life presented with such care and devotion, and the vastness and mystery of nature juxtaposed to and intertwined with the spirit of man. We sense everywhere a gracious acceptance of life and a serenity of spirit. The artist shows us his joy and pleasure in color, form, and movement, and shares with us the beauty of an object well made.

13
Meissen's Exotic Pagodas and Callots

The taste for the exotic and grotesque, that flourished in Western Europe in entertainment and the arts, showed no sign of abating as the seventeenth century turned into the eighteenth. On the contrary, it received new impetus through the discovery of porcelain manufacture at Meissen. Preoccupation with fabled and foreign characters and distant places repeatedly spurred their artistic representation in various media, and the contribution of porcelain, vigorously modeled and finely painted, quickly commanded attention.

Figural representation derived from the Italian comedy whose stock characters entertained the royal courts and attendant nobility in *opera buffa* and lively improvisations such as masquerades and pageants. Closely related were the obligatory court jesters kept exclusively to amuse royalty, an incredible and bizarre custom to modern minds.

Quaint "pagoda" figures reflected a fascination with the Orient, particularly intriguing because of its remoteness and inaccessibility and known to most only through several seventeenth century travel accounts. These works, such as the one by Joan Nieuhof,* proved informative, but interpreted

* Nieuhof, Joan, *Het Gesantschap der Neerlandtsche Oost-Indische Compagnie, aan den grooten Tartarischen Chan, den tegenwoordigen Keizer van China;* see Selected Bibliography.

foreign cultures rather than picturing them with accuracy. Fertile and imaginative European minds, drawing upon these illustrated reports, created a fantastic world that could scarecely be called a reliable replica of faraway lands. The resulting creations perhaps tell us as much about the Europeans of that time as about the lands and peoples they supposedly represented.

A series of "Callot" figures mirrored the aristocracy's predilection for strange Levantine characters as well as for numerous domestic types whose occupations or physical deformities were caricatured for the amusement of the upper class.

Though a few rare and impressive *commedia dell' arte* figures were modeled in Böttger's brown stoneware, prior to the successful firing of white-glazed porcelain, these characters' full effectiveness was not realized until Kaendler brilliantly recreated them in white and polychromed Meissen porcelain about two decades later. During the first experimental years, before Meissen's most gifted modelers boldly struck out and mastered their medium, the possibilities porcelain offered were tentatively tested and explored. This is why a period of magnificent porcelain decoration under Höroldt preceded the era of great modeling.

Thus during Meissen's initial phase, modeling

Three pagoda figures, white-glazed and variously deco-rated with gilding; porcelain of Meissen, 1715 (Böttger period)-1720.

Three pagoda figures, imaginatively and exotically deco-rated in colors; one (right), seated on an oblong base, in Indian garb; porcelain of Meissen, 1720-1730.

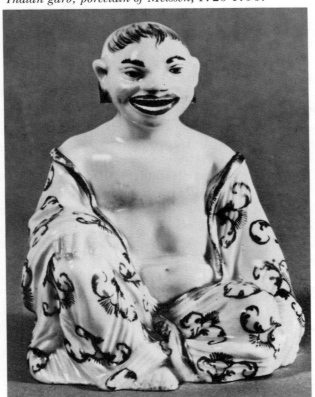

A pagoda figure decorated with gilding; porcelain of Meissen, ca. 1720.

A figure of a Callot dwarf, openmouthed and gesturing with outstretched hand, standing on an oblong base; white-glazed porcelain of Meissen, ca. 1720.

played a secondary role and remained generally modest and limited in scope. Rather than meeting the challenge of precariously balancing out-stretched limbs and picturing their subjects in abrupt motion, the early modelers cautiously re-strained themselves to more static positions. Their success depended on subtlety of detail, such as facial expression, and on the strength or fluidity achieved by a simple line or fold to lighten an essentially rather solid, though small, composition.

The first group of these extraordinary and rare objects were a variety of crouching pagoda figures, so-called after the Oriental temples, with open mouths and pierced ears that were intended for use as incense burners. Since brown stoneware models are so very rare, these figures were probably not made before 1715 to 1720, when white-glazed porcelain gradually began to replace Böttger's stoneware. Freely modeled after the Chinese deity Pu-tai Ho-shang, the god of contentment, the figures always appeared friendly and benevolently

Veith Schöberl, von Gumpendriel gebürthig,
der grossen Hollhippen Fabrica im Crabatendörffl,
Niderlags Verwandter.

So lang noch waß im Korb, ist mir still spill mein Kauff
Zahl aus! Zahl mir praff aus! daß Cräml geht schö drauff
Wan ich bin aus gespillt, werd ich mit schimpff u. hohn,
Gehaut, getaüfst, genent, Ein seiner Huren sohn

Model for preceding figure; Veith Schöberl, born in Gum-
pendriel, from Callots Neueingerichtetes Zwergenkabinett.

(Left) A figure of a drinking Callot dwarf standing on a waisted oval base; (right) a figure of a Callot dwarf standing on a hexagonal base, wearing a pouch suspended from a shoulder strap; white-glazed porcelain of Meissen, ca. 1720.

smiling. Another obligatory characteristic was the protruding belly that somehow complemented the plainly jovial facial expression. Fatness was admired in China, and to exhibit his generous girth, the god, according to Nieuhof, effectively "sits quite naked from top to bottom, showing breast and abdomen." In the Meissen models his left hand was sometimes hidden under the loose folds of his garment, the right rested lightly on his covered right knee. A few models, placed on a flat base, featured a tea set in front of the figure. How well the artist captured the serenity of the deity's pose, how relaxed the hands and fingers seem to follow and blend with the cloth!

The beauty of the porcelain and modeling was perhaps most directly expressed in the first white-glazed figures. Others were enhanced with gilt patterns on the cloth garment, or with larger totally gilded areas, that immediately changed the figure's overall appearance. Later touches of polychrome enamels transformed the early modest and tranquil pagoda into cheerful specimens that were colorful and amusing. It is easily understandable why some connoisseurs make a point of collecting the same model in white, as well as variously decorated. Each finely modeled and uniquely painted version exudes its own individual charm. These miniature Oriental deities of European manufacture and interpretation with their pseudo-Oriental faces are a special delight to the modern, more enlightened, and sophisticated Western eye.

Like the squat little pagodas, perhaps even more so, the Callot figures were distinct oddities. Their actual association with the engraver is several times removed. In 1622 Jacques Callot published in Nancy his *Varie figure gobbi*, a series of twenty-one engravings that had originally been conceived during his stay in Florence six years earlier. They

102

(Left) A figure of a Callot dwarf as a masked woman, standing on a tiered square base; decorated with gilding, her hands and face flesh-tinted; (right) a figure of a Callot dwarf as a pock-marked, grimacing woman, gesturing with her hands and holding a blue pouch; her conical skirt terminating in a flat round base; the skirt decorated with silver ornaments (now oxidized black), double iron-red lines, and a gilt border on the base; porcelain of Meissen, ca. 1720.

featured a motley assemblage of dwarfs, hunchbacks, and cripples pictured as musicians playing bagpipes, violins, guitars, and tambourines, as fencers wielding rapiers, and as comedians, dancers, and beggars.

Callot's creations emerged as caricatures of various types rather than conveying any psychological insights or inviting compassion. His was a cool observer's perspective that turned feared and painful infirmities or physical defects into jokes. Callot's work was much copied everywhere; variations appeared and eventually served as models for wood carvings and terra cotta figures. The endless imitations utterly distorted and finally obscured Callot's original conceptions.

Almost a century later, when the vogue had been just about exhausted, another gifted engraver, Wilhelmus Koning, culled from Callot and his imitator's work, added his own ideas and synthesized all the elements into a collection of fifty-seven newly invented grotesque types. Their only true relationship to the original was a reference in the title *Il Callotto resuscitato*, published in Amsterdam in 1716. Soon afterwards editions appeared in Augsburg and Vienna.* The subtitle explained, *"Le Monde est plein de sots joieux / Les plus Petits sont les mieux"* (The world is full of happy idiots, the smallest are the best). Appropriately amusing and at times devastating rhymed commentary accompanied each plate in German, Dutch, and French. An elaborate ornamental baroque border interspersed with small grotesque figures, animals, mascarons,

---

* Illustrations for this chapter are from Fraenger, Wilhelm, editor, *Callots Neueingerichtetes Zwergenkabinett*, a German facsimile edition; see the Selected Bibliography.

A figure of a Callot dwarf as a peasant woman, standing on an tiered oval base, holding a jug; decorated with gilding; porcelain of Meissen, ca. 1720.

Ursula Schleglin, servant at the Bluntzingen Manor, from Callots Neueingerichtetes Zwergenkabinett.

A covered teapot with a modeled mascaron spout, painted in colors with Callot dwarfs and enhanced with latticework borders and gilding; porcelain of Meissen, ca. 1722.

Reverse of teapot.

Model for figure on teapot: Monsieur le Marquis de Sauterelle, described as the high commissioner making a declaration of love, from Callots Neueingerichtetes Zwergenkabinett.

foliage, and baskets of fruit framed every page.

The assorted Lilliputians in this collection mockingly represented nationalities, social classes, and occupations, complete with suitable costumes and attributes. Callot's bizarre and brazen entertainers had diminished into a *petite bourgeoisie*, cast as misshapen dwarfs. The engraver depicted

and satirized a specific era with all its attendant paraphernalia.

Since none of the Callot figures are extant in Böttger stoneware and the *Callotto resuscitato* was not published until 1716, one may deduce with certainty that they were not made until sometime after that date.

Model for figure on teapot: Ruffanella, the shepherd-ess, who spurns the enamored Ploriander, from Callots Neueingerichtetes Zwergenkabinett.

The models of the extremely rare, small, thickly set figures are ascribed to Georg Fritzsche. Essentially unattractive because of their uniformly dwarfish appearance and various other deformities, the Callot figures nevertheless impress us as astonishing achievements. Human frailties, so exaggerated in these gnomes, that they would normally repel and cause us to turn our eyes away, tend to amuse instead, as we accept the characterizations so aptly demonstrated by expert modeling. Cleverly the modeler has transformed disabilities into assets.

A more than ample bosom, a hunched back, a grossly featured grinning face disperse our dread of such a reality; we admire the artistry that has recreated it. Though the modeling can hardly be called as audacious as that of the later Kaendler figures, the aim is swift and pointed.

For the most part the Callot figures are white-

106

glazed though a number are partly gilded, a decoration that, in some instances, may have been applied in Augsburg. Some have a tinted flesh color, or slight touches of polychrome.

A later series of dwarfs, probably modeled by Johann Christoph Ludwig von Lücke about 1728 or 1729, would prove the acclaim won by the originals. They were so popular that when factories were established elsewhere, as at Vienna and Venice, some notable and equally rare Callot figures were created at these porcelain centers.

14
Elegant Chantilly

The productions of the royal factory of Sèvres range from simple and attractive wares to those which are ornate and overwhelming in their splendor. The porcelains of Saint-Cloud belong to the most classic and dignified. The productions of Mennecy are especially appealing because of their modest soft pastel-like quality. But the aristocrat among French soft-paste procelains is undoubtedly that of Chantilly, remarkable for its singularly consistent perfection of form and decoration, evident in every piece.

Louis-Henri de Bourbon, Prince de Condé, one of the less illustrious members of that noble lineage and minister to Louis XV until his dismissal and retirement to his château at Chantilly, was instrumental in establishing a porcelain factory. Deficient in statecraft, he was, instead, an avid collector of Japanese porcelains and shared with other wealthy and prestigious noblemen and sovereigns of his time the desire to be able to produce his own porcelains, imitating prized Oriental examples.

When Cicaire Cirou, who may previously have been associated with the Saint-Cloud manufacture, began porcelain experiments at Chantilly in 1725, the Prince de Condé gladly subsidized his attempts. After ten years, the Prince granted Cirou a concession to manufacture porcelain. The Dubois brothers, Robert, who like Cirou is said to have

A teapot painted in polychrome in the Kakiemon style with the banded hedge pattern; a peach-shaped cup, with a green twig handle, painted in colors in the Kakiemon style with two boys in a rowboat; soft-paste porcelain of Chantilly, second quarter of the eighteenth century.

A bouquetier painted in colors in the Kakiemon style with the banded hedge and flying fox design; soft-paste porcelain of Chantilly, second quarter of the eighteenth century.

A double-handled bowl, painted in colors in the Kakiemon style with quails, herons, and a butterfly; soft-paste porcelain of Chantilly, second quarter of the eighteenth century.

An octagonally formed ewer and basin, painted in colors in the Kakiemon style with flowering branches; soft-paste porcelain of Chantilly, second quarter of the eighteenth century.

A covered vase with polychrome flower decoration in the Kakiemon style; soft-paste porcelain of Chantilly, second quarter of the eighteenth century.

A sugar bowl painted in polychrome in the Kakiemon style with children at play; soft-paste porcelain of Chantilly, second quarter of the eighteenth century.

A quadrilobed covered bowl and underdish, the finial formed of three polychromed flowers; painted in colors in the Kakiemon style with sprigs of flowers and insects; soft-paste porcelain of Chantilly, second quarter of the eighteenth century.

A cachepot with serpent-shaped handles, decorated in polychrome with Oriental figures and a border of floral ornamentation; soft-paste porcelain of Chantilly, second quarter of the eighteenth century.

A mug painted in colors in the Kakiemon style with the banded hedge pattern and flowering trees; soft-paste porcelain of Chantilly, second quarter of the eighteenth century.

An écuelle *with a flower finial and twig handles terminating in molded blossoms on the bowl; painted in polychrome with a profusion of flowers; soft-paste porcelain of Chantilly, second quarter of the eighteenth century.*

A cachepot with mascaron handles, painted in colors with Orientally inspired flowers; soft-paste porcelain of Chantilly, second quarter of the eighteenth century.

rel, wheat sheaf, and playing children patterns, were delicately painted against a sketched background or placed freely and asymmetrically on the porcelain, calculated to leave large areas of the softly gleaming, white-glazed surface. Floral decoration most frequently featured peonies, jonquils, and chrysanthemums. Sometimes figures appeared in a carefully drawn landscape.

The dainty, playful, polychrome decoration was often outlined in black. Large expanses of undecorated porcelain were neatly and charmingly interrupted with a deceptive casualness by an insect or a butterfly, expertly spaced to hold the eye.

The elegance of the Japanese porcelain decoration, added to the asymmetry practiced by both the Japanese painters and the French rococo artists, created a uniquely harmonious and restrained rococo style. Several of the Japanese patterns were copied secondhand from Meissen models, such as the "red dragon" motif and the Kakiemon reserved panels in a yellow or blue ground.

The startling beauty of the porcelain was enhanced by the novel application of a tin glaze, usually reserved for faïence. Later a creamy, yellowish lead glaze was introduced and used concurrently with the tin glaze. Chantilly's coloring, in iron red, blue, yellow, green, and aubergine, was soft and brilliant as applied on shapes that, like the decoration, were obviously imitated from the Japanese. Hexagonal and octagonal cups, saucers, and bowls; lobed and fluted dishes; gourd, pomegranate, and melon-shaped or paneled teapots; and cups and

A large urn with scroll handles, decorated with molded, polychromed festoons of flowers; soft-paste porcelain of Chantilly, second quarter of the eighteenth century.

worked at Saint-Cloud, and Gilles, assisted in managing the factory until 1738, when they left for Vincennes. Cirou retained the direction until his death in 1751. The manufacture continued to produce distinguished soft-paste porcelains into the 1770s.

The Prince's collection of Japanese porcelains of Kakiemon design served ideally as model and inspiration for the earliest Chantilly decoration. The scant but exquisite compositions, consisting of the popular flower, banded hedge, stork, quail, squir-

A pair of leaf-shaped dishes with serrated rims and molded veins, decorated in colors with insects and blossoms in the Kakiemon style; a plate with a molded basket-weave border and three reserved panels painted in colors with landscapes, the center with polychrome flower sprigs; a lozenge-shaped and notched dish painted in colors in the Kakiemon style with exotic birds and flowering sprigs; all soft-paste porcelain of Chantilly, second quarter of the eighteenth century.

saucers in peach or leaf form predominated over the shapes derived from French faïence and silver objects, such as gracefully scalloped dishes, shallow tureens and bowls, and pear-shaped or globular jugs and drug jars.

All the forms were of striking simplicity with clean, uncluttered lines. The result was an exquisite blending of the best of Japanese and French taste. Sometimes flower, fruit, or animal knobs elegantly topped and highlighted the shapes of tureens and pots. Bonbonnieres and snuffboxes were produced in the conventional round and oblong shapes or modeled into exceptionally fine and often amusing figures and animals. Other small objects included delightfully painted cane handles and knife hafts.

Figures were rare, but their modeling was distinctive, usually in imitation of Oriental types such as serenely smiling, seated Buddhas. An unusual exception is a charming pair of musicians. Their dress, facial expressions, and the slight stiffness in their bearing somewhat resemble the *commedia dell' arte* figures modeled at the German factory of Fürstenberg. Figures of animals, sometimes a mixture of fantasy and naturalism, were equally rare. An example is a wolf, ferociously baring his teeth, whose long, bushy tail lies forward, terminating between his forefeet and cleverly forming the base.

Gradually the Vincennes influence replaced Oriental designs on cachepots, bowls, pitchers, covered dishes, and other table wares. Molded rococo foliage and ornaments, applied flowers, and garlands of flowers and leaves were introduced at Chantilly as new decorative themes. European flower painting in the manner of Vincennes, Sèvres, and Meissen became fashionable. A variety of attractive service pieces was produced, especially numerous plates with diverse modest but charming floral designs.

Although several large and handsome specimens, including vases, flower holders, and figures of Chinese, were mounted in gilded bronze to stress their value and importance, Chantilly soft-paste porcelains steadfastly escaped ostentatiousness. Rather than obviously intruding on the eye of the beholder, their subtle aesthetic appeal invites discovery and its subsequent delights.

15

The Pastel Glow of Mennecy

The smaller French soft-paste procelain manufactures, of which Saint-Cloud, Chantilly, and Mennecy are the most distinguished, were established as fashionable fancies rather than commercial ventures of noblemen who were patrons of the arts. Their productions generally were intended to please the distinctive taste of a small minority—a few wealthy connoisseurs. The unpretentious objects made startled and delighted the viewer with their simplicity and delicacy instead of overpowering him with sumptuousness and magnificence.

Like the connoisseurs of the period when these factories were founded, today's discriminating collectors are well aware and appreciative of the merits of French soft-paste porcelains, often professing a preference for one or another of these diverse eighteenth century productions. One will admire the somewhat greenish paste of Saint-Cloud, the style of its objects still weighing heavily on the side of the baroque; another may be enchanted by the effect of Chantilly's Orientally inspired, colorful decoration and the effect of the porcelain's unique tin glaze.

Many collectors, however, will agree that Mennecy's soft paste is the most creamy, its modeling the softest, and its coloring the daintiest among the French porcelains. The Mennecy productions seemed to be appropriately timed to combine the best characteristics of Saint-Cloud and Vincennes in a subdued and refined rococo, before the impending predominance of Sèvres's opulent style.

The Mennecy factory was established in 1734 under the protection of Louis-François de Neufville, Duke of Villeroy. The manufacture was at first located in the Rue de Charonne in Paris. In 1748, perhaps because of exclusive royal privileges conferred on the Vincennes factory, the establishment was transferred to Mennecy. In 1773 it was ultimately moved to Bourg-la-Reine.

Since the same mark was used during the Paris and Mennecy phases of the Villeroy undertaking, and there was no noticeable change in its productions, it is impossible to distinguish between the two periods, excepting perhaps, when a question of style is involved. When Bourg-la-Reine pieces are unmarked, it is equally difficult to determine their origin with absolute certainty. It is a fact, however, that a gradual decline in quality set in during the Bourg-la-Reine operation.

The *faïencier*, Francois Barbin, who remains known only for his porcelains, was in charge of the Mennecy factory. Barbin's son, Jean-Baptiste, joined the management in 1751. After both father and son died in 1765, the factory was purchased by a

A covered jar with molded prunus blossom decoration; white-glazed soft-paste porcelain of Mennecy, second quarter of the eighteenth century; silver mounting.

A cup and saucer painted with flowers in polychrome; soft-paste porcelain of Mennecy, middle of the eighteenth century.

A custard cup with fine spiral reeding and a fruit finial; white-glazed soft-paste porcelain of Mennecy, second quarter of the eighteenth century.

A covered sauceboat with an interlaced twig handle and a ladle; decorated in colors with flower arrangements; soft-paste porcelain of Mennecy, middle of the eighteenth century.

A cup with an interlaced twig handle; painted in polychrome with birds and fruit; soft-paste porcelain of Mennecy, middle of the eighteenth century.

A mustard jar with an attached underdish, painted in colors with bouquets and sprigs of flowers; soft-paste porcelain of Mennecy, middle of the eighteenth century; gilded metal mounting.

An asymmetrically rococo-shaped and fluted sugar bowl, the cover terminating in a conch finial, with a ladle and underdish; decorated in colors with bouquets of flowers, the borders outlined in purplish rose; soft-paste porcelain of Mennecy, middle of the eighteenth century.

A set of three urns on quadrangular pedestals, painted in colors with sprigs of flowers; each urn filled with bouquets of polychromed flowers mounted on metal stems; soft-paste porcelain of Mennecy, middle of the eighteenth century; gilded bronze mountings.

A figure of a man seated beside a tree; white-glazed soft-paste porcelain of Mennecy, middle of the eighteenth century.

sculptor, Joseph Jullien, and a painter, Charles-Symphorien Jacques, who since 1763 had been managing the factory of Sceaux. Thus not only the porcelains of Mennecy and Bourg-la-Reine, but those of Sceaux as well, were closely related. In 1772 the two artists relinquished the Sceaux factory to Richard Glot, who, a year later, registered the Sceaux mark. The manufacture at Mennecy was officially abandoned in 1773, when Jullien and Jacques commenced working at Bourg-la-Reine.

The lambrequin decoration of Rouen and Saint-Cloud and the Kakiemon patterns of Chantilly experienced a passing fancy at Mennecy. Various forms, including teapots, figural snuffboxes, and pastille burners, produced by Mennecy, were similar or even identical to those created by the earlier soft-paste porcelain establishments. A Chantilly melon-shaped teapot, painted in colors in the Japanese style, appears with slight variations in a Mennecy version in glazed white porcelain decorated with prunus blossoms applied in relief. Mennecy models of *objets de vitrine,* such as cane handles, snuffboxes, as well as knife and fork handles, often resembled those of Saint-Cloud and Chantilly.

The wares produced were designed mainly for the lady's dressing table or for dessert and afternoon tea. Custard and sherbet cups and pomade jars with a smooth surface or spiral reeding were common. Among the most elaborate productions ranked a variety of potpourri vases or pastille burners, ranging from small, delicate pieces closely set all over with applied blossoms to the larger ones in the shape of a basket laden with fruit or flowers. Individual flowers were modeled as at the other soft-paste factories, Vincennes in particular. In Mennecy, left white or exquisitely painted in pastel colors, they were frequently mounted on metal stems and set into porcelain vases and urns.

Many of Mennecy's productions, like those of Saint-Cloud, were simply glazed white, showing off to best advantage the clear, shining glaze and the superior quality of the lustrous, creamy soft paste. Gently curved globular teapots, pear-shaped coffeepots, tall coffee cups, and shallow tea bowls were ornamented in the Saint-Cloud and Meissen manner with applied prunus blossoms or with garlands of flowers in relief. Fine fluting and basket-weave molding were executed on a variety of objects.

The simplicity, gracefulness, and balance inherent in Mennecy's shapes was also achieved in the painted decoration. Since the factory at Vincennes, and later at Sèvres, enjoyed a monopoly under the patronage of King Louis XV, other factories were at various times proscribed the use of polychrome decoration and, at all times, of gilt ornamentation. Only the gilding interdict applied to the Mennecy factory, which resorted to unobtrusive, attractive border outlines of rose and bright blue.

After having exhausted the fleeting Oriental influences, imitated secondhand from Saint-Cloud and Chantilly, the Mennecy manufacture's own style emerged. Not altogether original, it was a sensitive interpretation of borrowed themes, translated into extremely appealing, modest, and muted decoration. The captivating, predominantly purplish-rose tones of cool, fresh, naturalistic German flowers blended perfectly with the delicacy of the softly glazed ivory paste. Green, yellow, lilac, and blue were added in pleasing combinations to enhance the rose color. The effect was fresh and delicate but never too sweet or sentimental. The factory's forced limitation in the use of colors eliminated any danger of overdecoration. Painting at Mennecy, especially of flowers, was free and relaxed in contrast to the more rigid, mannered style practiced at Sèvres. Exceptionally fine naturalistic bird painting also ornamented service pieces. These Mennecy porcelains created a feeling of intimacy and informality.

Considering the relatively small output of the factory, figure modeling was impressive and immensely varied. Models of figures were characterized by uniquely soft rounded contours and expressive faces. Chinese, grotesque dwarfs, and comedy characters were of striking and original conception, their dress sometimes decorated in the Kakiemon style. A number of figures engaged in various tasks were also produced. They were daintily painted in colors that fused with the soft paste and glaze. Figures of children and groups of children in biscuit, glazed white or decorated in polychrome were popular. Sometimes in a burst of rococo fantasy, reminiscent of Johann Joachim Kaendler at Meissen, a modeler might create a *putto*, who supports a shell-shaped sweetmeat dish resting on a rockwork base.

A fine distinctive sense of artistry prevailed at Mennecy. Producing wares chiefly designed to satisfy the eager interest and collecting zeal of the Duke of Villeroy and his friends, the artists were permitted the freedom of imaginative play. The results were objects of exceptional quality, treasured by a few connoisseurs in a localized area, long before they achieved enduring international recognition.

16

Myth, Allegory, and Religion

The eighteenth century often looked back to antiquity for its inspiration in the arts. It was a time when humanism was still very much alive. Scholars were fluent and conversed in Latin; Virgil and Ovid were considered important authors who were actually read and exerted a pervasive influence on the century. An indispensable part of the education of princes and noblemen consisted of a journey to France or Italy; most of them spent some time studying at the old respected Italian universities. The educated *bourgeoisie*, which emerged and achieved prominence during the eighteenth century, was equally well acquainted with the gods and heroes of antiquity. Seventeenth and eighteenth century poets at the various royal courts frequently compared their sovereign to Mars, his consort to Juno, and his mistress to Venus. This was the ultimate tribute.

But not society alone was well-informed about Parnassus and its glories. It was a requirement for the porcelain modelers at the many European manufactures, beginning with Meissen, to be familiar with the heroes of antiquity. When the youthful artists were engaged by the factories, their education in all probability was scant, not having included the poets of antiquity. However, they acquired an

A bowl painted in purple and iron red with Venus and cupids, surrounded by lacework borders enhanced with gold; porcelain of Meissen, 1720-1725; Hausmalerei by Auffenwerth.

A teapot painted in purple and iron red with Apollo and his lyre in a landscape, surrounded by lacework borders enhanced with gold; porcelain of Meissen, 1720-1725; Hausmalerei by Auffenwerth.

A pair of figures of Psyche (La Nymphe Falconet, 1761) and Cupid (L'Amour Falconet garçon, 1758); soft-paste biscuit of Sèvres; models by Falconet.

A plate decorated in purple monochrome with bacchantes, putti, and satyrs, and enhanced with a gilt Laub und Bandelwerk *border; porcelain of Vienna, Du Paquier period; signed and dated on the back:* Carolus Ferdinandus Wolfsburg et Wallsdorf, 1731, eques Silesia pinx. Vienna Austria.

A group of figures representing Pygmalion; *soft-paste biscuit of Sèvres, 1763; model by Falconet.*

118

A saucer decorated in sepia and gold with a hunting scene, allegorical of November; porcelain of Vienna, Du Paquier period, ca. 1720; Hausmalerei, probably Bohemian, in the Benckertt manner.

A saucer decorated in sepia and gold with a woman kindling a fire, allegorical of December; porcelain of Vienna, Du Paquier period, ca. 1720; Hausmalerei, probably Bohemian, in the Benckertt manner.

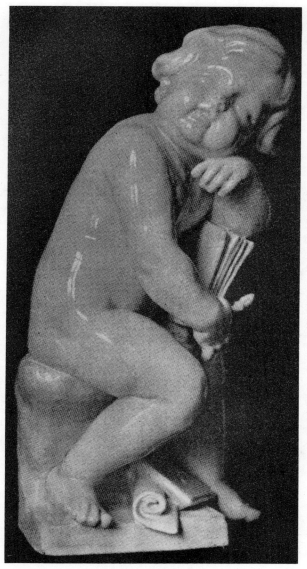

A figure of a putto, *allegorical of Art; white-glazed faïence of Brussels, middle of the eighteenth century.*

elementary knowledge essential for their artistic creations from a wealth of copper engravings frequently used as models for figures, groups of figures, and painted decoration. Furthermore, interested and erudite patrons of porcelain manufactures, such as King Frederick the Great of Prussia at Berlin, saw to it that the modelers and painters received the proper education, stimulation, and direction toward the execution of their work.

Even Johann Joachim Kaendler, an educated man, who in his youth had successfully studied the literature of the ancient poets, for many years after he had been appointed to his important and respon-

sible position of chief modeler at Meissen, still took daily lessons for the elucidation of the more difficult mythological poets.

Mythological subjects were favored by Meissen and the other factories subsequently established in the course of the eighteenth century, regardless of changes in style. They remained popular through the baroque, rococo, and neoclassical eras, unlike *chinoiseries* and Japanese influences which enjoyed brief—though strong and significant—fashionable phases.

The painting of mythological, allegorical, and religious subjects on porcelain had its precedents in

119

An apothecary jar with serpent handles terminating in lion heads; decorated in blue on a light blue ground with foliage and floral ornaments; in the center the monogram of Christ in yellow and blue, and a band with an inscription; majolica of Venice, ca. 1600.

A group of figures of putti, allegorical of Spring, decorated in colors and gold; the rococo base outlined in rose purple; porcelain of Frankenthal, ca. 1760; model by Lanz.

A small bowl painted in colors with the Virgin and Child and a winged angel's head, surrounded by a border of foliage and ornaments; lustered majolica of Deruta, sixteenth century.

A tall figure of Saint John Nepomuk, carrying a crucifix and palm branch; white-glazed porcelain of Meissen, ca. 1745; model by Kaendler and Reinicke.

A crucifix, the figure finely modeled and naturalistically touched with color; porcelain of Höchst, 1770-1775; model by Melchior; mounted on a dark wooden cross with base of the period.

A tankard decorated in colors with a biblical scene: the two scouts returning from Canaan; German faïence, eighteenth century; hinged pewter lid.

the decoration of early Italian majolicas and other European potteries from the fifteenth through the seventeenth centuries. But it was actually during the first period at Meissen and Vienna, and in the various *Hausmaler* workshops outside the factories, that such painting excelled and figured most prominently on individual small tablewares and rare coffee and tea services.

In figure modeling an immense variety of mythological representations was created, frequently with delightful, imaginative, and original twists. Sometimes the interpretations were clever, in other instances charmingly naive. Gods and goddesses, winged cupids and plump *putti*, Tritons and mermaids, nymphs and satyrs, heroes and Muses were modeled singly and more often in pairs or series. Large groups depicted specific mythological scenes or events.

Kaendler was the leader in recreating the world of classical mythology in porcelain. His models ranged from individual small figures to a large imposing centerpiece depicting Apollo with Pegasus and the nine Muses. Other Meissen models included numerous familiar subjects such as figures of Hercules, Diana, and Neptune carrying a fountain on his back, and groups of figures of Apollo and Daphne, Aeneas and Anchises, Bacchus and satyrs or sileni, and the Rape of Proserpine. At one time Kaendler portrayed the Marquise de Pompadour and Prince Charles de Rohan in the guise of Acis and Galatea, after an engraving by Charles-Nicolas Cochin.

The sculptor Johann Wilhelm Ludwig Beyer at Ludwigsburg modeled important, gracefully tall and long-limbed figures of Cupid and Psyche, Venus and Adonis, the Medici Venus, the Three Graces, and playing bacchantes. Konrad Linck at Frankenthal achieved impressive results with his groups of Meleager and Atalanta, and Boreas carring off Orithya. At Nymphenburg, Franz Anton Bustelli's delightfully conceived diverging rococo version of the ancient gods was a series of chubby yet daintily modeled *putti*, each equipped with the attribute of a deity.

These are just a few important and well known examples. Innumerable other specimens exist, created at different factories by artists of varying temperaments and abilities. Mythology became a suitable subject to celebrate the apotheosis of a ruler although the resulting work of art might by today's taste be judged somewhat awkward, heavy-handed, or even mawkish.

One such porcelain sculpture was an elaborate group modeled by Frankenthal's artist Konrad Linck for the Elector Karl Theodor, protector of the factory, after his recovery from a serious illness in 1774. Entitled "The Wishes of the Palatinate Come True," it pictures on the right a female figure personifying the Palatinate, kneeling beside a flaming altar, with the province's heraldic emblem, a lion recumbent, behind her. She is appealing to the gods for help. A weeping *putto,* bent over a palette and marble bust, symbolizes the arts mourning for their beloved patron. But the group of figures to the left of the altar shows that the prayers have already been answered: Pallas Athena descends from Mount Olympus with Hygiea, the goddess of health, who with her foot crushes the dragon of illness. A joyous second *putto* lifts a drapery from the portrait of Karl Theodor. An inscription on the altar reads *Vita Palatinatus exaudita.*

As in this complex composition, mythology and allegory sometimes overlapped or merged. However, quite independently, allegorical subjects were produced in perhaps even greater numbers than those models devoted to classical mythology. Personifications of the virtues, five senses, four elements, four seasons, twelve months, four continents, time and eternity, fame and victory, war and peace, and the arts and professions were extremely popular.

Mostly the abstract concepts represented were easily recognizable, but sometimes the attributes of the figures were too insignificant or obscure to enable one to define with certainty, or even to guess, the ideas personified. Garbed in classical costume or in the momentary prevailing fashion of the period, the figure's manner of dress often provided a clue toward identification. A muff or fur indicated winter. A scantily clad, barefoot girl with a wreath of flowers might represent summer. If the figure carried a bunch of grapes, and garlands of vine leaves served to decorate the rococo trellises and base, it would signify autumn. A warmly dressed child blowing on a fire would most certainly represent winter. A figure of a musician, however, standing on a base on which also rested a basket of grapes and other fruit, might not necessarily be identified as autumn until one saw the remaining three figures of the series with their respective attributes.

Nymphenburg's small busts on pedestals, depicting the seasons, featured a young girl as spring, a woman as summer, a youth as autumn, and an old man as winter. Linck at Frankenthal used four busts of women—of slightly noticeable varying ages—on pedestals to portray the seasons. Spring is bareheaded, but for a few sprigs of green in her hair; summer wears a wide-brimmed hat with flowers; autumn has a wreath of grapes and vine leaves entwined in her hair; winter, elderly and somewhat mournful-looking but beautiful, wears a black scarf loosely tied around her head, while a fur covers her shoulders.

Large attractive groups of *putti,* with the attributes of sculpture, painting, or music, were modeled at the Vienna factory. Karl Gottlob Lück at Frankenthal created a charming group of figures representing architecture: the cavalier holds a blueprint, the lady part of a column.

Large vases modeled with recognizable attributes, frequently with ornate covers and handles enhanced with figures, depicted the four seasons, elements, and other allegories. Large and small pyramids with applied trophies of war and music celebrated victories and fame.

These elaborate compositions of popular eighteenth century subject matter graced the mantelpiece of many elegant salons. The huge allegorical and mythological centerpieces in the form of temples crowded with figures decorated the banquet tables of sovereigns and wealthy noblemen. Many individual figures, now in museums or still available on the market, were once part of such impressive porcelain sculptures, that were dismantled because of changes in fortune and fashion, or in times of war.

The many different porcelain factories also drew on the Bible for inspiration. From the beginning of its existence Meissen, for example, produced models based on biblical subject matter, such as the figures of the apostles by Kaendler and Kirchner, although religious themes never elicited an exceptional response on the part of the public. Beautifully and tastefully executed, these sacred representations were received with serious and respectful admiration, but they could not compete with the popular appeal of mythological and, even less, of allegorical subjects, that continued to flourish. Delight and enthusiasm were reserved for these clever, more frivolous, entertaining, and idealized themes.

17
Neglected Spanish Faïence

Curiously a lack of interest in Spanish pottery still seems to prevail. This is surprising because stylistically the predominating strong characteristic features of sixteenth through eighteenth century Spanish faïences should prove attractive to modern taste.

Apart from the early Hispano-Moresque potteries, whose exotic lusters and finely detailed diaper patterns deriving from Eastern designs are much admired, desired, and quite costly, Spanish faïences remain little known and appreciated. It is the gradual emergence of a truly domestic product, during and after the decline of the Moorish influence, that is particularly interesting in the history and rewarding in the study of Spanish pottery manufacture. Collectors seem strangely uncertain and even unaware when it comes to this large unexplored terrain of ceramic art, while unquestioningly accepting the importance of Italian majolica, or Delft, French, and German faïences.

The progress and far-reaching impact of other European ceramic centers penetrated Spain after the Moorish style had been thoroughly exhausted. Italian, Dutch, and French influences, in turn, left their mark on Spanish wares but, simultaneously, strong and distinct Spanish characteristics developed.

Although Moorish styles persisted into the seventeenth century, the first major change in Spanish pottery production occurred during the sixteenth century with the introduction of colorful Renaissance motifs used on Italian majolica of high quality. This refined and diversified art form of enameling earthenware was entirely different from the restricted Hispano-Moresque technique and readily adopted as itinerant workmen from Italy came to Spain.

In the beginning of the sixteenth century the Italian tile painter Nicoloso Pisano settled in Seville where his majolica tile pictures, used for wall decoration in place of hangings, became very popular. Seville soon provided tiles for the needs of most of Spain and Portugal. However, polychrome and blue and white tiles were also produced in quantity at Toledo and at most other Spanish faïence manufactures somewhat later.

During the early part of the sixteenth century, objects with distinctly non-Moorish floral and armorial designs were being made concurrently with the prevailing Arab oriented wares in the famous luster centers such as Valencia. Simple circular patterns, gold stylized ornaments, and European heraldry replaced or added variety to the intricate, mazelike motifs of the Saracens. A primitive earthiness, zest,

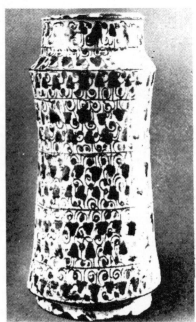

An albarello *decorated in cobalt blue and gold luster with a stylized leaf design; Hispano-Moresque lusterware, fifteenth century.*

A tazza painted in vivid blue with a land and seascape; faïence of Catalonia, eighteenth century.

An albarello *decorated in colors with foliage, berry, and ribbon motifs, and an inscription in the center medallion; faïence of Alcora, eighteenth century.*

124

A large tankard decorated in blue with a Tree of Life in the center, surrounded by stylized foliage and ornaments; faïence of Hamburg, dated 1639.

and forcefulness supplanted the tight, formal delicacy of net and lacelike overall designs. Cool, striking blue and white decoration, or a rare beautiful combination of manganese purple and blue, contrasted sharply with the warmth of the golden luster potteries.

Talavera de la Reina, with the neighboring Puente del Arzobispo, became the leading center of faïence production in a representative Spanish style. In the seventeenth century, after having absorbed Italian trends of majolica workmanship, Talavera turned to the Dutch for inspiration of iron scrollwork designs as well as bird and floral motifs. But at the same time, through the wide distribution of Savona faïences, an Italian influence once more became apparent. Popular *chinoiserie* subjects were copied secondhand in blue and white from Delft and Savona wares.

Most significant, however, was the vital development of Spanish features. Very large plaques, vases, drug jars, gadrooned dishes, bowls, basins and ewers, and smaller objects of handsome, vigorously modeled baroque shapes were painted with bold, free brush strokes in greyish or deep blues and polychromes—green, orange, yellow, blue, and manganese purple.

A great variety of scenes and subjects indigenous to Spain and its people predominated. Sports such as hunting, fishing, falconry, and bullfighting were depicted with facile, swift strokes, often with amusing results. Battle scenes were frequently pictured.

Often a portrait of a lady, a dog, bird, or building, or a figure busy at some task, painted in an easy, stylized manner, occupied the center of a large round plaque, whose border consisted of primitive, powerfully executed foliage and scroll ornaments. The attraction and charm of this decoration is contained in its naïveté and directness. The painting style is artless and lacks refinement but grips with its strength and frequent humor.

Religious and mythological subjects occurred less often, but were imaginatively and masterfully conceived. Though simple and straightforward in execution, the resulting decoration always emerged with stunning intensity.

Some objects, such as large, covered, double-handled vases, were painted more elaborately with continuous overall decoration, picturing in detail gallants and their ladies in a sketchy landscape with fir trees, or several figures in conversation and at diverse occupations.

In the eighteenth century, Talavera reflected baroque shapes fashionable in France and Italy, featuring shell and acanthus-leaf designs. Talavera objects lost their simplicity and assumed a more ornate look. Variations of the distintive lacelike Bérain patterns were attempted.

During this period when faïence production in Europe reached its zenith, other Spanish pottery centers that manufactured an unusual variety of exceptional wares, particularly in blue and white, flourished in Catalonia and Aragon.

The establishment of a faïence factory at Alcora, in Valencia, eventually led to the decline of Talavera. Founded in 1726 by Don Buenaventura Pedro de Alcantara, Count of Aranda, the manufacture's products were strongly influenced by the current French style. For some time two French artists from Moustiers, Joseph Olérys and Edouard Roux, were associated with Alcora. In emulation of prized imported Chinese porcelains, the production of blue and white wares ranked highly, as at most other European factories. The polychrome palette included green, orange, yellow, brown, and blue.

Alcora produced drug jars, tureens, centerpieces, platters, and other smaller useful wares. Under the direction of Olérys, until 1739, his blue and white and polychrome designs of grotesques after Jacques Callot engravings were effectively rendered on Spanish faïence. Similarly his wreath, flower, and ribbon motifs were introduced. Later they were to achieve notable success at the factory he founded in Moustiers. Miniature scenes within medallions and fantastic animals were well-painted. More attention was paid to form; an extensive array of flamboyant shapes was modeled after baroque and rococo silver examples, as in other parts of Europe.

At the same time Spanish characteristics persisted, thus distinguishing Alcora objects from those made at Moustiers. The body of the Spanish faïence was heavier; many specimens, in particular *albarelli* and vases, featured Spanish heraldic decoration framed by rococo ornaments.

The factory continued until about 1770, producing faïences of ambitious rococo forms including lavabos, figures, and busts. Mention should also be made of beautiful flower painting and elaborate rococo embellishments, often in the French manner of Marseilles and Moustiers. With Alcora's decline, original, interesting, and fine-quality faïence production in Spain came to an end.

One group of potteries that deserve attention

here are those of the seventeenth century, generally attributed to the city of Hamburg, that in the body of the earthenware and its blue and white or polychrome decoration, have more in common with Spanish or Portuguese rather than German wares.

Recent and current investigations are attempting to determine whether these objects were not actually made in Spain or Portugal, perhaps commissioned by wealthy Hamburg traders or merchants.

18
Castelli Majolica

Castelli was a latecomer among Italian majolicas. When the glories of Florence, Faenza, Castel Durante, Urbino, and Venice among others were past, the Castelli workshops began to florish.

The collective name Castelli conveniently includes a number of factories existing at the leading artistic and industrial center Castelli, and at Naples, Bussi, Atri, and Teramo, all situated in the Abruzzi region. Although several outstanding painters during the seventeenth and eighteenth centuries impressed their artistry on the majolicas produced at these workshops, the similarity of the wares makes it difficult to assign them to a specific place and factory, particularly because of the absence of factory marks. The signature of an artist on some objects is the only clue toward identification beyond the general area of their origin.

Different eras prescribe different styles and tastes. Castelli majolicas are easily recognizable by their colors. They are pale and light and do not possess the depth of the brilliant and vibrant colors applied to the potteries of earlier periods. However, the mild color palette used in the Castelli region is very lovely and harmonious. The striking boldness of Renaissance majolica painting has been replaced by a delicate, modest manner of decoration, with sensitive, subtle nuances, in blue, yellow, manganese brown and purple, green, ochre, and orange. The colors were painted on a white ground and fired in a high-temperature kiln. Sometimes the spare and skillful use of gold heightened the lustrous and warm effect of a finely painted piece. Among the earliest objects ascribed to Castelli are a few painted in blue and white.

The attractiveness of Castelli decoration was much strengthened and enhanced through well-balanced compositions and attention to details. The choice of subject matter and ornamental motifs had also undergone a change. Formerly limited almost entirely to mythological and religious themes, and portraits of nobility or a few other personages of importance, majolica painting now encompassed a far wider range.

Scenes from country life and animal painting in the manner of Nicolas Berghem became popular. Landscapes, often with ruins from antiquity, winding streams, and strolling figures were most successfully rendered. Naturalistic painting of figures engaged in various tasks was attractively conceived and executed. For figural subjects from mythology and religion, contemporary engravings, usually by Italian masters, frequently served as models.

Purely decorative designs, so popular on earlier majolicas, were apparently not used at all. Orna-

A plaque painted in yellow, blue, green, and brown with Moses and Aaron in the desert pointing to manna falling from Heaven, as the Israelites collect it from the ground; majolica of Castelli, seventeenth century.

*A platter with a molded and scalloped border, decorated in
yellow, orange, green, and blue with an arrangement of
fruit and foliage; faïence of Alcora, eighteenth century.*

A saucer painted in polychrome with a bird perched on a branch and an ornamental border; porcelain of Oude Loosdrecht (Mol), ca. 1775. A saucer decorated in colors with an East Indian flower arrangement and enhanced with an ornamental border; porcelain of Meissen, ca. 1730.

A large dish painted in polychrome with a swirling design of phoenixes, clouds, and ornaments around the border, and flowering shrubs and chrysanthemums in the center; porcelain of Arita, Japan, ca. 1700.

An octagonally shaped basket with two handles, the sides with vertical openwork outlined in green and gold and with molded entwining ribbons in rose purple; the bottom, inside, painted in polychrome with a bouquet of flowers and butterflies; the rim with gilt ornamentation on a brown ground; porcelain of Berlin, ca. 1790.

A pair of finely modeled figures of birds, one (left) with a turquoise glaze and shadings of brown, the other with a mottled aubergine glaze with red and blue highlights; the brown bases unglazed; Kuang-tung stoneware, China, eighteenth century.

A heart-shaped inkstand, decorated in green, turquoise, and blue with floral sprigs; faïence of Strasbourg, ca. 1745.

A bouquetier in the shape of a commode decorated in colors; faience of Montpellier, eighteenth century.

*A pair of cachepots painted in colors with sprigs of flowers
in reserves and with foliage, pearls, and dotted gilt
ornaments on bands of purplish pink, purplish brown,
and blue; soft-paste porcelain of Sèvres, 1790; painters:
Choisy and Fontaine; gilder: Henri Marin Prévost.*

A large plaque painted in yellow, blue, green, orange, and brown with the Creation of Eve, the border elaborately decorated with three adoring putti *and a bird amidst flowers, foliage, and ornamental scrollwork; majolica of Castelli, first quarter of the eighteenth century.*

A pair of albarelli *painted in dark brown, white, blue, green, and yellow with a nun and a monk at prayer in a landscape, framed by yellow and blue bands and an ornamental border in blue; majolica of Castelli, ca. 1720; painted by Dr. Francesco Antonio Grue.*

mental motifs consisting of acanthus leaves, scrollwork, naturalistic flowers, trophies, mascarons, and *putti* were tastefully combined and arranged to form decorative borders on dishes, commonly featuring a mythological or allegorical scene in the center.

Objects produced in the Castelli workshops included large and small dishes, drug jars, vases, decorative round and rectangular wall plaques or tiles, and some unusual small specimens such as saltcellars, *trembleuses*, inkstands, and boxes.

One of the first known painters at Castelli, Antonio Lollo, whose subject matter on dishes and bowls was drawn from mythology, allegory, and the Bible, was active during the second quarter of the seventeenth century. His style is identified through a signed piece depicting the Judgment of Paris, painted in yellow and brown with manganese outlines, that is preserved in the San Martino Museum at Naples. Lollo often surrounded his subjects with scroll and leaf borders.

The most famous name associated with Castelli is that of a family of painters called Grue. The earliest known specimen decorated by a member of the family is a tile picturing the Madonna of Loreto, signed by Francesco Antonio Grue and dated 1647. His son Carlo Antonio (1655-1723) is by some considered to be one of Castelli's best painters of figural compositions. Some of his signed dishes featured ornamental borders of *putti* among flowers and baroque foliage motifs.

Among Carlo Antonio's four sons, Francesco Antonio (1686-1746) was an outstanding artist noted for his landscapes as well as figures. He had studied philosophy and theology and occasionally included his doctoral title on majolicas bearing his signature. He was politically active and is said to have spent eight years in a Neapolitan jail. Several majolicas signed with his name and *Napoli* from the years 1718 and 1722 are extant.

Dr. Grue's brothers specialized in diverse subject matter. Anastasio (1691-1743) became known for landscapes, Aurelio (1699-1744) for animal and peasant scenes. Fine figural decoration with gold highlights is attributed to the fourth brother Liborio (1701-1776). A signed bowl after Annibale Caracci

A large dish decorated in green, blue, orange, yellow, brown, and white with Venus and Cupid in a landscape, framed by a molded rosette border painted in blue and white; majolica of Castelli, first quarter of the eighteenth century.

A set of three plates painted in green, yellow, brown, blue, and orange with mountainous landscapes, castles, and strolling figures; at the top a cardinal's hat and coat of arms; majolica of Castelli, first quarter of the eighteenth century.

A cup and saucer (trembleuse) *painted in blue, green, yellow, orange, brown, and white: the depressed saucer with a* putto, *basket of flowers, and cornucopias spilling fruit, surrounded by a decorative border; the cup with a* putto *in a continuous landscape; majolica of Castelli, first quarter of the eighteenth century.*

A plaque decorated in green, yellow, orange, blue, brown, and manganese purple with a woman on horseback in a landscape with a classical ruin; majolica of Castelli, first quarter of the eighteenth century.

is in the Victoria and Albert Museum in London.

Francesco Saverio Grue (born in Naples in 1731), a son of Dr. Francesco Antonio, fully signed an oval wall plaque with a classical landscape *Saverio Grue fece in Castelli 1747*. He later became the director of the royal porcelain manufacture at Capodimonte.

Another famed family of Castelli painters were the Gentili. The earliest recorded piece is a Crucifixion panel in the San Martino Museum, signed by Bernardino Gentili and dated 1670. His son Carmine (1678-1763), who was a pupil of Carlo Antonio Grue, excelled at religious themes.

The Gentili family members, like the Grues, became known for one or another specialty. A son of Carmine Gentili, Giacomo (1717-1765), might be singled out as an exceptional landscape painter, whose compositions on plaques frequently featured figures in contemporary dress. Another son, Bernardino (1727-1813), was a prolific majolica painter of diverse subjects.

Several other artists in the Castelli workshops achieved prominence, among them Matteo Borselli who painted a large plaque with the birth of Christ after Agostino Caracci. Some painters are known only by the initials with which they signed their work. But most Castelli majolicas that have survived are unsigned and one can only conjecture regarding the artists who may have painted them. Ultimately it is the object and its quality that counts, not the signature or lack of it.

The factories in Castelli and the surrounding region thrived until about the middle of the eighteenth century. With their decline ended the last distinctive period of qualitative and truly beautiful majolica production in Italy.

PART IV

Collecting for Decorative Purposes

19
Living with Porcelain and Faïence

The collector of porcelain or faïence, who prefers to decorate his home with his acquisitions rather than display them in cabinets, may well be in a quandary because of the wealth and variety of art objects available which, both functional and attractive, will purposefully fit into modern living arrangements.

A collector's individual taste ultimately determines his choices. A catholic taste in clothes, music, or food may extend to one's surroundings. An expansive person might be casual in his choices, mixing objects in a manner that would shock his sophisticated neighbor whose discriminately assembled furnishings are a prerequisite to his formal way of life. But the pleasure of selecting and collecting, and perhaps, in a change of fancy, eventually rejecting a specimen for replacement, is unlimited and entirely personal. The novice collector who asks what to collect should seriously search his own mind, consider his life style and surroundings, and, of course, his financial state.

Tradition dictates that Delft faïence, English porcelain and pottery, or Chinese export procelain most properly enhance eighteenth century English and American furniture, while Chinese, French, and German porcelains more suitably decorate French furniture. There is no reason why such arbitrary, unwritten rules should be strictly ob-

A handleless cup and saucer decorated with a battle scene in Schwarzlot *and gold; porcelain of Vienna, Du Paquier period, ca. 1730;* Hausmalerei.

A double-handled cup and saucer decorated in colors with fantastic animals and East Indian flowers; porcelain of Meissen, 1730-1735.

137

A plate decorated in colors with a shepherd scene surrounded by floral ornaments; porcelain of Meissen, ca. 1735; Hausmalerei by Mayer of Pressnitz, ca. 1750.

A bowl painted in colors with botanical flowers and insects; porcelain of Meissen, ca. 1740.

A plate painted in colors with a Watteau scene surrounded by a border of putti, *branches of fruit tied by ribbons, and shell ornaments; porcelain of Meissen, ca. 1735;* Hausmalerei *by Mayer of Pressnitz, ca. 1750.*

A bowl decorated in colors and gold over underglaze blue with birds, fruit, and flowers; porcelain of Meissen, ca. 1725; Hausmalerei by Ferner, ca. 1750.

served. Why not consider the much neglected, sturdy baroque and elaborate rococo furniture crafted in eighteenth century Holland and Germany? Or the many decorative possibilities offered by Viennese, Italian, and Thuringian porcelains, among others, of the same period?

And where do all the magnificent and playful rococo faïences find their proper place? Though generally they are characterized by an earthy quality, many in their own way are as finely modeled and painted as porcelain. They can serve with equal effectiveness in elegant or informal surroundings.

The independent art lover and collector will follow his own instincts and preferences, and delight in his choices. One might mention that for a majestic sweep, for nobility and simplicity of form, and for dazzling color, the coolness of Chinese porcelain is unsurpassable. It speaks for itself, in silence and strength, requiring no explanation.

Similarly, brilliance and clarity of color, precision of shape, boldness of movement, and unflagging attention to every artistic detail characterize the first Meissen porcelains.

An incandescent luminous glow, an understated elegance of style, and subtlety of decoration mark the early French soft-paste porcelains of Saint-Cloud, Chantilly, Mennecy, and Vincennes.

Once several porcelain factories had been founded, crosscurrents established by itinerant workers created interesting relationships and variations on common themes. Meissen, Venice, and Vienna's Chinese fantasies, Meissen's German flowers, Vienna's foliage and ribbon designs, and all the imaginative decorative ideas that followed soon became public property, surfacing everywhere,

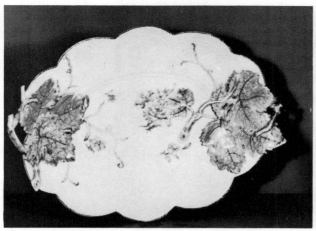 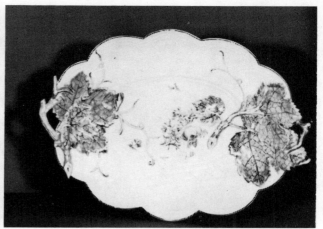

A pair of dishes with a scalloped border and molded green leaves terminating in brown twig handles; painted in colors with bouquets and sprigs of flowers; porcelain of Chelsea, red-anchor period, ca. 1755.

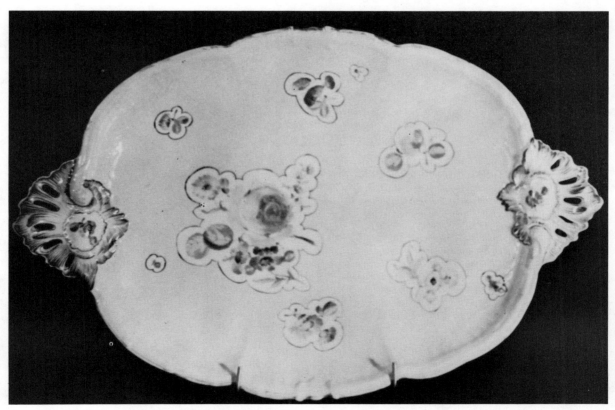

An oblong yellow-ground tray with a molded scalloped border and elaborate openwork handles accented with rose purple; painted within irregularly shaped reserves with flowers in polychrome; porcelain of Berlin, 1760-1770.

A large, oblong jardinière with twisted rope-handles, standing on four feet; painted in green, blue, brownish yellow, and manganese purple with Chinese, Italian comedy figures, fantastic birds, flowers, and insects; faïence of Samadet, ca. 1760.

A bidet decorated in blue with an Orientally inspired border and a large bouquet of flowers; faïence of Rouen, eighteenth century.

A tall, slender vase painted in polychrome in the Chinese manner with figures, birds, and flowering shrubs, and with richly ornamental borders at the neck and base; faïence of Delft, ca. 1700.

A pair of vases decorated with foliage ornamentation in underglaze blue; porcelain of China, K'ang Hsi period, 1662-1722; overdecorated in Holland with chinoiseries in lacquer colors; early eighteenth century.

A tall bottle-shaped vase with an iron-red rim; decorated in colors with blossoming trees; porcelain of Kutani, Japan, late seventeenth century.

An octagonally shaped vase, its bulbous bottom tapering to a slender neck and slightly flared rim; painted in polychrome in the Chinese manner with ornamental bands around the neck and with alternating panels of figures and potted plants; faïence of Delft, ca. 1700.

A tureen and underdish with a yellow ground, the reserved panels painted in colors in the Oriental manner with roosters, hens, and blossoming sprigs; porcelain of Meissen, ca. 1730.

A large jar with a molded collar; painted in underglaze blue with men and children at play in a landscape traversed by a stream; porcelain of Hirado, Japan, late eighteenth century.

141

An écuelle *with a finely modeled finial and elaborate openwork handles; decorated with blossoms and foliage in relief; white-glazed soft-paste porcelain of Saint-Cloud, ca. 1730.*

A peach-shaped covered dish with a twig handle terminating in modeled foliage and blossoms; painted in polychrome with bouquets and sprigs of German flowers; porcelain of Meissen, ca. 1745.

A tureen with stem handles terminating in modeled female heads; decorated with molded prunus blossoms; white-glazed porcelain of Bow, ca. 1750.

An oval tureen with a modeled pear finial, naturalistically colored; painted in manganese purple, blue, green, and ochre with large carnations and sprigs of flowers; faïence of Crailsheim, ca. 1755.

A tankard with an engraved coat of arms enhanced with colors and gold; polished brown Böttger stoneware, Meissen, ca. 1720; pewter mounting.

A large tankard painted in polychrome with chinoiseries; *porcelain of Vienna, Du Paquier period, ca. 1730; metal cover.*

whether faithfully copied or in delightful and amusing transformations.

Majolicas and faïences, as a group, were more informal and rustic. In contrast to the sharply etched porcelain forms, their contours were engagingly rounded as prescribed by the softer medium. The gentler outlines and blurriness of shape induced gifted modelers to tone down rococo extravaganzas to suit these special requirements of faïence.

These somewhat muted potteries work their magic, providing sheer delight in the proper setting of a modern home. Whether of Dutch, German, French, Italian, Spanish, Belgian, Swiss, Swedish, or other Western European origin, simple vases, bowls, and jars, more intricately modeled useful wares, and purely decorative figural centerpieces can readily be placed in a number of variously furnished period and contemporary rooms.

Blue and white or polychrome Spanish and Italian *albarelli* of the seventeenth and eighteenth centuries—or earlier, more precious examples—handsomely complement rooms of furniture of the same origin and period, whether used as decorations or flower vases. However, there is no rule that restricts these unusual, colorful objects to areas decorated with furniture of the same epoch.

Thus the collector, who wants to surround himself with basically decorative utilitarian ceramic art such as jars or vases, can choose from objects of distinct national or regional character. The varieties of shapes modeled throughout the seventeenth and eighteenth centuries, from late Renaissance or early baroque styles through the neoclassical period, as well as the subject matter and colors used for decoration are endless and all-encompassing. Brilliant primary colors eventually gave way to softer pastels; subject matter changed with time and taste in the course of the eighteenth century.

On bulbous or slender forms, ornate or plain, the painting of garden flowers, ornithological subjects, animals, children at play, scenes after Watteau engravings, peasants at rest or work, shepherds, workmen, mythological subjects, and allegorical scenes reflected the life style of a particular era, its dreams, aspirations, and predilections. The artists strove for naturalistic representation, and whatever struck their fancy was recreated on faïence and porcelain. Sometimes imaginative ornamental designs of intertwined stylized foliage and ribbon motifs, originally derived from Oriental subject

A tankard decorated in purple monochrome with continuous shipping scenes and classical ruins; porcelain of Meissen, ca. 1740; Hausmalerei.

A tankard decorated in Schwarzlot with Judah and Tamar; faïence of Nuremberg, early eighteenth century; Hausmalerei by Matthias Schmid; pewter mounting.

A tankard painted in colors with chinoiseries; German faïence, middle of the eighteenth century; pewter mounting.

A tall Enghalskrug, the grey body partly covered with a mottled aubergine salt-glaze; applied with stylized rosettes and floral reliefs around the coat of arms of Bishop Franz von Ingelheim, Elector of Mainz, surrounded by an inscription, within an octagonal field; highlighted with touches of blue; Rhenish stoneware, Grenzhausen, Westerwald, dated 1680.

A group of three small tankards, variously decorated in colors with landscapes, floral designs, and buildings; German faïence, seventeenth to eighteenth century; pewter mountings.

Two small tankards decorated in colors with a village and a floral design; German faïence, eighteenth century; pewter mountings.

A large jug in the shape of a man, "Jacquot," seated on a grassy mound; decorated in colors; faïence of Lille, eighteenth century; metal spigot and lid.

matter and adapted to European taste, were the sole decoration enhancing a ceramic object.

These diverse, colorful themes and variations extended to and were multiplied on sets of plates and service platters made of ordinary round, oval, and quadrangular form, shaped with valanced and fluted rims, modeled with pierced latticework, or molded with rococo motifs such as shells and asymmetrical curves, waves, and rockwork striations. Because each object was individually painted, no two are absolutely identical. Close scrutiny will reveal that even pairs of plates, serving dishes, or other objects will bear differentiating identifying marks in subtle decorative details, or in minor nuances in shape or color resulting from firings.

Such tablewares, while usually displayed in cabinets, may be handsomely arranged singly, in pairs, or in garnitures atop commodes, side tables, wall brackets, shelves, or console tables. Since they are not affected by atmospheric changes, beautifully painted large and small plates can very successfully take the place of oil paintings or other conventional pictures. What could be more cheerful and inviting than a set of Meissen, Frankenthal, or Ludwigsburg plates decorated with a variety of fruit or vegetables, attractively hung on the wall of a dining room?

Large, boldly designed majolica plaques, painted in characteristic sunny colors; pairs of blue and white Delft plates of diverse decoration; or Chelsea, Sèvres, and Chantilly dinner plates, airily painted with a variety of simple flower bouquets against the background of gleaming white porcelain offer just three wide-ranging choices of ceramic wall decoration.

A small collection of saucers, enhanced with different subjects, a sampling from several factories and countries, constitutes a delightful and unusual wall arrangement. Unity is provided by the approximate sameness of shape and size. From time to time the collection can easily be enlarged and rearranged.

There are, of course, numerous porcelain and faïence plaques of equal diversity that were intended to be hung like paintings, either as they are or framed. Some have molded ceramic frames simulating wood. Most European factories produced such tiles or pictures in faïence and porcelain.

Ideally, for table decoration, there is the covered tureen, the porcelain example usually more elegant than its faïence counterpart. If it is of rococo shape, the tureen is intricately and delightfully ornate in its

A pair of covered bowls decorated in the Imari style with floral motifs in iron red, blue, and gold; porcelain of China, early eighteenth century; mounted in French gilded bronze of the period.

A set of three flowerpots filled with large bouquets of modeled flowers, decorated in polychrome; porcelain of Bow, ca. 1760.

147

details of modeling and painted decoration. Often the handles and finial boast special features, cleverly enhancing the entire object, such as simulated curving twigs with applied leaves and shaped flowers. Sometimes the finial is fully modeled as a miniature basket of fruit, as a single fruit on a leaf, or perhaps as a *putto* bearing a horn of plenty spilling fruit.

In faïence such tureens will convey a warmer tone in color and a softness of line and form, in comparison to the august, cool appearance of porcelain. Modeled with particular flair and success were the showpiece tureens in the shape of fruits, vegetables, and birds. A pigeon or cabbage tureen as a dining room centerpiece may well be the most striking and handsome object in a room.

For the fancier of flowers an arrangement placed in an appropriate container as a room's major eye-catching attraction may be more desirable and useful. Here again choices of bowls, cachepots, pitchers, or other improvised flower holders abound, and every taste can find satisfaction.

A discriminating collector can be selective and indulge his taste and checkbook. But another's more limited, modest choice, that is primarily bright and cheerful, may be equally pleasing. In the case of Sèvres soft-paste porcelain, the first may demand rare, costly, fan-shaped *rose-Pompadour* ground-color containers, the second might prefer simple round white-glazed bowls painted with polychrome floral sprigs. In faïence the choice may vary from delicately painted or finely modeled all-white German or French bouquetiers and cachepots, to vividly ornamented, sturdy, oval jardinières with modeled twig, fruit, or twisted rope-handles. Each specimen serves decorative purposes while reflecting the connoisseur's judgment. More ostentatiously, a porcelain or faïence tureen bowl will be a useful flower holder while the cover is casually put aside. These objects remain as silent witnesses of the collector's taste long after the flowers have faded or wilted.

One collector may place his set of Meissen dinner plates on display stands in a cabinet, while another will use and enjoy them and his tureen with his guests at the dinner table.

Other decorative collector's objects might include a rare inkstand on a desk with a Saint-Cloud knife handle next to it serving as a letter opener, and various rococo-inspired shell or leaf-shaped dishes and covered sugar bowls as containers for sweets and nuts.

An array of tankards on a shelf, cupboard, fireplace, or bookcase, ranging from finely painted specimens of early Meissen manufacture to more provincial, robust examples of German faïence with amusing, often primitive, decoration always proves imposing, handsome, and distinctive, expressive of an individualistic collector's preference.

Assorted bibelots or small sculptures such as figures and groups of figures, birds, and animals will attractively and uniquely divide bookshelves into desired sections.

Corner shelves and small hanging cabinets are ideal for displaying collections of cups and saucers, tea caddies, snuffboxes, or miniature vases, at the same time brightening a room with movement and color. Large, important, costly figures of birds and other animals are perhaps most effectively placed on carved wood brackets, console tables, or pedestals.

The neophyte collector should never feel restrained because of uncertainty. There are no rules except that he search for and find the genuine article. With some imagination the possibilities are endless and the decorative results for the collector most gratifying as he lives with and among his treasures, truly enjoying them in full measure.

Selected Bibliography

Ballu, Nicole. *La Porcelaine française*. Paris: Charles Massin & Cie., 1958.

Berges, Ruth. *Collector's Choice*. South Brunswick and New York: A.S. Barnes and Company, 1967.

———. *From Gold to Porcelain*. New York and London: Thomas Yoseloff, 1963.

Berling, Karl. *Das Meissner Porzellan und seine Geschichte*. Leipzig: F.A. Brockhaus, 1900.

Bourgeois, Emile. *Le Biscuit de Sèvres au XVIIIe siècle*. Paris: Goupil et Cie., 1909.

———. *Le Biscuit de Sèvres, recueil des modèles de la manufacture de Sèvres au XVIIIe siècle*. Paris: P. Lafitte et Cie., 1914.

Brinckmann, Justus. *Führer durch das Hamburgische Museum für Kunst und Gewerbe*. Hamburg: Verlag des Museums für Kunst und Gewerbe, 1894.

Brunhammer, Yvonne. *La Faïence française*. Paris: Editions Charles Massin, no date.

Chavagnac, Xavier de, and Grollier, Gaston de. *Histoire des manufactures françaises de porcelaine*. Paris: Alphonse Picard et Fils, 1906.

Christ, Hans. *Ludwigsburger Porzellanfiguren*. Stuttgart and Berlin: Deutsche Verlagsanstalt, 1921.

Dansaert, G. *Les Anciennes faïences de Bruxelles*. Brussels and Paris: Van Oest et Cie., 1922.

Doenges, Willy. *Meissner Porzellan*. Berlin: Marquardt & Co., 1907.

Ducret, Siegfried. *Fürstenberger Porzellan*. Braunschweig: Klinkhardt und Biermann, 1965.

———. *German Porcelain and Faïence*. New York: Universe Books, 1962.

———. *Meissner Porzellan bemalt in Augsburg von 1718 bis um 1750*. 2 vols. Braunschweig: Klinkhardt und Biermann, 1971.

———. *Unknown Porcelain of the 18th Century*. Translated by John F. Hayward. Frankfurt/Main: Lothar Woeller Verlag, 1956.

———. *Zürcher Porzellan des 18. Jahrhunderts*. Zurich: Fretz & Wasmuth, 1945.

Eberlein, Harold Donaldson, and Ramsdell, Roger Wearne. *The Practical Book of Chinaware*. New York: Halcyon House, 1925.

Escriva de Romani, Manuel. *Historia de la céramica de Alcora*. Madrid: Aldus, 1945.

Falke, Otto von. *Majolika*. Berlin: Georg Reimer, Handbücher der königlichen Museen zu Berlin, 1907.

Fraenger, Wilhelm, ed. *Callots Neueingerichtetes Zwergenkabinett*. Erlenbach-Zurich: Eugen Rentsch Verlag, 1922 (facsimile edition of the German version of *Il Callotto resuscitato*).

Frothingham, Alice W. *Capodimonte and Buen Retiro Porcelains. Period of Charles III*. New York: The Hispanic Society of America, 1955.

———. *Lustreware of Spain*. New York: The Hispanic Society of America, 1951.

———. *Talavera Pottery*. New York: Catalog of The Hispanic Society of America, 1944.

Fuchs, Eduard, and Heiland, Paul. *Die deutsche Fayence-Kultur*. Munich: Albert Langen Verlag, no date.

Giacommotti, Jeanne. *French Faïence*. New York: Universe Books, 1963.

Graul, Richard, and Kurzwelly, Albrecht. *Altthüringer Porzellan*. Leipzig: E.A. Seemann, 1909.

Hannover, Emil. *Pottery and Porcelain, A Handbook for Collectors.* Edited by Bernard Rackham. 3 vols. New York: Charles Scribner's Sons, 1925.

Haug, Hans. *Les Faïences et porcelaines de Strasbourg.* Strasbourg: A. & F. Kahn, 1922.

Hayward, John F. *Viennese Porcelain of the Du Paquier Period.* London: Rockliff, 1952.

Hofmann, Friedrich H. *Frankenthaler Porzellan.* Munich: F. Bruckmann, 1911.

————. *Geschichte der bayerischen Porzellan-Manufaktur Nymphenburg.* 3 vols. Leipzig: Karl W. Hiersemann, 1921-1923.

————. *Johann Peter Melchior, 1742-1825.* Munich: F. Schmidt, 1921.

Honey, William Bowyer. *The Ceramic Art of China and other Countries of the Far East.* London: Faber and Faber, Ltd., 1945.

————. *Dresden China.* London: A. & C. Black, Ltd., 1934.

————. *European Ceramic Art from the End of the Middle Ages to about 1815.* 2 vols. London: Faber and Faber, Ltd., 1949-1952.

————. *French Porcelain of the 18th Century.* London: Faber & Faber, Ltd., 1950.

————. *German Porcelain.* London: Faber and Faber, Ltd., 1947.

————. *Old English Porcelain.* New York: McGraw-Hill Book Co., 1946.

Hudig, Ferrand W. *Delfter Fayence.* Berlin: Richard Carl Schmidt & Co., 1929.

Hughes, Bernard and Therle. *English Porcelain and Bone China, 1743-1850.* New York: The Macmillan Company, 1955.

Hyde, J.A. Lloyd. *Oriental Lowestoft.* Newport, Monmouthshire: The Ceramic Book Company, 1954.

Jenyns, Soame. *Japanese Porcelain.* London: Faber and Faber, Ltd., 1965.

————. *Later Chinese Porcelain.* London: Faber and Faber, Ltd., 1959.

————. *Ming Pottery and Porcelain.* London: Faber and Faber, Ltd., 1953.

Jonge, Caroline H. de. *Delft Ceramics.* London: Pall Mall Press, 1969.

Koetschau, Karl. *Rheinisches Steinzeug.* Munich: Kurt Wolff Verlag, 1955.

Köllman, Erich. *Berliner Porzellan, 1763-1963.* 2 vols. Braunschweig: Klinkhardt und Biermann, 1965.

Lane, Arthur, *French Faïence.* New York: Pitman Publishing Corp., 1946.

————. *Italian Porcelain.* London: Faber and Faber, Ltd., 1954.

Lenz, Georg. *Berliner Porzellan: Die Manufaktur Friedrichs des Grossen, 1763-1786.* 2 vols. Berlin: Reimar Hobbing, 1913.

Litchfield, Frederick. *Pottery and Porcelain.* New York: The Macmillan Company, 1925.

Liverani, Giuseppe. *Five Centuries of Italian Majolica.* New York: McGraw-Hill, 1960.

Lukomsky, Georgii. *Russisches Porzellan, 1744-1923.* Berlin: Verlag Ernest Wasmuth, 1924.

Meister, Peter Wilhelm. *Porzellan des 18. Jahrhunderts, Meissen, Höchst, Frankenthal, Ludwigsburg—Sammlung Pauls.* 2 vols. Frankfurt/Main: Verlag Osterrieth, 1967.

Miller, Roy Andrew. *Japanese Cermics.* Tokyo: Toto Shuppan Company, Ltd., 1960.

Nieuhof, Joan. *Het Gesantschap der Neerlandtsche Oost-Indische Compagnie, aan den grooten Tartarischen Chan, den tegenwoordigen Keizer van China.* Amsterdam: Jacob van Meurs, 1665.

Pazaurek, Gustav Eduard. *Deutsche Fayence und Porzellan-Hausmaler.* 2 vols. Leipzig: Karl W. Hiersemann, 1925.

Petrasch, Ernst, ed. *Durlacher Fayencen, 1723-1847.* Karlsruhe—Schloss: Catalog of the exhibition, June 20-September 28, 1975, Badisches Landesmuseum.

Phillips, John Goldsmith. *China-Trade Porcelain.* Cambridge, Massachusetts: Harvard University Press, 1956.

Rackham, Bernard. *Italian Majolica.* London: Faber and Faber. Ltd., 1952.

Riesebieter, O. *Die deutschen Fayencen des 17. und 18. Jahrhunderts.* Leipzig: Klinkhardt und Biermann Verlag, 1921.

Röder, Kurt, and Oppenheim, Michel. *Das Höchster Porzellan.* Mainz: L. Wilckens, 1930.

Rückert, Rainer. *Meissener Porzellan, 1710-1810, Katalog der Ausstellung im Bayerischen Nationalmuseum, München.* Munich: Hirmer Verlag, 1966.

Sauerlandt, Max. *Deutsche Porzellanfiguren des 18. Jahrhunderts.* Cologne: Marcan-Block-Verlag, 1923.

Savage, George. *18th Century English Porcelain.* New York: The Macmillan Company, 1952.

————. *Porcelain through the Ages.* Harmondsworth, Middlesex: Penguin Books, 1954.

Scherer, Christian. *Das Fürstenberger Porzellan.* Berlin: Georg Reimer Verlag, 1909.

Schmidt, Robert. *Frühwerke europäischer Porzellanmanufakturen, Sammlung Otto Blohm.* Munich: F. Bruckmann, 1953.

————. *Das Porzellan als Kunstwerk und Kulturspiegel.* Munich: F. Bruckmann, 1925.

Schnorr von Carolsfeld, Ludwig. *Porzellan der europäischen Fabriken des 18. Jahrhunderts.* Berlin: Richard Carl Schmidt & Co., 1920.

Stetten, Paul von. *Erläuterungen der in Kupfer gestochenen Vorstellungen aus der Geschichte der Reichsstadt Augsburg.* Augsburg: 1765.

Stoehr, August. *Deutsche Fayencen und deutsches Steingut.*

Berlin: Richard Carl Schmidt & Co., 1920.

Swoboda, Franz. *Mosbacher Fayencen, 1770-1836.* Mannheim: Städtisches Reiss-Museum, 1970.

Tilmans, Emile. *Faïences de France.* Paris: Editions de Deux-Mondes, 1954.

———. *Porcelaines de France.* Paris: Editions de Deux-Mondes, 1953.

Walcha, Otto. *Meissner Porzellan.* Edited by Helmut Reibig. Dresden: Verlag der Kunst, 1973.

Zimmermann, Ernst Albert. *Die Erfindung und Frühzeit des Meissner Porzellans.* Berlin: Georg Reimer, 1908.

———. *Meissner Porzellan.* Leipzig: Karl W. Hiersemann, 1926.

Index